CW01582520

ASTERIX AND THE LAUREL WREATH

TEXT BY GOSCINNY

DRAWINGS BY UDERZO

TRANSLATED BY ANTHEA BELL AND DEREK HOCKRIDGE

HODDER DARGAUD
LONDON SYDNEY AUCKLAND

ISBN 0 340 72755 1

This compilation copyright © Dargaud Editeur 1998, by Goscinny and Uderzo

First published 1998

10 9 8 7 6 5 4 3 2 1

All rights reserved. No part of this publication may be reproduced or transmitted in any form or by any means, electronically or mechanically, including photocopying, recording, or any information storage and retrieval system, without either prior permission in writing from the publisher or a licence permitting restricted copying. In the United Kingdom such licences are issued by the Copyright Licensing Agency, 90 Tottenham Court Road, London W1P 9HE.

Published by Hodder Dargaud Ltd,
338 Euston Road, London NW1 3BH

Printed in Belgium by Proost International Book Production

Asterix and the Laurel Wreath

Copyright © Dargaud Editeur 1972, Goscinny-Uderzo
English language text copyright © Hodder and Stoughton Ltd 1974
(now Hodder Children's Books)

The year is 50 BC. Gaul is entirely occupied by the Romans. Well, not entirely . . . One small village of indomitable Gauls still holds out against the invaders. And life is not easy for the Roman legionaries who garrison the fortified camps of Totorum, Aquarium, Laudanum and Compendium . . .

a few of the Gauls

Asterix, the hero of these adventures. A shrewd, cunning little warrior; all perilous missions are immediately entrusted to him. Asterix gets his superhuman strength from the magic potion brewed by the druid Getafix...

Obelix, Asterix's inseparable friend. A menhir delivery-man by trade; addicted to wild boar. Obelix is always ready to drop everything and go off on a new adventure with Asterix – so long as there's wild boar to eat, and plenty of fighting.

Getafix, the venerable village druid. Gathers mistletoe and brews magic potions. His speciality is the potion which gives the drinker superhuman strength. But Getafix also has other recipes up his sleeve...

Cacofonix, the bard. Opinion is divided as to his musical gifts. Cacofonix thinks he's a genius. Everyone else thinks he's unspeakable. But so long as he doesn't speak, let alone sing, everybody likes him...

Finally, Vitalstatistix, the chief of the tribe. Majestic, brave and hot-tempered, the old warrior is respected by his men and feared by his enemies. Vitalstatistix himself has only one fear; he is afraid the sky may fall on his head tomorrow. But as he always says, 'Tomorrow never comes.'

ANOTHER SUNNY DAY HAS JUST DAWNED UPON THE GREATEST CITY IN THE UNIVERSE
ROME.
ALTHOUGH, BY CAESAR'S DECREE, TRAFFIC IS NOT ALLOWED ON THE STREETS IN THE DAYTIME, THE CITY IS INCREDIBLY NOISY, CROWDED WITH SHOPKEEPERS AND STREETSELLERS CRYING THEIR WARES... FRUCTUARII, PEPONARII, OLITORES, PISCATORES, VINARII, SILIGINARII, PASTILLARII...
EAT MORE FRUIT!
RIPE JUICY MELONS!
TRY MY VEGETABLES! NICE WHOLESOME VEG!
FISH! GOOD FRESH FISH!
CAKES!
SWEETS!
THE PASSERS-BY ARE BESET BY BEGGARS AND FLAG SELLERS...
HAVE PITY ON A POOR GLADIATOR IN REDUCED CIRCUMSTANCES!
DON'T YOU WANT TO SUPPORT A GOOD CAUSE THEN?
TOURISTS FROM ALL OVER THE WORLD, THRACIANS, GOTHS, BRITONS, EGYPTIANS, SICAMBRES, ETHIOPIANS, NUMIDIANS, ALL ADD TO THE LOCAL COLOUR...
AND HERE WE HAVE THE CIRCUS MAXIMUS...
AND HERE WE HAVE THE CIRCUS MAXIMUS...
and here we have the Circus Maximus
IN FACT, EVERYTHING LEADS US TO BELIEVE THAT WE MAY SEE EVEN STRANGER SIGHTS AROUND THE NEXT CORNER...

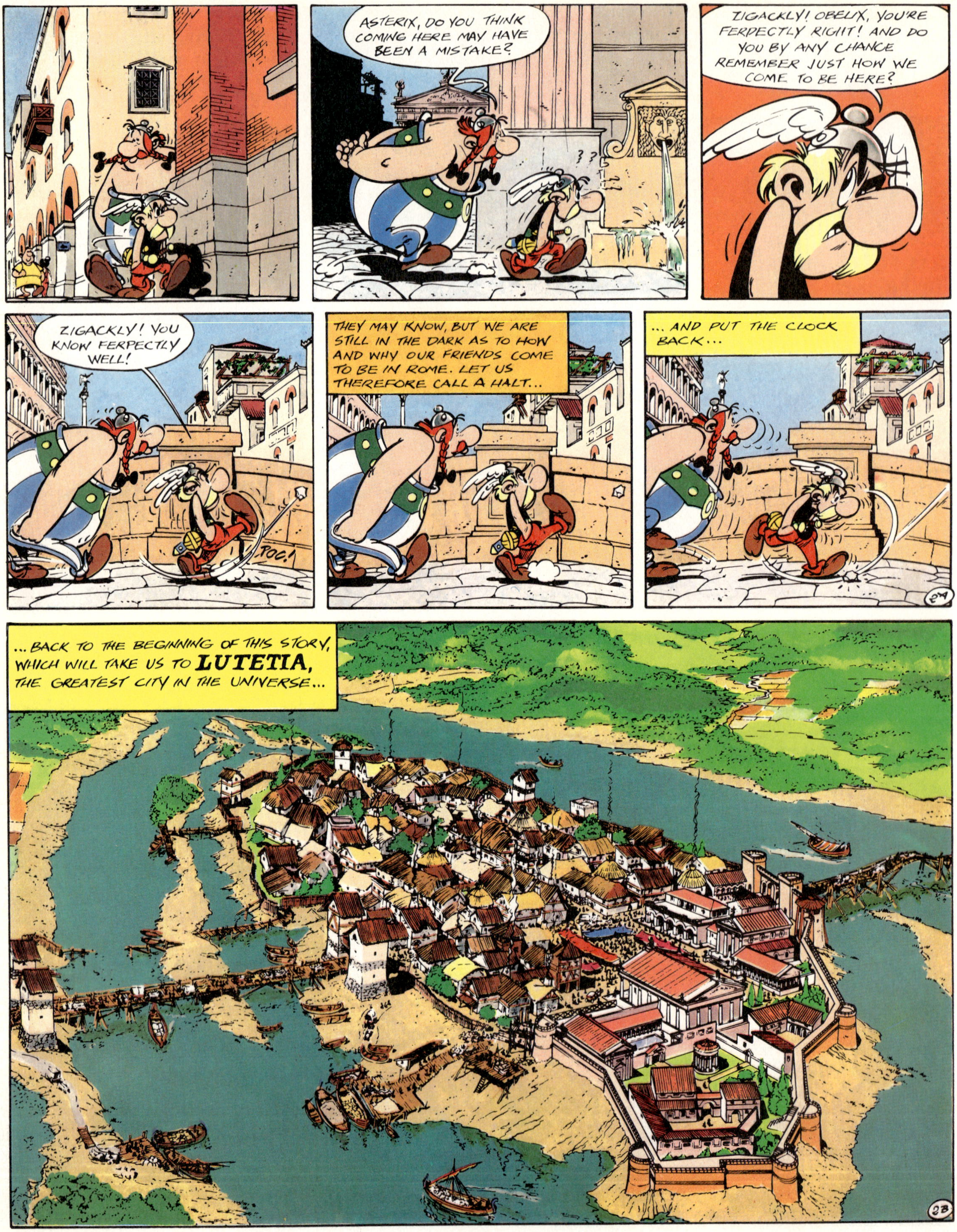
ASTERIX, DO YOU THINK COMING HERE MAY HAVE BEEN A MISTAKE?
??
ZIGACKLY! OBELIX, YOU'RE FERDECTLY RIGHT! AND DO YOU BY ANY CHANCE REMEMBER JUST HOW WE COME TO BE HERE?
ZIGACKLY! YOU KNOW FERPECTLY WELL!
POC!
THEY MAY KNOW, BUT WE ARE STILL IN THE DARK AS TO HOW AND WHY OUR FRIENDS COME TO BE IN ROME. LET US THEREFORE CALL A HALT...
... AND PUT THE CLOCK BACK...
... BACK TO THE BEGINNING OF THIS STORY, WHICH WILL TAKE US TO LUTETIA, THE GREATEST CITY IN THE UNIVERSE...

IN SPITE OF THE FACT THAT TRAFFIC IS FORBIDDEN, THE STREETS OF LUTETIA ARE NOISY. NOISY BUT CHEERFUL, THANKS TO THE INSPIRED REPARTEE SO TYPICAL OF THE LUTETIAN SENSE OF HUMOUR...
I'VE GOT A JOB TO DO, I HAVE!
FOOL!
IDIOT!
YOUNG HOOLIGAN!
HALF-WIT!
MORON!
GO ON, YOU CAN GET THROUGH!
NO, I CAN'T!
I'M TELLING YOU YOU CAN!
DO YOU REALLY THINK SO?
THERE, WHAT DID I TELL YOU?
LET US TAKE A CLOSER LOOK AT THIS LITTLE GROUP OF VISITORS UP FROM THE COUNTRY...
LOOK HERE, IMPEDIMENTA, COMING TO LUTETIA TO DO YOUR SHOPPING IS ONE THING, BUT GOING TO SEE HOMEOPATHIX IS ANOTHER! DO WE REALLY HAVE TO?
WELL, I CAN HARDLY VISIT LUTETIA WITHOUT CALLING ON MY BROTHER, CAN I? ANYWAY, HE'S INVITED US TO DINNER.
YOU KNOW VERY WELL HOMEOPATHIX AND I DON'T GET ON!
OH, OF COURSE, WHEN IT'S A MEMBER OF MY FAMILY...
HOMEOPATHIX HAS GOT TO THE TOP, HE HAS! HIS WIFE DOESN'T LIVE IN A VILLAGE OF MADMEN, SURROUNDED BY ROMANS.
AND DID YOU HAVE TO ASK THOSE TWO TO COME ALONG?
?
I MAY NOT HAVE GOT TO THE TOP, BUT I AM A CHIEF! AND A CHIEF NEEDS HIS ESCORT... ASTERIX AND OBELIX ARE MY BEST MEN! MY GUARD OF HONOUR!
WELL, I HOPE YOUR GUARD OF HONOUR KNOWS HOW TO BEHAVE ITSELF, THAT'S ALL. HERE WE ARE!
RHUBARBRHUBARBGUARDOFHONOUR RHUBARBRHUBARBRHUBARBRHUBARB RHUBARBANDDOYOUKNOWWHATMY GUARDOFHONOURSAYSTOYOU...
H
KNOCK! KNOCK! KNOCK!

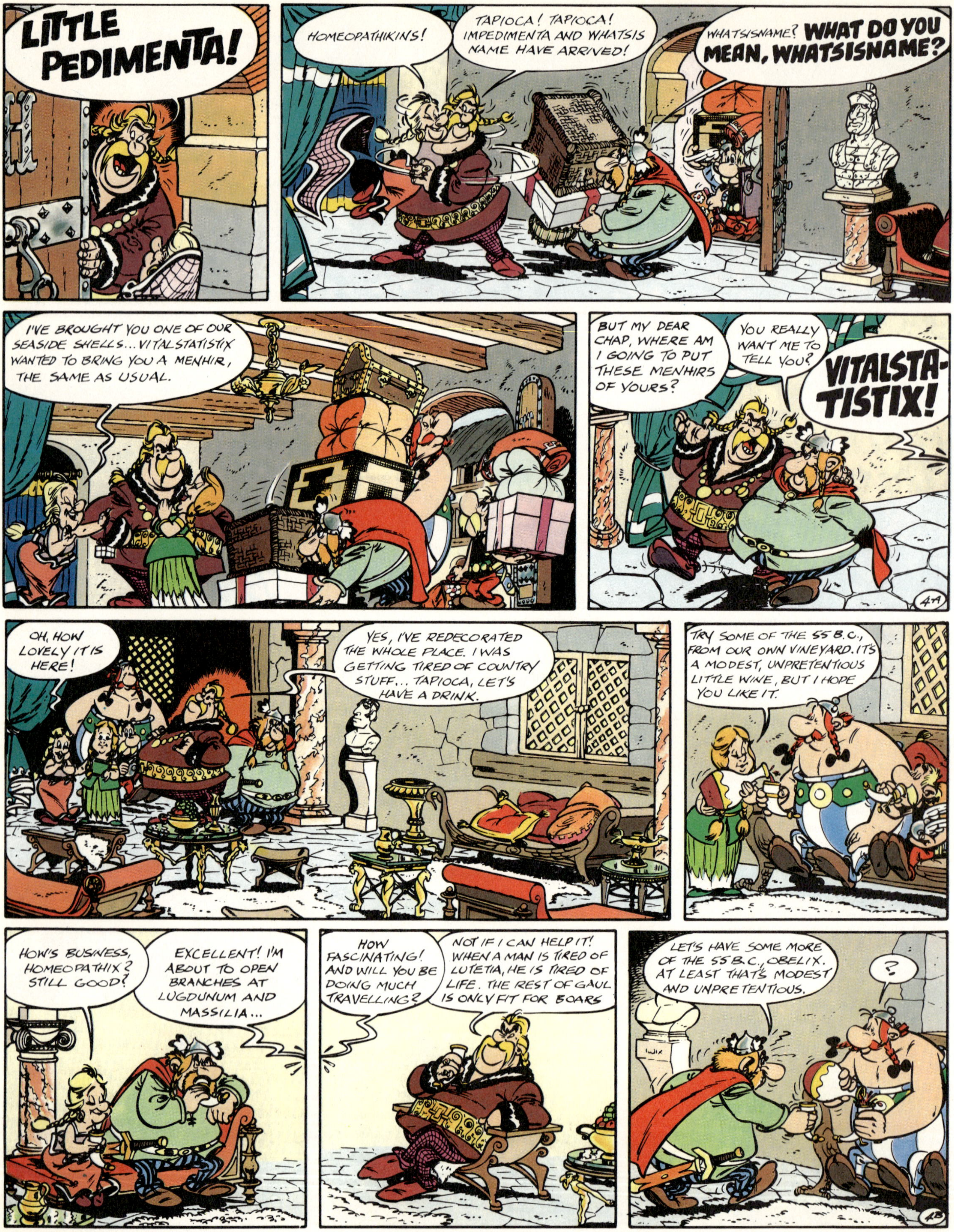

LITTLE PEDIMENTA!
HOMEOPATHIKINS!
TAPIOCA! TAPIOCA! IMPEDIMENTA AND WHATSIS NAME HAVE ARRIVED!
WHATSISNAME? WHAT DO YOU MEAN, WHATSISNAME?
I'VE BROUGHT YOU ONE OF OUR SEASIDE SHELLS... VITALSTATISTIX WANTED TO BRING YOU A MENHIR, THE SAME AS USUAL.
BUT MY DEAR CHAP, WHERE AM I GOING TO PUT THESE MENHIRS OF YOURS?
YOU REALLY WANT ME TO TELL YOU?
VITALSTA-TISTIX!
OH, HOW LOVELY IT IS HERE!
YES, I'VE REDECORATED THE WHOLE PLACE. I WAS GETTING TIRED OF COUNTRY STUFF... TAPIOCA, LET'S HAVE A DRINK.
TRY SOME OF THE 55 B.C., FROM OUR OWN VINEYARD. IT'S A MODEST, UNPRETENTIOUS LITTLE WINE, BUT I HOPE YOU LIKE IT.
HOW'S BUSINESS, HOMEOPATHIX? STILL GOOD?
EXCELLENT! I'M ABOUT TO OPEN BRANCHES AT LUGDUNUM AND MASSILIA...
HOW FASCINATING! AND WILL YOU BE DOING MUCH TRAVELLING?
NOT IF I CAN HELP IT! WHEN A MAN IS TIRED OF LUTETIA, HE IS TIRED OF LIFE. THE REST OF GAUL IS ONLY FIT FOR BOARS
LET'S HAVE SOME MORE OF THE 55 B.C., OBELIX. AT LEAST THAT'S MODEST AND UNPRETENTIOUS.
?

CENA IS SERVED!
OH, TAPIOCA, HOW WONDERFUL!
OF COURSE, IT MUST BE A BIT OF A CHANGE FROM THE STUFF YOU GET TO EAT AT HOME!
AND WHAT'S WRONG WITH WHAT WE GET TO EAT AT HOME?
NOTHING, EXCEPT I DON'T OFTEN HAVE BEAVERS' TAILS IN STRAWBERRY SAUCE AT HOME!
HEY, OBELIX! PASS THE WINE, WILL YOU?
NOW, WHATSYOURNAME, HOW ABOUT SOME COW'S HOOF MOULD? I BET YOU'VE NEVER HAD ANYTHING LIKE THIS...
YOU DON'T IMPRESS ME WITH YOUR COW'S HOOF MOULD! YOU'RE JUST MAKING PIGS OF YOURSELVES!
VITALSTATISTIX, DON'T BE SUCH A BOOR!
WELL, AT LEAST I CAN BRING HOME THE BACON!
HOMEOPATHIX!
DID MADAM CALL?
YES. MORE WINE, PLEASE.
WELL, I MAY NOT HAVE YOUR MONEY, BUT I DO HAVE HONOUR AND GLORY INSTEAD!
AND DOES HONOUR AND GLORY PROVIDE YOU WITH COW'S HOOF MOULD, DEAR BROTHER-IN-LAW?

HONOUR AND GLORY IS WORTH A LOT MORE THAN FOW'S COOF.. I MEAN HOW'S MOOF... I MEAN ALL THIS ROT!
YOU COME TO MY VILLAGE, YOU AND SEMOLINA... TAPIOCA! I'LL GIVE YOU A MEAL. AND WHAT A MEAL! ONE YOUR MONEY COULD NEVER BUY! HIC!
AND WHAT EXACTLY WILL THIS GOURMET MEAL CONSIST OF?
AHA! A STEW... OUT-OF-THIS-WORLD... SEASONED WITH...
CAESONED WITH CAESAR'S LAUREL WREATH! HIC!
PRRFFFF!
TAKE NO NOTICE. HE'S HAD A DROP TOO MUCH.
THAT'S ALL RIGHT, IMPEDIMENTA. HE'S VERY AMUSING.
AMUSING, EH? HIC! ALL RIGHT THEN, YOU WAIT AND SEE! I'M SENDING MY MEN TO ROME TO BRING ME CAESAR'S LAUREL WREATH, TO SEASON THE STEW I SHALL GIVE YOU WHEN YOU VISIT MY VILLAGE!
ZIGACKLY! WHATSISNAME ISH FERPECTLY RIGHT! HIC!
?!?
LET GO OF ME, ASTERIX! WE'RE GOING TO ROME TO BRING BACK CHAESHAR'S LAUREL WREATH! ZIGACTLY!
COME TO MY ARMS, OBELIX!
HOMEOPATH-IKINS!
NO! SINCE THIS BIGHEADED WARRIOR OF YOURS IS SO CLEVER, I'LL ACCEPT HIS INVITATION!
BUT I HAVE HIS WORD OF HONOUR THAT IT REALLY WILL BE CAESAR'S LAUREL WREATH IN THE STEW, DON'T I?
THASH FERPECTLY RIGHT!
IMPEDIMENTA, DARLING... D-DID YOU SEE ANYTHING NICE IN LUTETIA?

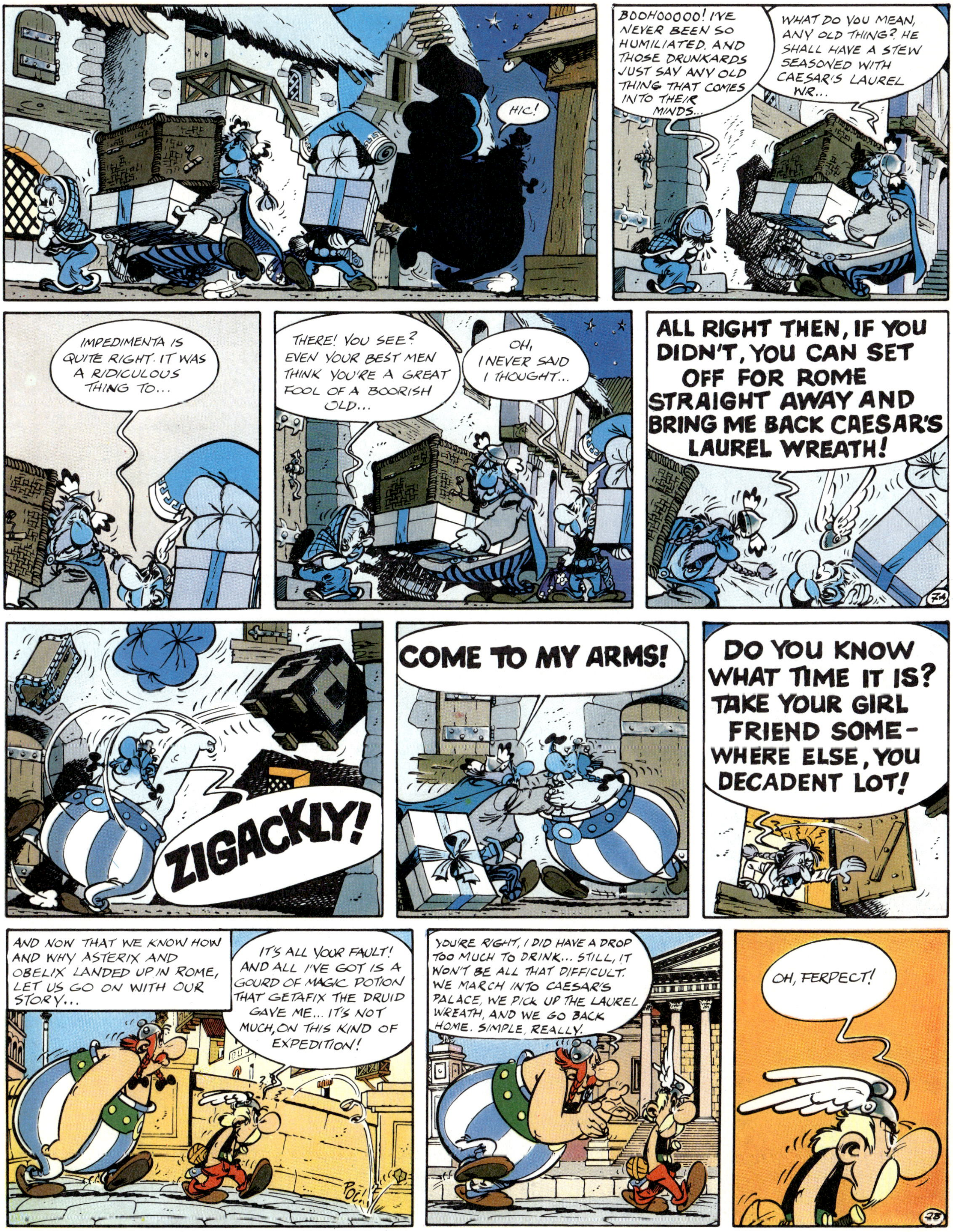
HIC!
BOOHOOOOO! I'VE NEVER BEEN SO HUMILIATED. AND THOSE DRUNKARDS JUST SAY ANY OLD THING THAT COMES INTO THEIR MINDS...
WHAT DO YOU MEAN, ANY OLD THING? HE SHALL HAVE A STEW SEASONED WITH CAESAR'S LAUREL WR...
IMPEDIMENTA IS QUITE RIGHT. IT WAS A RIDICULOUS THING TO...
THERE! YOU SEE? EVEN YOUR BEST MEN THINK YOU'RE A GREAT FOOL OF A BOORISH OLD...
OH, I NEVER SAID I THOUGHT...
ALL RIGHT THEN, IF YOU DIDN'T, YOU CAN SET OFF FOR ROME STRAIGHT AWAY AND BRING ME BACK CAESAR'S LAUREL WREATH!
ZIGACKLY!
COME TO MY ARMS!
DO YOU KNOW WHAT TIME IT IS? TAKE YOUR GIRL FRIEND SOMEWHERE ELSE, YOU DECADENT LOT!
AND NOW THAT WE KNOW HOW AND WHY ASTERIX AND OBELIX LANDED UP IN ROME, LET US GO ON WITH OUR STORY...
IT'S ALL YOUR FAULT! AND ALL I'VE GOT IS A GOURD OF MAGIC POTION THAT GETAFIX THE DRUID GAVE ME... IT'S NOT MUCH, ON THIS KIND OF EXPEDITION!
POC!
YOU'RE RIGHT, I DID HAVE A DROP TOO MUCH TO DRINK... STILL, IT WON'T BE ALL THAT DIFFICULT. WE MARCH INTO CAESAR'S PALACE, WE PICK UP THE LAUREL WREATH, AND WE GO BACK HOME. SIMPLE, REALLY.
OH, FERPECT!

SEE THAT? THAT'S JULIUS CAESAR'S PALACE.
SO WE JUST MASSACRE THE GUARD, AND ONCE INSIDE THE PALACE WE ASK OUR WAY TO CAESAR'S LAUREL WREATH, WHICH WE NEED TO SEASON A STEW...
...AND HAVING GOT OUR HANDS ON THE LAUREL WREATH WE SIMPLY BASH OUR WAY OUT AND GO HOME. RIGHT?
RIGHT! COMING?
OBELIX, THOSE LEGIONARIES IN CAESAR'S PALACE ARE A TOUGHER PROPOSITION THAN THE SORT WE GET AT HOME!...AND THE MAGIC POTION DOESN'T MAKE US INVULNERABLE. WE MUST THINK OF SOMETHING ELSE.
THAT MAN JUST CAME OUT OF THE PALACE. HE MIGHT BE ABLE TO TELL US HOW TO GET IN. LET'S FOLLOW HIM.
BUT... HE MAY KNOW THE WAY OUT, BUT THAT DOESN'T MEAN TO SAY HE KNOWS THE WAY IN, AND...
EXCUSE ME! WE'RE STRANGERS HERE, AND WE'D LIKE TO ASK YOU A FEW QUESTIONS.
I'M A BUSY MAN GAUL...
TABERNA BIBULUS
HOW ABOUT GOING IN HERE FOR A LITTLE DRINK?
I DON'T REALLY KNOW IF I CAN...
JUST AS I THOUGHT! HE CAN GET OUT OF PLACES ALL RIGHT, BUT HE'S NOT SO GOOD AT GETTING IN.

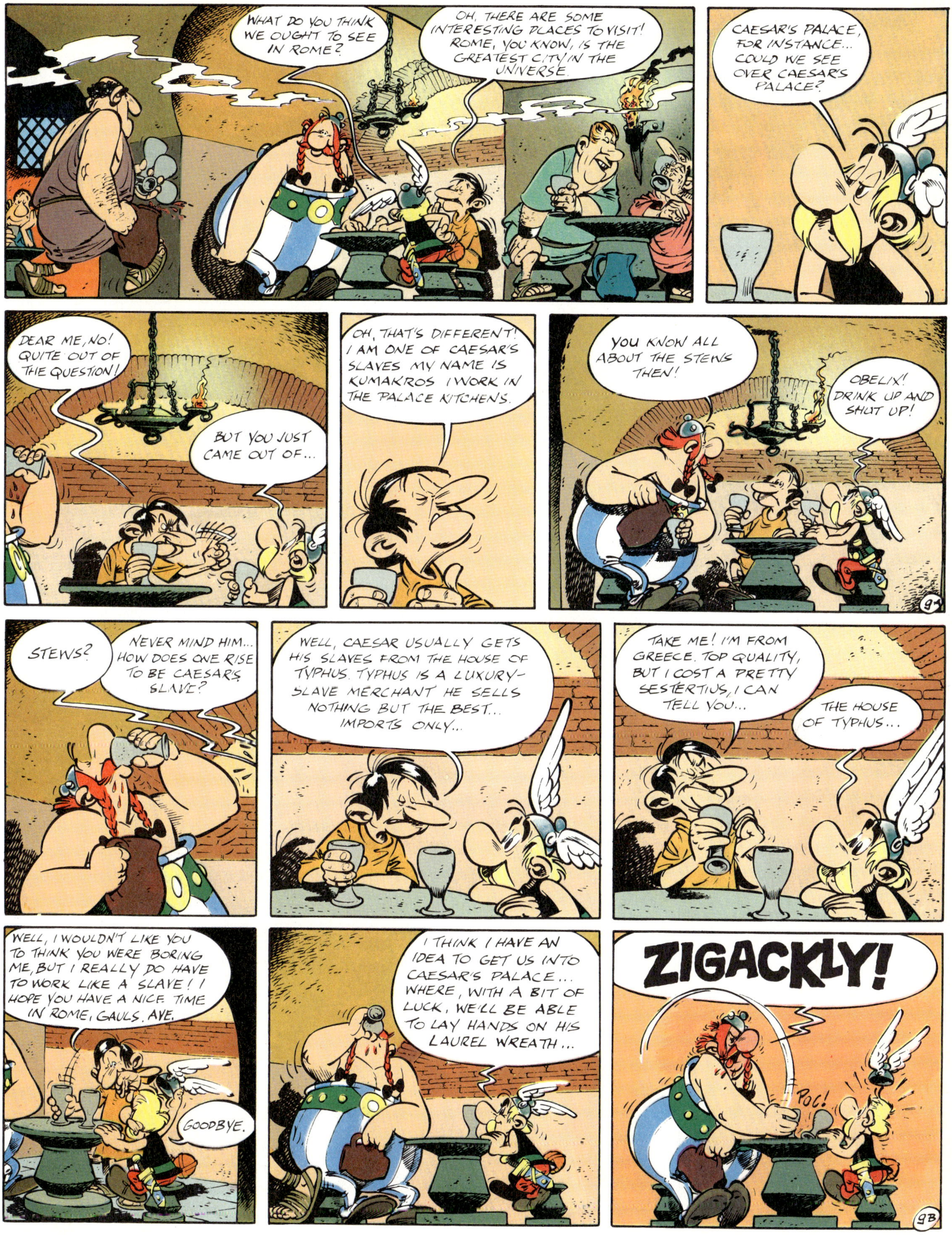

WHAT DO YOU THINK WE OUGHT TO SEE IN ROME?
OH, THERE ARE SOME INTERESTING PLACES TO VISIT! ROME, YOU KNOW, IS THE GREATEST CITY IN THE UNIVERSE.
CAESAR'S PALACE, FOR INSTANCE... COULD WE SEE OVER CAESAR'S PALACE?
DEAR ME, NO! QUITE OUT OF THE QUESTION!
BUT YOU JUST CAME OUT OF...
OH, THAT'S DIFFERENT! I AM ONE OF CAESAR'S SLAVES. MY NAME IS KUMAKROS. I WORK IN THE PALACE KITCHENS.
YOU KNOW ALL ABOUT THE STEWS THEN!
OBELIX! DRINK UP AND SHUT UP!
STEWS?
NEVER MIND HIM... HOW DOES ONE RISE TO BE CAESAR'S SLAVE?
WELL, CAESAR USUALLY GETS HIS SLAVES FROM THE HOUSE OF TYPHUS. TYPHUS IS A LUXURY-SLAVE MERCHANT. HE SELLS NOTHING BUT THE BEST... IMPORTS ONLY...
TAKE ME! I'M FROM GREECE. TOP QUALITY, BUT I COST A PRETTY SESTERTIUS, I CAN TELL YOU...
THE HOUSE OF TYPHUS...
WELL, I WOULDN'T LIKE YOU TO THINK YOU WERE BORING ME, BUT I REALLY DO HAVE TO WORK LIKE A SLAVE! I HOPE YOU HAVE A NICE TIME IN ROME, GAULS. AVE.
GOODBYE.
I THINK I HAVE AN IDEA TO GET US INTO CAESAR'S PALACE... WHERE, WITH A BIT OF LUCK, WE'LL BE ABLE TO LAY HANDS ON HIS LAUREL WREATH...
ZIGACKLY!
POC!

LOOK! THAT MAN SHOULD BE ABLE TO DIRECT US.
WHAT MAKES YOU THINK SO?
THE SLAVE MARKET? I'VE JUST LEFT IT. IT'S THAT WAY.
SLAVES! SLAVES! FINE UPSTANDING SLAVES!
WHO'LL BUY MY GOTHS? NICE FRESH GOTHS!
NUUUMIDIANS! NUUUMIDIANS!
HEAVY-DUTY NIMBLE HOPLITES!
BELGIANS! BELGIANS! BELGIANS! BELGIANS!
YOU'LL NEVER WANT TO GET SHOT OF MY PARTHIANS!
DANCING-GIRLS! DANCING-GIRLS! THIS WAY FOR THE DANCING-GIRLS!
AH! THIS MUST BE IT.
THE HOUSE OF TYPHVS
BY APPOINTMENT TO JULIUS CAESAR
ARE YOU INTERESTED IN OUR WARES? WOULD YOU LIKE TO SEE THE CATALOGUE?
ARE YOU TYPHUS?
NO, THAT'S ME.
WHAT CAN I DO FOR YOU? WE'VE JUST HAD A DELIVERY OF REALLY TOP QUALITY BRITONS...

WE DON'T WANT TO BUY, WE WANT TO SELL.
SELL! OH, THAT'S DIFFERENT...
IF YOU'RE IN THE TRADE I CAN ONLY SEE YOU FIRST THING IN THE MORNING... WELL, AND WHO DID YOU HAVE TO OFFER ME?
US.
YOU? I DON'T GO BUYING ANY OLD THING.
WE'RE NOT ANY OLD THING!
THIS ONE SMELLS OF WINE.
SNIFF SNIF!
WELL, YES, BUT HE ONLY INDULGES ONCE IN A WHILE... AND HE'S VERY STRONG.
SHOW US HOW STRONG YOU ARE OBELIX!
RIGHT
PAF!
YES, YES... BUT I SPECIALIZE IN ELEGANT STUFF I'M EXPECTING THE PALACE MAJOR-DOMO ANY MINUTE, LET ME TELL YOU. HE'S COMING TO BUY SOME SLAVES...
SCHLONK!
I'M VERY STRONG TOO. WANT ME TO SHOW YOU?
NO! NO! DON'T BOTHER... MAFTER, I'M FURE THEY WON'T FPOIL THE DIFPLAY...
RIGHT, I'LL TAKE YOU, BUT ONLY ON SALE OR RETURN. IF I DON'T SELL YOU TODAY, YOU CAN GO AND GET SOLD SOMEWHERE ELSE.

THE HOUSE OF TYPHVS
BY APPOINTMENT TO JULIUS CAESAR
COME ON! UP ON THE PLATFORM! LET'S SEE A BIT OF CLASS! WE'RE NOT FLOGGING ANY CHEAP MASS-PRODUCED SLAVES HERE, YOU KNOW!
HMPH... I CAN SMELL THE FUMES OF WINE!
WHERE? WHERE?
PAY NO ATTENTION, MY DEAR. IT MUST BE REMNANT DAY... ONLY AN ADVERTISING GIMMICK. JUST JUNK!
JUNK? WHO'S JUNK?
SHUT UP, OBELIX!
YOU ARE, YOU SECOND-HAND PIECE OF GOODS!
FLAWED, AT THAT.
YOU'LL BE FLOORED TOO IF YOU'RE NOT CAREFUL!
SHUT UP, YOU FREE GIFT!
SCHLAFF!
WHERE DO YOU THINK YOU ARE? DON'T DISTURB THE DISPLAY!
YOU SAW THAT? MY FRIEND HERE IS STRONG TOO!
I SAY, SO HE IS, OLD BOY! JOLLY GOOD SHOW!
YOU SHUT UP, BRITON, OR I'LL SELL YOU AT A DISCOUNT!
AND YOU GET OUT, GAULS!
YOU MAY FIND A DEPARTMENT STORE OR SUPERMARKET TO TAKE YOU. YOU'RE FREE!
OH NO, WE'RE NOT! AND IF NECESSARY WE'LL FIGHT TO LOSE OUR FREEDOM!
GET THESE GOODS OUT OF HERE! I'M EXPECTING CAESAR'S MAJOR-DOMO ANY MINUTE.

SUCH GOINGS-ON ARE MOST DEGRADING! I PROTEST, IN THE NAME OF THE ENTIRE STOCK!
TCHONC!
TCHAC!
HOW MUCH FOR THOSE TWO GAULS?
?
YOU... YOU WANT TO BUY THEM?
I THINK THEY'RE QUITE AMUSING.
PAF!
OF COURSE HE WANTS TO BUY US! AND HE'LL BE MAKING A GOOD DEAL, WON'T HE, OBELIX?
QUITE RIGHT! WE'RE A GOOD DEAL OF A GOOD DEAL, TOO!
THAT DEPENDS HOW MUCH DO YOU COST?
NAME YOUR PRICE! HE'LL TAKE IT.
NO, GO ON, DO! YOU NAME A PRICE.
FIVE SESTERTII THE PAIR, ALL RIGHT?
OH, COME NOW! WAIT A MINUTE...
OH, I SAY! THIS IS RIDICULOUS, EH, WHAT? SELLING AT A PRICE LIKE THAT WILL DEVALUE THE WHOLE STOCK!
HOW ABOUT SIX THEN?
MAY I GET A WORD IN EDGEWAYS?
TEN! BRITONS NEVER, NEVER, NEVER SHALL BE CUT-PRICE SLAVES!
VS JULIUS CAES
DONE!
HERE YOU ARE!
OH, NO! ALLOW ME!
WELL, IF YOU INSIST. I'LL DO AS MUCH FOR YOU ONE OF THESE DAYS

FOLLOW ME.
THE HOUSE OF TYPHUS
ONCE INSIDE CAESAR'S PALACE, WE'LL SET ABOUT LOOKING FOR HIS LAURELS!
SO LONG AS HE ISN'T RESTING ON THEM!
SOON AFTERWARDS...
HERE WE ARE.
HEY, ASTERIX... THIS ISN'T CAESAR'S PALACE, IS IT?
PERHAPS HE HAS SEVERAL...
FIBULA! TIBIA! NITWIT! COME AND LOOK AT THIS!
SEE THESE GAULS? I GOT THEM FROM THE HOUSE OF TYPHUS.
THE HOUSE OF TYPHUS? YOU MUST BE MAD, OSSEUS! HE'S TERRIBLY EXPENSIVE.
AND WHEN I THINK OF THE FUSS THEY KICK UP IN THIS DOMUS WHEN I WANT TO BUY A NEW TOGA!
IS THAT WHAT ALL THE SHOUTING WAS ABOUT?
I THOUGHT IT WOULD BE A NICE SURPRISE.. THEY'RE RATHER AMUSING.
OH WELL, I'M GOING BACK TO MY CUBICULUM TO GET A BIT OF SLEEP.
YOU'VE BEEN OUT DRINKING ALL NIGHT WITH YOUR FRIENDS AGAIN! YOU'LL FIND YOURSELF IN MY LIBRI NIGRI* IF YOU DON'T WATCH OUT!
I SAY... ISN'T THIS CAESAR'S PALACE?
* BLACK BOOKS
CAESAR'S PALACE?
YOU'RE RIGHT, THEY ARE AMUSING!

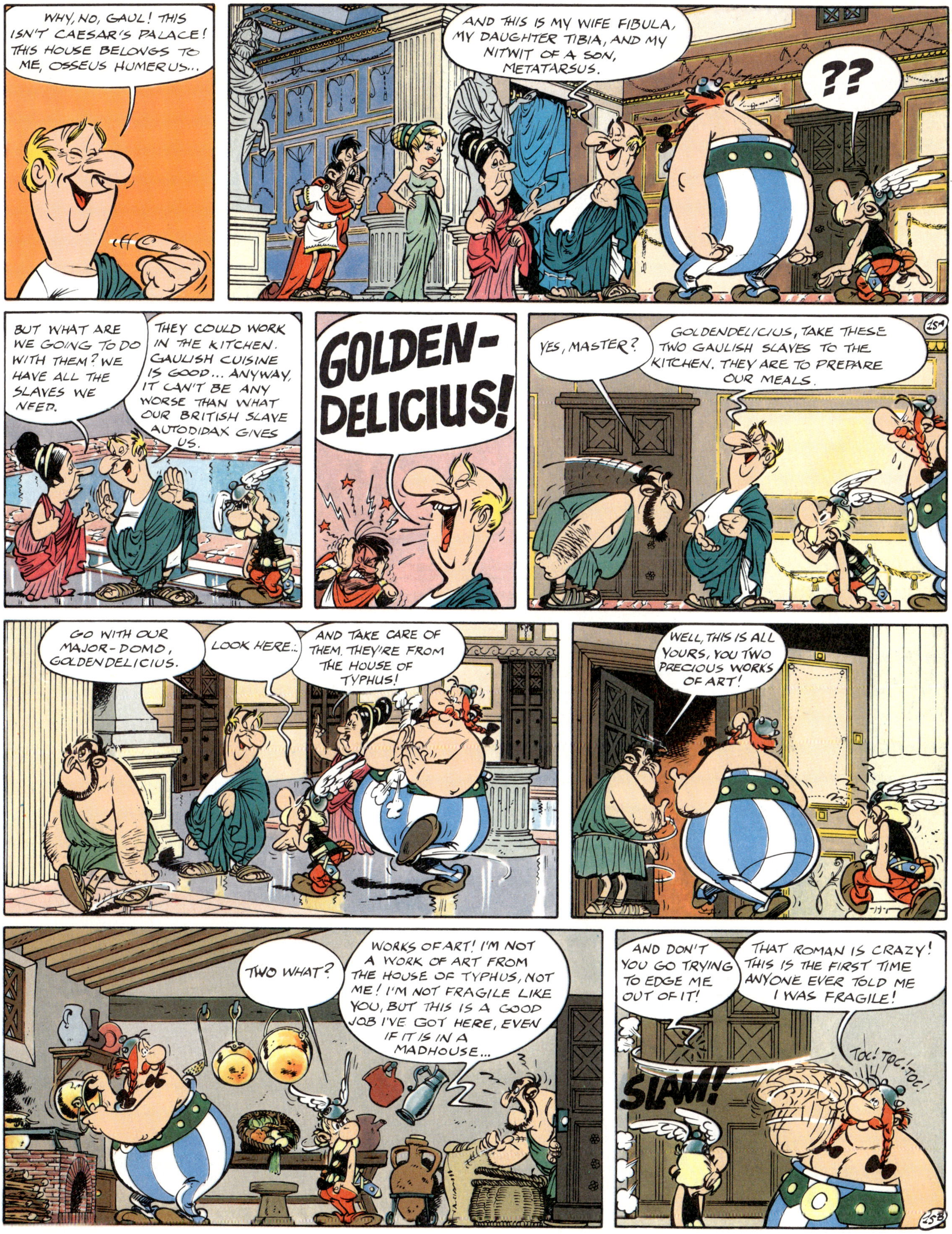
WHY, NO, GAUL! THIS ISN'T CAESAR'S PALACE! THIS HOUSE BELONGS TO ME, OSSEUS HUMERUS...
AND THIS IS MY WIFE FIBULA, MY DAUGHTER TIBIA, AND MY NITWIT OF A SON, METATARSUS.
??
BUT WHAT ARE WE GOING TO DO WITH THEM? WE HAVE ALL THE SLAVES WE NEED.
THEY COULD WORK IN THE KITCHEN. GAULISH CUISINE IS GOOD... ANYWAY, IT CAN'T BE ANY WORSE THAN WHAT OUR BRITISH SLAVE AUTODIDAX GIVES US.
GOLDEN-DELICIUS!
YES, MASTER?
GOLDENDELICIUS, TAKE THESE TWO GAULISH SLAVES TO THE KITCHEN. THEY ARE TO PREPARE OUR MEALS.
GO WITH OUR MAJOR-DOMO, GOLDENDELICIUS.
LOOK HERE...
AND TAKE CARE OF THEM. THEY'RE FROM THE HOUSE OF TYPHUS!
WELL, THIS IS ALL YOURS, YOU TWO PRECIOUS WORKS OF ART!
TWO WHAT?
WORKS OF ART! I'M NOT A WORK OF ART FROM THE HOUSE OF TYPHUS, NOT ME! I'M NOT FRAGILE LIKE YOU, BUT THIS IS A GOOD JOB I'VE GOT HERE, EVEN IF IT IS IN A MADHOUSE...
AND DON'T YOU GO TRYING TO EDGE ME OUT OF IT!
SLAM!
THAT ROMAN IS CRAZY! THIS IS THE FIRST TIME ANYONE EVER TOLD ME I WAS FRAGILE!
TOC! TOC! TOC!

WE'VE MADE A MISTAKE... ALL THIS IS ONLY TAKING US FURTHER AWAY FROM CAESAR'S LAUREL WREATH.
WELL THEN, LET'S GO.
NO. WE'RE SLAVES. IF WE RUN AWAY WE'LL NEVER HAVE A CHANCE OF GETTING INTO CAESAR'S PALACE.
WE MUST PERSUADE HUMERUS TO RETURN US TO TYPHUS TO BE RESOLD.
JUST LIKE THE PEOPLE WHO BUY YOUR MENHIRS AND BRING THEM BACK BECAUSE THEY'RE NOT SATISFIED.
ALL MY CUSTOMERS ARE SATISFIED!
AH, BUT YOUR MENHIRS DON'T DO THE COOKING...
WE'LL MAKE THEM A MEAL THEY WON'T FORGET IN A HURRY, BY TOUTATIS! BRING ME EVERYTHING YOU CAN FIND IN THE LARDER!
HERE YOU ARE! JAM, BLACK PEPPERCORNS, SALT, KIDNEYS, CARBOLIX SOAP, A CHICKEN, HONEY, RED PEPPERS, BLACK PUDDING, EGGS, AND POMEGRANATE SEEDS!
I'VE FOUND SOME MORE RED PEPPERS AND BLACK PEPPERCORNS... WE'LL FLING IT ALL IN THE POT!
HOW ABOUT THE CHICKEN? SHALL I PLUCK IT?
WHY BOTHER?
SOON AFTERWARDS...
IT'S NEARLY DONE.
CAN I HAVE A TASTE?

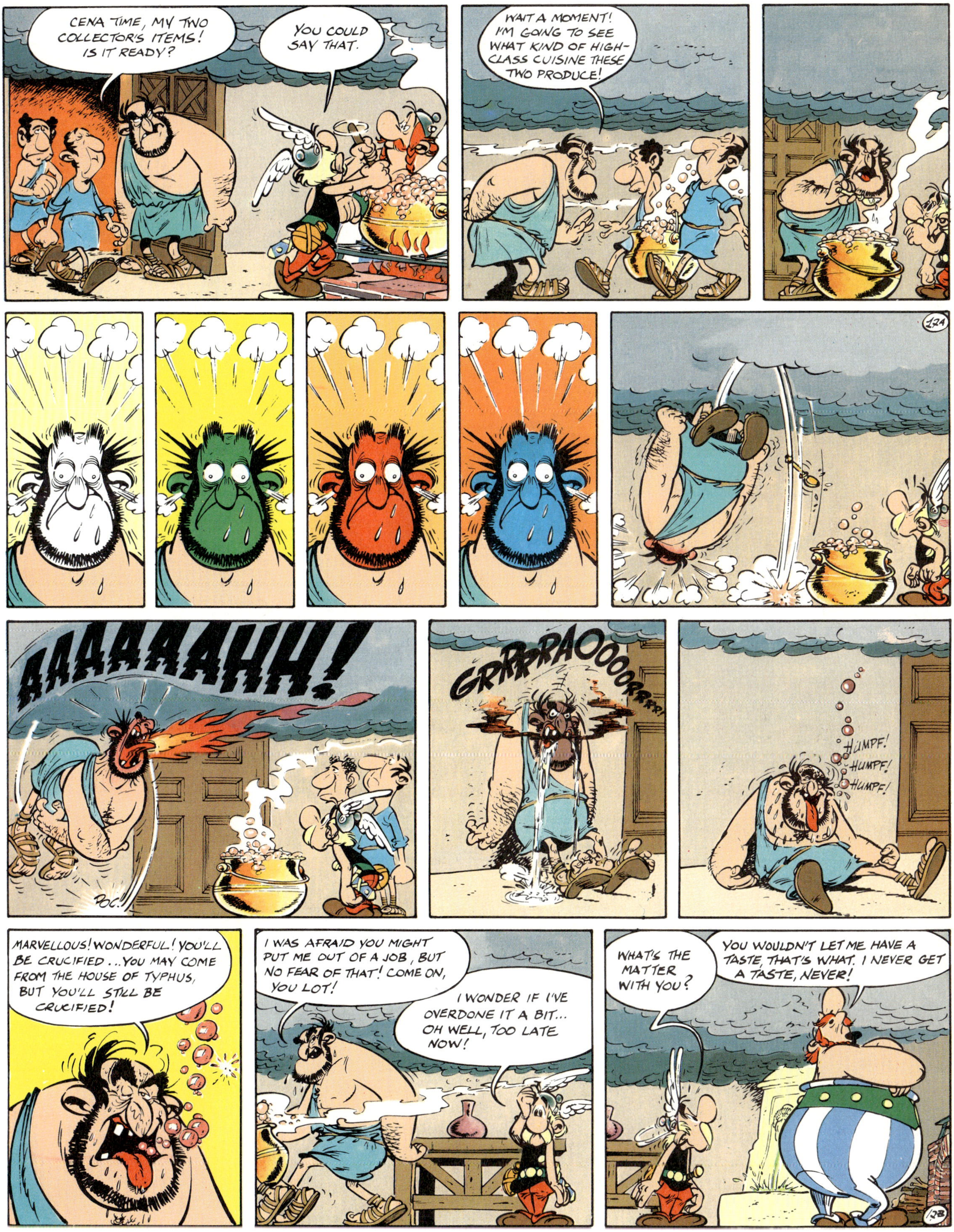
CENA TIME, MY TWO COLLECTOR'S ITEMS! IS IT READY?
YOU COULD SAY THAT.
WAIT A MOMENT! I'M GOING TO SEE WHAT KIND OF HIGH-CLASS CUISINE THESE TWO PRODUCE!
AAAAAAHH!
POC!
GRRRRAOOOORRR!
HUMPF! HUMPF! HUMPF!
MARVELLOUS! WONDERFUL! YOU'LL BE CRUCIFIED ... YOU MAY COME FROM THE HOUSE OF TYPHUS, BUT YOU'LL STILL BE CRUCIFIED!
I WAS AFRAID YOU MIGHT PUT ME OUT OF A JOB, BUT NO FEAR OF THAT! COME ON, YOU LOT!
I WONDER IF I'VE OVERDONE IT A BIT... OH WELL, TOO LATE NOW!
WHAT'S THE MATTER WITH YOU?
YOU WOULDN'T LET ME HAVE A TASTE, THAT'S WHAT. I NEVER GET A TASTE, NEVER!

METATARSUS! GET OUT OF YOUR CUBICULUM AND COME INTO THE TRICLINIUM! CENA IS SERVED!
LOOK, I'LL DO ANYTHING, ANYTHING, ONLY DON'T SHOUT LIKE THAT... I'D FEEL BETTER FLAT ON MY CUBILE, BUT IF...
THE FACT THAT YOU HAVE MANAGED TO DECUBILATE YOURSELF GIVES YOU NO RIGHT TO BEHAVE BADLY. LIE DOWN TO THE TABLE PROPERLY.
IT DOES SMELL FUNNY...
NOT FOR ME, THANKS.
THIS MEAL WAS COOKED BY MY TWO GAULS FROM THE HOUSE OF TYPHUS! YOU'LL EAT IT AND LIKE IT!!!
GLOP!
etc...
TEEHEE HEE!
SCRUNCH! SCRUNCH!
WHERE ARE THEY? WHERE ARE THEY?
OBELIX, I RATHER THINK THE MOMENT HAS COME TO SELL OUR LIVES DEARLY!
DIDN'T WE SELL THEM BEFORE?

?
COME TO MY ARMS!
!?
YOUR MIRACULOUS DISH HAS CURED ME LIKE A SHOT!
THANKS TO YOU TWO, I'LL BE ABLE TO SPEND THE NIGHT DRINKING AND MAKING MERRY WITH MY FRIENDS, HAPPY IN THE KNOWLEDGE THAT NEXT DAY YOU WILL COOK UP THIS EXCELLENT CONCOCTION TO MAKE A NEW MAN OF ME!
COME ON! COME ON! THE FAMILY WANTS TO CONGRATULATE YOU!
HEY, PATER, PATER! WE DON'T OFTEN SEE OCULUS TO OCULUS, BUT YOU REALLY WERE INSPIRED WHEN YOU BOUGHT THESE TWO THEY'RE MARVELS!
WHAT A WONDERFUL RECIPE!
GLAD YOU LIKED IT, MY BOY... YES, EXCELLENT, BUT IT IS A BIT STRONG... WE WON'T ASK THE GAULS TO DO ANY MORE COOKING EXCEPT ON SPECIAL OCCASIONS. AND NOW LET'S GO TO BED...
I DON'T UNDERSTAND... HOW CAN THEY HAVE LIKED IT?
YOUR'E RIGHT...
IT WAS A BIT INSIPID.
?!

YOU MAY HAVE GOT AWAY UNCRUCIFIED, BUT I'LL HAVE YOU THROWN TO THE LIONS YET... THEY DON'T OFTEN TASTE CHOICE TITBITS FROM THE HOUSE OF TYPHUS, POOR THINGS!
MEANWHILE, SLEEP TIGHT, MY WORKS OF ART! WE RISE AT DAWN IN THIS HOUSE, AND I SHALL KEEP YOUR NOSES TO THE GRINDSTONE!
ASTERIX, DO YOU THINK WE'LL END UP AS CHOICE TITBITS FED TO THE LIONS?
I DON'T KNOW ABOUT THAT, OBELIX, BUT I HAVE AN IDEA THAT WILL MAKE THE ROMANS FED UP WITH US!
WE'LL KEEP THEM AWAKE ALL NIGHT... AND SINCE THE ROMANS RISE AT DAWN, THEY WON'T LIKE THAT.
WE'LL BE SOLD BACK FIRST THING TOMORROW.
IT'S TIME!
HGMFFF– FKHGPFFF!
WE NEED SOMETHING TO MAKE A LOUD NOISE. LET'S TRY THE KITCHEN.
COULDN'T WE MAKE A LOUD NOISE BY SNORING?
BLOING! CLANG!
BLOMMM!
BLOING!
CLANG!

CLANG! BLOIMM! CLANG! BLOIMM! CLANG!
WHAT'S GOING ON?
THE BARBARIANS! IT'S THE FALL OF THE ROMAN EMPIRE!
BLOIMM! CLANG! BLOIMM! CLANG! CLANG!
WHAT ARE YOU DOING, BY JUPITER?
WE JUST CAN'T HELP IT, WE GAULS, IT'S IN OUR BLOOD! WE HAVE TO MAKE MERRY AT NIGHT!
MASTER, WOULD YOU LIKE ME TO HAVE THEM WHIPPED?
WHIP SLAVES FROM THE HOUSE OF TYPHUS? DO YOU THINK GAULS GROW ON TREES?
CLANG! BLOIMM!
WHAT'S ALL THIS? EVERYONE AWAKE?
IS THIS THE SORT OF HOUR YOU CHOOSE TO COME HOME, YOU DISSOLUTE BOY?
JUST IN TIME, TOO! I SEE YOU'RE HAVING SOME FUN IN THIS DOMUS FOR ONCE!
OH YES! LET'S HAVE FUN, LIKE THE GAULS!
I'M GOING TO FIND MY FRIENDS! THEY CAN'T HAVE GOT FAR, NOT IN THE STATE THEY'RE IN!
BUT...
OH YES, OSSEUS DARLING! LET'S HAVE A SURPRISE ORGY, LIKE WHEN WE WERE YOUNG!
CLANG! CLANG! CL...
?!?
GOLDENDELICIUS! LIGHT THE LAMPS! FETCH SOME WINE! SEND FOR MUSICIANS AND BRING ON THE DANCING-GIRLS!
SOON AFTERWARDS...
BLING! HAHAHA HIHIHI!
I SAY, ASTERIX, DO YOU THINK WE COULD RESELL THESE ROMANS?

THE SUN RISES UPON A HOUSE WHICH HAS FINALLY FALLEN SILENT...
COME ON, YOU LOT! BRING OUT YOUR MAPPAE AND SCOPAE! *
* FLOORCLOTHS AND BROOMS
CLEAN THE PLACE UP! I'M GOING TO WAKE THE MASTER.
22A
MASTER, THE SUN IS ALREADY HIGH IN THE SKY. AM I TO SEND FOR THE TONSOR TO SHAVE YOU?
NO! AND TELL ALL THOSE OTHER IDIOTS THAT IF THEY GO ON MAKING THAT NOISE I'LL SELL THEM OFF AS A JOB LOT, WITH YOU AND THE TONSOR THROWN IN!
OOOOH! MY HEAD...
ER... MASTER... MAY I REMIND YOU THAT YOU HAVE AN IMPORTANT ENGAGEMENT AT THE PALACE THIS MORNING? AM I TO GO AND SAY YOU'RE ILL?
HMM? NO... I'LL SEND MY GAULS FROM THE HOUSE OF TYPHUS, THAT WILL LOOK MORE ELEGANT. NOW LEAVE ME ALONE. I FEEL A BIT EX COLORE. CLEAR OFF!
22B
OH, SO THEY'VE SUPPLANTED ME! SO THEY'RE GOING TO THE PALACE INSTEAD, EH? RIGHT! I HAVE AN IDEA!...

THERE'S ONLY ONE WAY OUT OF THIS: WE'LL HAVE TO BUY OURSELVES BACK FROM HUMERUS. THEN WE'LL THINK OF A PLAN TO GET INTO CAESAR'S PALACE. GIVE ME ALL THE MONEY YOU'VE GOT.
THERE YOU ARE... DO YOU THINK THAT WILL BE ENOUGH?
WE ARE FROM THE HOUSE OF TYPHUS AFTER ALL... PERHAPS WE'RE BEYOND OUR MEANS.
WE'LL BEAT HIM DOWN.
HEY, YOU GAULS! THE MASTER WANTS TO SEE YOU IN HIS TABLINIUM.*
HE'S TIMED THAT WELL!
* STUDY
AH, MY DEAR GAULS... WE REALLY DID HAVE A GOOD TIME WITH YOU LAST NIGHT...
... BUT I'M FEELING A LITTLE TIRED TODAY. I'VE GOT AN IMPORTANT APPOINTMENT. WILL YOU GO TO THE PALACE FOR ME AND TELL THEM I'M INDISPOSED...
TO JULIUS CAESAR'S PALACE?
YES. ASK FOR LOCUS CLASSICUS, ONE OF CAESAR'S SECRETARIES.
WAIT A MOMENT. WE WERE GOING TO BEAT YOU DOWN...
NO, NO, NO!
AND HURRY BACK, SO WE CAN TRY YOUR FANTASTIC RECIPE AGAIN!
WHAT A STROKE OF LUCK, BY TOUTATIS!
WHAT A STROKE OF LUCK, BY MERCURY!

NOW WHAT'S HAVE WE GIVEN UP THE IDEA OF BUYING OURSELVES BACK?
WE DON'T NEED TO! WE'VE GOT A GOOD EXCUSE TO GET INTO CAESAR'S PALACE NOW!
ONCE INSIDE, WE'LL FIND A WAY TO GATHER CAESAR'S LAURELS!
WHAT A PITY! I SHOULD HAVE LIKED TO BUY US... WE WOULD HAVE MADE A NICE SOUVENIR TO TAKE HOME FROM OUR TRIP.
HALT! QUO VADIS?
WE HAVE COME ON BEHALF OF OUR MASTER, OSSEOUS HUMERUS, WITH A MESSAGE FOR...
...FOR LOCUS CLASSICUS, CAESAR'S SECRETARY. COME IN, COME IN! YOU'RE EXPECTED.
TEEHEEHEE-HEE!
?
HE LET US VADERE QUO WE WANTED TO GO VERY READILY... THIS IS EASY!
TOO EASY... HOW DOES HE KNOW WE'RE EXPECTED?
HOLD IT THERE, GAULS!!
?!?

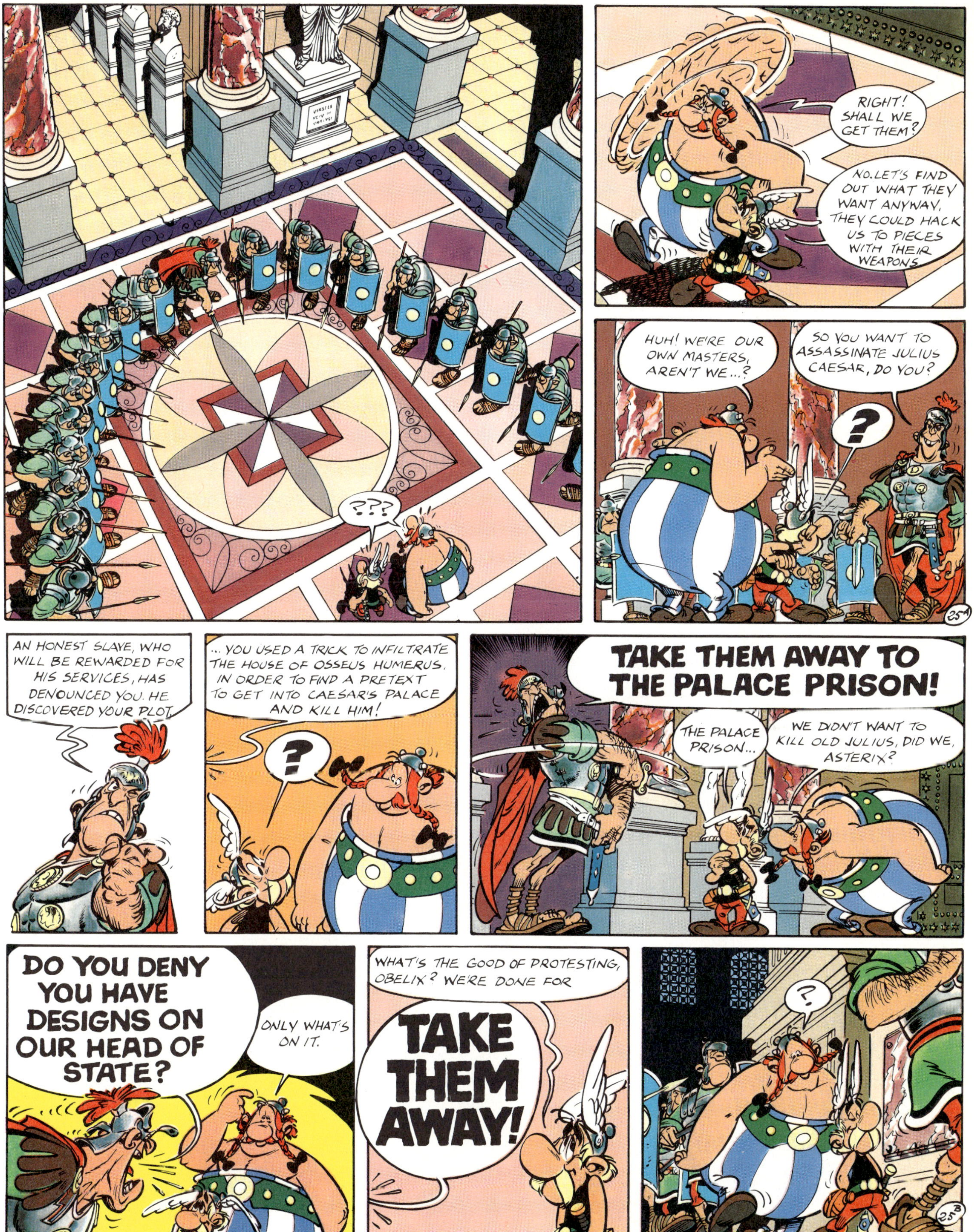
VIRTUS VCIV ET CAVIVS
???
RIGHT! SHALL WE GET THEM?
NO. LET'S FIND OUT WHAT THEY WANT ANYWAY. THEY COULD HACK US TO PIECES WITH THEIR WEAPONS.
HUH! WE'RE OUR OWN MASTERS, AREN'T WE...?
SO YOU WANT TO ASSASSINATE JULIUS CAESAR, DO YOU?
?
AN HONEST SLAVE, WHO WILL BE REWARDED FOR HIS SERVICES, HAS DENOUNCED YOU. HE DISCOVERED YOUR PLOT.
... YOU USED A TRICK TO INFILTRATE THE HOUSE OF OSSEUS HUMERUS, IN ORDER TO FIND A PRETEXT TO GET INTO CAESAR'S PALACE AND KILL HIM!
?
TAKE THEM AWAY TO THE PALACE PRISON!
THE PALACE PRISON...
WE DIDN'T WANT TO KILL OLD JULIUS, DID WE, ASTERIX?
DO YOU DENY YOU HAVE DESIGNS ON OUR HEAD OF STATE?
ONLY WHAT'S ON IT.
WHAT'S THE GOOD OF PROTESTING, OBELIX? WE'RE DONE FOR
TAKE THEM AWAY!
?

?
IN YOU GO!
I DON'T UNDERSTAND, ASTERIX! WHY ARE WE LETTING THEM TREAT US LIKE THIS? THEY'RE ONLY ROMANS, AFTER ALL!
VLAN!
BUT THIS IS WONDERFUL, OBELIX! WE'RE IN THE PALACE! TONIGHT WE CAN GET OUT OF OUR CELL AND LOOK AROUND FOR CAESAR'S LAUREL WREATH AT OUR LEISURE!
WHAT! WE DON'T GET ANY SLEEP TONIGHT EITHER?
VERITAS ODIUM PARIT
NO SEDITIOUS GRAFFITI
GLORIA VICTIS
DEATH TO THE LIONS
AND SO, THAT NIGHT...
OPEN THE DOOR AS QUIETLY AS POSSIBLE.
?
CLONG!
CLANG!
BIFF!
THEY MAKE MORE NOISE COMING DOWN THAN GOING UP
LET'S GO!

WE'LL SEARCH EVERYWHERE, AS QUIETLY AS POSSIBLE.
PIF! POF!
PIF! POF!
PIF! POF!
PIF! POF!
PIF! POF!
PIF! POF!
THIS GUARD'S A BIG ONE!
STILL NO SIGN OF IT. THE PALACE IS ENORMOUS, AND A LAUREL WREATH ISN'T VERY BIG.
I'LL JUST DUMP THESE HERE... WE SEEM TO BE GETTING ON TOP OF ONE ANOTHER. THEN WE CAN GO ON.
NO, NO. IT'S NEARLY DAYLIGHT. LET'S GET BACK TO OUR CELL. WE'LL CARRY ON TOMORROW NIGHT.
WHEN ARE WE GOING TO GET SOME SLEEP? THEY WON'T LET US LIE IN, I BET!

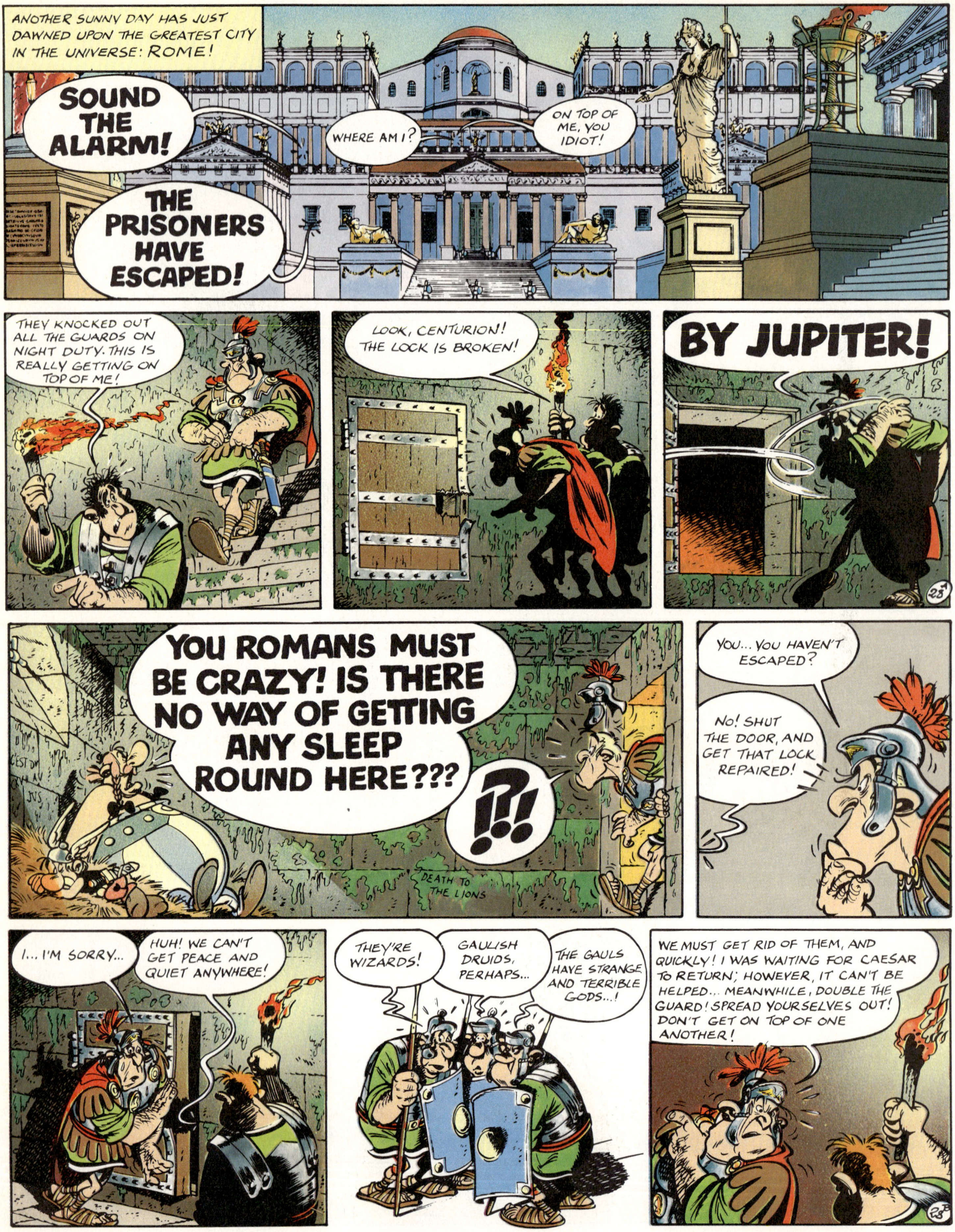
ANOTHER SUNNY DAY HAS JUST DAWNED UPON THE GREATEST CITY IN THE UNIVERSE: ROME!
SOUND THE ALARM!
THE PRISONERS HAVE ESCAPED!
WHERE AM I?
ON TOP OF ME, YOU IDIOT!
THEY KNOCKED OUT ALL THE GUARDS ON NIGHT DUTY. THIS IS REALLY GETTING ON TOP OF ME!
LOOK, CENTURION! THE LOCK IS BROKEN!
BY JUPITER!
YOU ROMANS MUST BE CRAZY! IS THERE NO WAY OF GETTING ANY SLEEP ROUND HERE???
!?!
DEATH TO THE LIONS
YOU... YOU HAVEN'T ESCAPED?
NO! SHUT THE DOOR, AND GET THAT LOCK REPAIRED!
I... I'M SORRY...
HUH! WE CAN'T GET PEACE AND QUIET ANYWHERE!
THEY'RE WIZARDS!
GAULISH DRUIDS, PERHAPS...
THE GAULS HAVE STRANGE AND TERRIBLE GODS...!
WE MUST GET RID OF THEM, AND QUICKLY! I WAS WAITING FOR CAESAR TO RETURN; HOWEVER, IT CAN'T BE HELPED... MEANWHILE, DOUBLE THE GUARD! SPREAD YOURSELVES OUT! DON'T GET ON TOP OF ONE ANOTHER!

I DON'T LIKE BIG TOWNS; I NEVER SLEEP WELL THERE. I FEEL HEMMED IN... SHUT UP...
WHAT WE MUST DO IS FIND CAESAR... HE'S GENERALLY TO BE FOUND JUST UNDERNEATH HIS LAUREL WREATH.
VERITAS ODIUM PARIT
DEATH TO THE LIONS
AH! SO THESE ARE MY CLIENTS!
YOUR CLIENTS?
YES, I'M YOUR LAWYER, TITUS NISIPRIUS.
YOU ARE GOING TO BE TRIED THIS VERY DAY, AND I'VE BEEN ASSIGNED TO YOU AS LEGAL AID. IT'S A GOOD BRIEF FOR ME. TWO GAULISH WIZARDS— THAT'LL ATTRACT A LARGE CROWD!
I HAVE A VERY FINE SPEECH PREPARED. IT BEGINS LIKE THIS: DELENDA CARTHAGO, SAID THE GREAT CATO...
ARE YOU GOING TO GET US SET FREE?
YOU MUST BE JOKING! LOTS OF WILD ANIMALS HAVE ARRIVED IN THE CIRCUS, AND THEY'VE HAD NOTHING SUBSTANTIAL TO GET THEIR TEETH INTO... SO YOU SEE, TWO GAULISH WIZARDS, JUST THINK! WHAT A SHOW!
DOES JULIUS CAESAR GO TO THESE SHOWS?
USUALLY, YES... DELENDA CARTHAGO, I SHALL SAY TO THEM...
AND WHEN HE GOES TO THE CIRCUS, DOES HE WEAR HIS LAUREL WREATH?
I'VE NEVER SEEN HIM IN A STRAW HAT, MY FRIEND... WHY DON'T YOU LISTEN TO MY PLEA FOR THE DEFENCE? DELENDA CARTHAGO, SAID THE GREAT CATO...
?
BONG! BONG!
BRING THE GAULISH WIZARDS BEFORE THE COURT!

THE DELATOR* WILL SPEAK FIRST.
* COUNSEL FOR THE PROSECUTION
DON'T WORRY.
DELENDA CARTHAGO, AS THE GREAT CATO SAID...
WH...WHAT THE...? DELENDA CARTHAGO? BUT I WAS GOING TO...
SILENCE! YOUR TURN WILL COME; YOU CAN SPEAK AFTERWARDS.
BANG!
MAY I NOW CONTINUE?

YOU MAY SPEAK, DELATOR.
SO IT IS CATO YOU HEAR, SPEAKING THROUGH ME... DELENDA CARTHAGO, AS I WAS SAYING, AND...
I WOULD REQUEST AN ADJOURNMENT IN ORDER TO RECONSIDER MY DEFENCE.
RHUBARBRHUBARBRHUBARBRHUBARBRHUBARBRHUBARBRHUBARBRHUBARBRHUBARBRHUBARBRHUB
SILENCE IN COURT! DELATOR, HAVE YOU ANY OBJECTIONS TO THE DEFENCE COUNSEL'S REQUEST?
NONE WHATSOEVER.
BANG! BANG! BANG!
32A
WELL, I HAVE BY TOUTATIS!
RHUBARBRHUBARBRHUBARBRHUBARBRHUBAR
BANG! BANG! BANG! BANG!
SILENCE! SILENCE, OR I'LL HAVE THE COURT CLEARED!
AND WHAT ABOUT THE WILD ANIMALS? THE POOR THINGS MUST BE FED. UNHAPPY CREATURES, THEY KNOW NOTHING OF THE COURSE OF HUMAN JUSTICE...!
WILL YOU ALLOW THIS? YOU SEE BEFORE YOU TWO FOREIGNERS OF DOUBTFUL REPUTATION...
... WHO HAVE ABUSED THE GOOD FAITH OF AN HONEST AND REPUTABLE SLAVE DEALER...!
32B

TWO FOREIGNERS WHO HAVE DECEITFULLY INFILTRATED A FAMILY HIGHLY RESPECTED IN THE CITY, WITH THE SOLE AIM OF FINDING A PRETEXT FOR A COWARDLY ATTEMPT ON THE LIFE OF THE ILLUSTRIOUS PERSON OF JULIUS CAESAR...
... AND YOU WASTE YOUR TIME IN FUTILE ARGUMENTS? IN ENDLESS SPEECHES?
I SAY NOOOO! JUDGES, I SAY NO! THROW THEM TO THE LIONS! TO THE LIONS, I SAY!
AND MAY CAESAR HIMSELF, WEARING THE LAUREL WREATH HE SO RICHLY DESERVES, WITNESS THE FEASTING OF THESE HARMLESS ANIMALS...
... WHOSE FANGS WILL THUS BECOME THE MIGHTY SWORD OF IMPERIAL JUSTICE... THAT IS THE CASE FOR THE PROSECUTION.
SNIFF! SNIFF! SNIFF! SNIFF! SNIFF! SNIFF! SNIFF! SNIFF! SNIFF! SNIFF!
SNIF!
I-I FIND THE ACCUSED GUILTY. I SENTENCE THEM TO BE THROWN TO THE LIONS IN THE CIRCUS MAXIMUS!
BANG!
BRAVO! BRAVO! HEAR, HEAR!
LONG LIVE THE PRISONERS! BRAVO!
BRAVO! HEAR, HEAR!
CLEAR THE COURT! LEGIONARIES, CLEAR THE COURT!
NOT EXACTLY A CLASSIC SUMMING-UP BUT SO MOVING!
THOSE WILD ANIMALS ARE LUCKY! VERY, VERY LUCKY!

ONE OF THE SINISTER CELLS IN THE CIRCUS MAXIMUS...
TYPHUS HAS SENT YOU THIS AMPHORA OF WINE, AND THESE DELICACIES ARE FROM THE HUMERUS FAMILY...
THAT ROAST BOAR WAS GOOD.
THAT'S THE ADVANTAGE OF BEING THROWN TO THE LIONS. YOU ALWAYS GET TASTY GOURMET DISHES...
WHEREAS THOSE THROWN FROM THE TARPEIAN ROCK GET SOLID, HEAVY FOOD.
THERE'S A FANTASTIC LINE-UP ON THE PROGRAMME: LIONS PANTHERS, LEOPARDS, TIGERS! ALL FINE SPECIMENS! THEY'VE EATEN NOTHING BUT LETTUCE FOR A WHOLE WEEK NOW!
SO YOU HAVE NO CAUSE FOR COMPLAINT! YOU REALLY ARE SPOILT!
CLANG!
ASTERIX, I'M SCARED.
SCARED? SCARED OF A FEW WILD ANIMALS?
OH, I'M NOT WORRIED ABOUT THE ANIMALS, IT'S THE PUBLIC! ALL THOSE PEOPLE!
YOU'LL BE ALL RIGHT IN THE ARENA...
I'M SURE THAT ONCE THE SHOW BEGINS OTHER PRISONERS FORGET THEIR STAGE FRIGHT TOO AND THINK OF NOTHING BUT THE ANIMALS.
I'M AFRAID OF LETTING THE... AUDIENCE DOWN... LOOKING SILLY...
EXCUSE ME, YOU WOULDN'T HAVE A DROP OF OIL TO RUB ME DOWN WITH, WOULD YOU - LIKE THE GLADIATORS? IT LOOKS GOOD.
OIL?
DON'T YOU THINK MUSTARD WOULD BE MORE APPROPRIATE.

THE CIRCUS MAXIMUS IS PACKED WITH THE USUAL ENTHUSIASTIC FIRST-NIGHT, OR IN THIS CASE LAST-NIGHT, AUDIENCE.
CREEEEAK!
AAAAAAAAAHHHH!
IT'S YOUR TURN NOW.
AT LAST!
WHAT'S THAT?
IT'S TO MAKE ME TASTE NICE.
YOU'RE A REAL PROFESSIONAL! ONLY THE GREAT ARTISTES THINK OF SMALL DETAILS LIKE THAT!
ARE MY PLAITS ALL RIGHT?
D'YOU KNOW, PEOPLE COME FROM ALL OVER THE PLACE TO BE EATEN HERE, AND THERE'S NEVER BEEN THIS MUCH EXCITEMENT!
WHAT A PITY JULIUS CAESAR ISN'T HERE FOR THIS PERFORMANCE!
WHAT'S THAT?
CREEEEAK!

CREEEAK
I SAID JULIUS CAESAR ISN'T HERE, AND...
WHERE IS HE?
HE'S FIGHTING A CAMPAIGN AGAINST THE PIRATES, I THINK... WELL, ON YOU GO, AND ALL THE BEST!
POF! POF!
IF JULIUS CAESAR ISN'T PRESENT, WE'RE NOT GOING ON! WE'LL WAIT FOR HIM!
WHAT DO YOU MEAN, WAIT FOR HIM?! YOU CAN'T DO THAT!
OH YES. WE CAN!
AND ALL THE BEST TO YOU TOO!
HEY, ARE THEY COMING ON? THE CROWD IS GETTING IMPATIENT, AND WE CAN'T HOLD THE ANIMALS ANY LONGER. ONE OF THE LIONS HAS ALREADY EATEN A PANTHER!
THEY DON'T WANT TO GO ON!
OH, THAT'S NOTHING NEW... WE'RE ALWAYS DEALING WITH BEGINNERS IN THIS JOB.
COME ALONG, NOW! THE AUDIENCE WON'T EAT YOU!
WE'RE NOT GOING ON.
AND THE BEST OF ROMAN LUCK TO YOU TOO!
LET'S FORCE THEM IN, JAILER!
RIGHT, ANIMAL TAMER!
GO ON, ASTERIX!
RIGHT! GO ON, OBELIX!
BIFF!
WILL YOU PICK UP THE WHIP, PLEASE, ASTERIX?
GUAARRARDS!

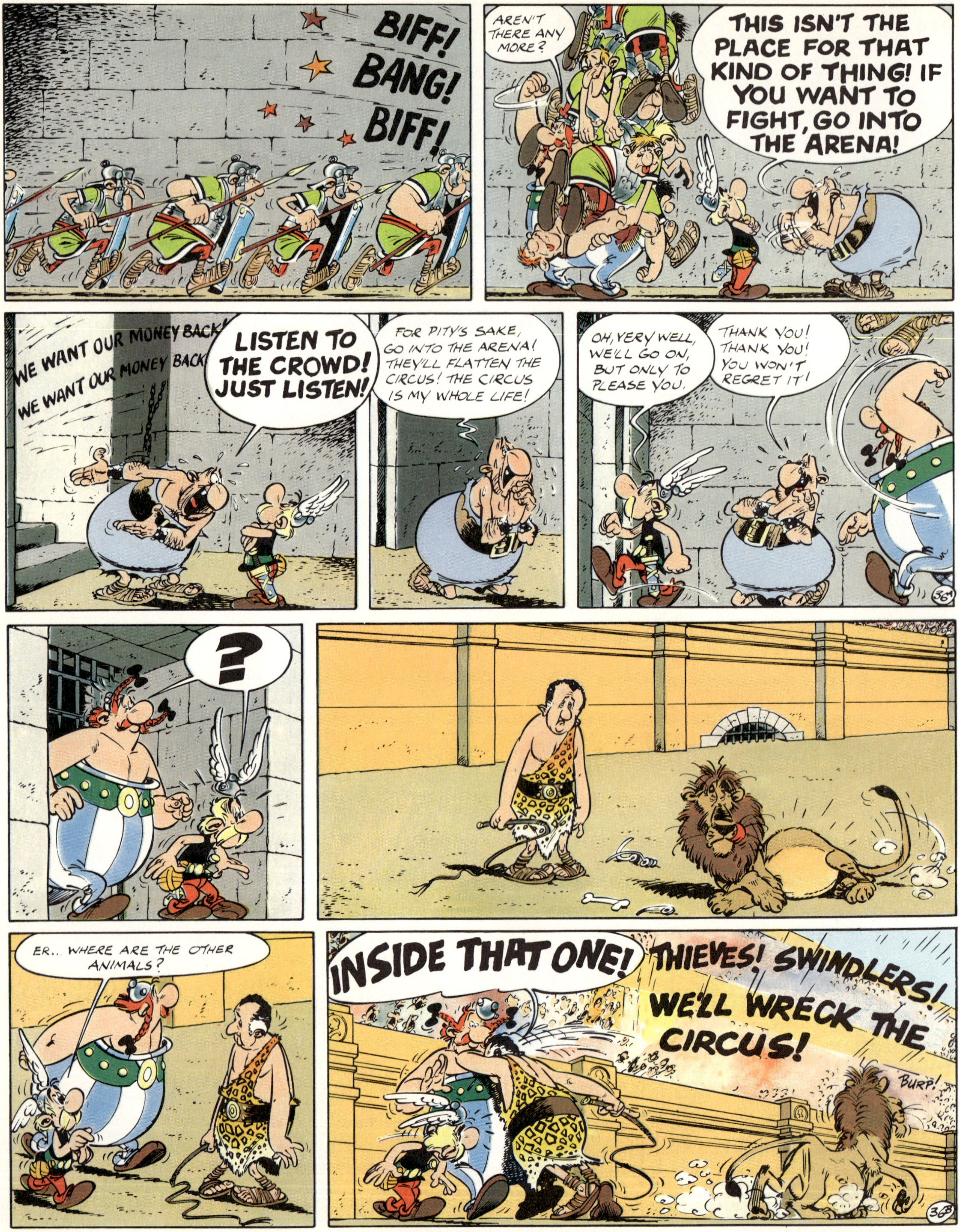
BIFF!
BANG!
BIFF!
AREN'T THERE ANY MORE?
THIS ISN'T THE PLACE FOR THAT KIND OF THING! IF YOU WANT TO FIGHT, GO INTO THE ARENA!
WE WANT OUR MONEY BACK!
WE WANT OUR MONEY BACK!
LISTEN TO THE CROWD! JUST LISTEN!
FOR PITY'S SAKE, GO INTO THE ARENA! THEY'LL FLATTEN THE CIRCUS! THE CIRCUS IS MY WHOLE LIFE!
OH, VERY WELL, WE'LL GO ON, BUT ONLY TO PLEASE YOU.
THANK YOU! THANK YOU! YOU WON'T REGRET IT!
?
ER... WHERE ARE THE OTHER ANIMALS?
INSIDE THAT ONE!
THIEVES! SWINDLERS! WE'LL WRECK THE CIRCUS!
BURP!

GUARDS! GET EVERYBODY OUT!
EVERYBODY OUT! EVERYBODY, BY JUPITER!
OUT! EVERYBODY OUT!
NOT US! HE DOESN'T MEAN US!
OH, SHUT UP, OBELIX!
THAT MIX-UP GAVE US GOOD COVER. WE'VE SEEN ENOUGH OF THIS PERFORMANCE. LET'S FIND A PEACEFUL SPOT TO SLEEP.
WHAT A GOOD IDEA!
WE SHOULD BE ALL RIGHT HERE. TOMORROW WE'LL THINK ABOUT OUR NEXT MOVE.
AT NIGHT THE ROMAN STREETS, INADEQUATELY PATROLLED BY THE SEBACIARIA (NIGHT WATCHMEN) ARE THE HUNTING GROUND OF SICARII, EFFRACTORES AND RAPTORES, MURDERERS, THIEVES AND MUGGERS OF ALL KINDS.
BY ALL THAT'S UNHOLY! HERE ARE TWO FINE FELLOWS SLEEPING OFF THEIR BOOZE! LET'S LIGHTEN THEIR PURSES!
RROOON!
DO YOU ROMANS NEVER SLEEP?!
BIF!

BANG!
BIF!
ER... YOU WOULDN'T BE THOSE TWO GAULS EVERYONE IS LOOKING FOR, WOULD YOU?
YES, THAT'S US. AND WHO ARE YOU?
HABEASCORPUS, CHIEF OF THE MOST FEARSOME BAND OF CUTTHROATS THE URBS HAS EVER KNOWN.
I HEAR YOU ARE MAGICIANS. YOUR STRENGTH SEEMS TO PROVE IT... WE COULD USE YOU.
WHY NOT? WE DON'T HAVE ANYWHERE TO GO.
PUT ME DOWN, THEN, AND FOLLOW ME.
38A
LET'S GET A MOVE ON. IT'S NEARLY DAYBREAK.
HERE'S OUR HIDE-OUT: THE CATACOMBS. IT'S QUITE SAFE. YOU'LL MAKE OLD BONES DOWN HERE.
TOMORROW NIGHT WE'LL LEAVE A SKELETON STAFF HERE, AND YOU CAN TRY YOUR HAND AT SKULDUGGERY...
WE WORK AT NIGHT AND SLEEP BY DAY.
GOOD DAY, THEN!
SO THAT'S HOW IT'S DONE!
38B

AFTER A PEACEFUL DAY, NIGHT HAS FALLEN ONCE MORE ON THE GREATEST CITY IN THE UNIVERSE*, AND SHADOWY FIGURES CREEP ALONG THE NARROW STREETS.
*ROME.
DIDO, DIDO, GIVE ME YOUR ANSWER, DO... HIC!... THERE'S AN OLD MOLA BY THE FLUMEN... HAEC! THE BELLS OF HADES GO TING-A-LING-A-... HOC!!
A DRUNK, FULL OF WINE AND GOLD! I'LL LEAVE HIM TO YOU TO SEE HOW YOU PERFORM.
RIGHT!
COME ALONG, OBELIX!
IF HE MAKES A FUSS... THE CHOP!
WE'RE NOT REALLY GOING TO GIVE HIM THE CHOP, ARE WE, ASTERIX?
OF COURSE NOT! ON THE CONTRARY WE'RE GOING TO SAVE HIM FROM THESE THUGS. WATCH OUT, HERE HE COMES...
LONG LIVE JULIUSH... HIC!
...CHAESHAR!
GO HOME, QUICKLY! YOU'RE IN GREAT DANGER! YOU...
METATARSUS! THE SON OF HUMERUS!
OUR COLLECTOR'S ITEMS! OUR WORKS OF ART FROM THE HOUSE OF TYPHUS!
QUICK! BEAT IT!
NOT ON YOUR LIFE! WE'LL NEVER PART AGAIN! I'LL DRINK TO THAT!
MY COLLECTOR'S ITEMS! MY OWN LITTLE WORKS OF ART! HIC!
WELL, HOW'S IT GOING? HE'LL ATTRACT THE SEBACIARA WITH ALL THAT ROW!
HE'S A FRIEND. NOBODY'S GOING TO HARM HIM!
WE'LL SOON SEE ABOUT THAT!

BANG!
BIF!
LONG LIVE JULIUSH CAESHAR!
SOON AFTERWARDS...
RIGHT, OFF YOU GO HOME, NOW. WHY DID YOU GET YOURSELF INTO SUCH A STATE, ANYWAY?
TO CELEBRATE THE RETURN OF JELIUS SOOS... ER... JULIUS CAESAR!
JULIUS CAESAR?
HE HAS RETURNED VICTORIOUS FROM HIS CAMPAIGN AGAINST THE PIRATES... TOMORROW THERE'S TO BE A TRIUMPH IN THE STREETS OF ROME!
ARE YOU SURE?
SURE I'M SURE! GOLDENDELICIUS TOLD ME. HE'S GOT HIS EAR TO THE GROUND, HAS OLD GOLDENDE... GOLDENDEWHATISINAME.
AFTER HE DENOUNCED YOU, THEY MADE HIM PERSONAL SLAVE TO JULIUS CAESAR AS A REWARD!
AH! AND WHERE IS GOLDENDELICIUS NOW?
HE STAYED ON IN THAT BAR OVER THERE, BUT WATCH OUT, HE'S AB-SO-LUTE-LY BLOTTO!
LET'S GO!
GOOD IDEA! LET'S GO!
NOT YOU! YOU GO HOME!
AT LEAST GIVE ME THE RECIPE OF THAT FANTASTIC DISH! I THINK I MIGHT BE ILL TOMORROW, AND THEN I WOULDN'T BE ABLE TO GO TO CAESAR'S TRIUMPH...
RIGHT. LISTEN CAREFULLY. AN UNPLUCKED CHICKEN, SOME CARBOLIX SOAP, KIDNEYS...
BAR AURIGARUM

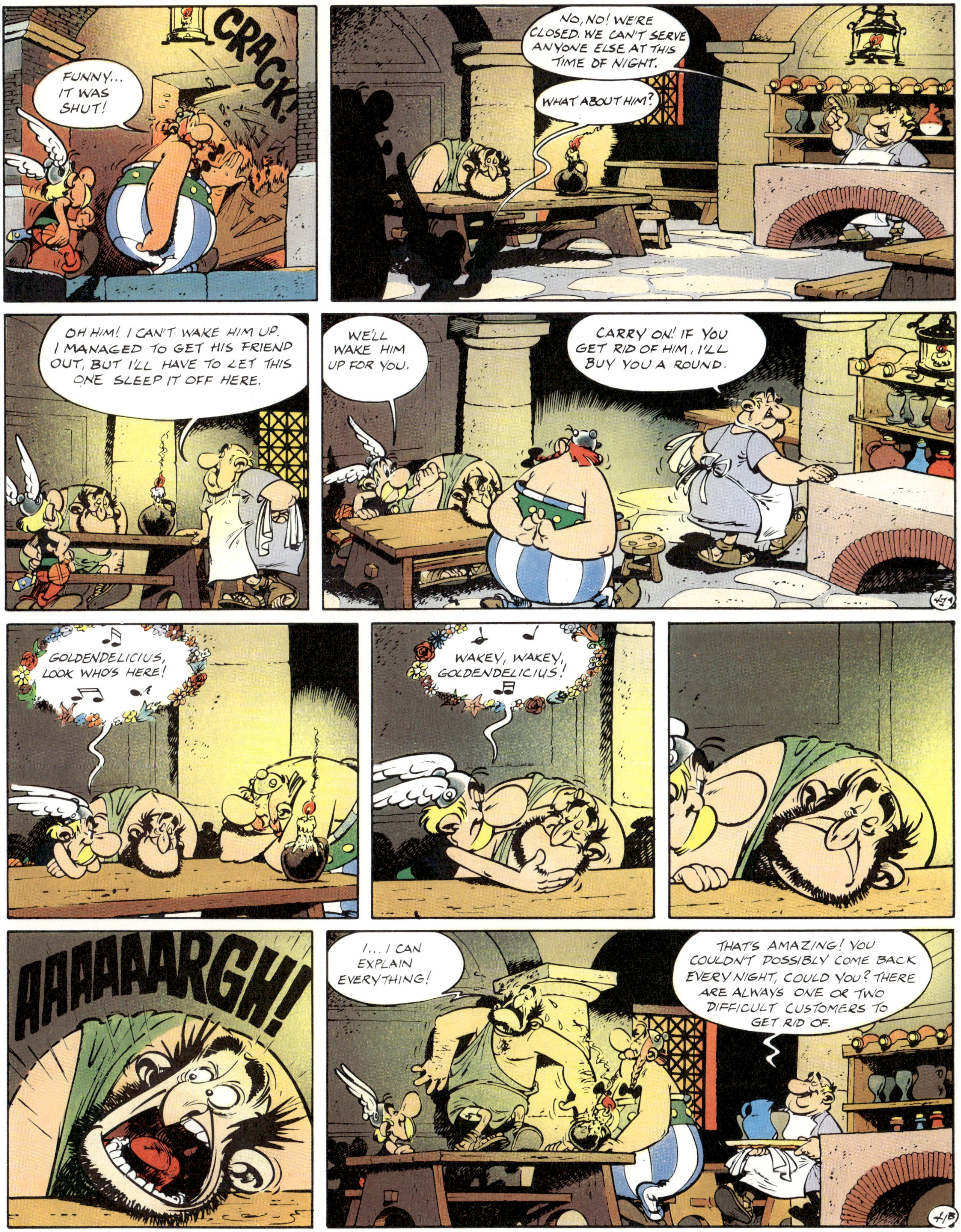

FUNNY... IT WAS SHUT!
CRACK!
NO, NO! WE'RE CLOSED. WE CAN'T SERVE ANYONE ELSE AT THIS TIME OF NIGHT.
WHAT ABOUT HIM?
OH HIM! I CAN'T WAKE HIM UP. I MANAGED TO GET HIS FRIEND OUT, BUT I'LL HAVE TO LET THIS ONE SLEEP IT OFF HERE.
WE'LL WAKE HIM UP FOR YOU.
CARRY ON! IF YOU GET RID OF HIM, I'LL BUY YOU A ROUND.
GOLDENDELICIUS, LOOK WHO'S HERE!
WAKEY, WAKEY, GOLDENDELICIUS!
AAAAARGH!
I... I CAN EXPLAIN EVERYTHING!
THAT'S AMAZING! YOU COULDN'T POSSIBLY COME BACK EVERY NIGHT, COULD YOU? THERE ARE ALWAYS ONE OR TWO DIFFICULT CUSTOMERS TO GET RID OF.

I WAS AFRAID YOU'D TAKE MY PLACE. THAT'S WHY I DENOUNCED YOU, BUT I'M VERY SORRY, YES, I REALLY AM, VERY SORRY! YOU DON'T KNOW HOW SORRY I AM!
I HEAR YOU ARE VERY CLOSE TO CAESAR NOW?
NOT HALF! TOMORROW I SHALL RIDE IN HIS CHARIOT AT HIS TRIUMPH!
IN HIS CHARIOT?
WHENEVER THERE'S A TRIUMPH, ONE SLAVE HAS THE JOB OF HOLDING THE LAUREL WREATH ABOVE CAESAR'S HEAD TOMORROW THAT SLAVE WILL BE ME!
CAESAR'S LAUREL WREATH! THAT'S WONDERFUL, BY TOUTATIS!
YOU'RE TELLING ME! FOR A SLAVE IT'S THE CROWNING GLORY! NOW I'M A COLLECTOR'S ITEM TOO!
LANDLORD, DO YOU HAVE ANY BAY LEAVES?
NO, BUT I'VE GOT SOME PARSLEY.
THAT'LL DO. BRING IT HERE, QUICK!
YOU'RE NOT GOING TO TAKE MY PLACE, ARE YOU?
NO! IT'S THAT LAUREL WREATH WE WANT! WE'LL DO A SWAP!
I'M GOING TO TELL YOU WHAT TO DO TOMORROW... IF YOU WANT TO SEE TOMORROW, THAT IS!
I... I DON'T FEEL TOO GOOD... I'VE HAD A DROP TOO MUCH... NOW I THINK ABOUT IT, I DON'T KNOW THAT I'LL BE ABLE TO MAKE THE TRIUMPH TOMORROW...
LANDLORD! BOIL UP AN UNPLUCKED CHICKEN, SOME CARBOLIX SOAP, JAM, BLACK PEPPERCORNS, SALT, KIDNEYS, FIGS, HONEY, BLACK PUDDING, POMEGRANATE SEEDS, EGGS AND RED PEPPERS!
SHALL I PUT THE PARSLEY IN?
NO! WE'RE GOING TO MAKE WREATHS WITH THAT PARSLEY, AREN'T WE, OBELIX?
FERPECTLY RIGHT!
BANG

AT DAWN, IN A NARROW STREET NEAR CAESAR'S PALACE...
HERE HE COMES!
YOUR POTION IS ABSOLUTELY MARVELLOUS!
TAKE IT- QUICK!
CAESAR'S LAUREL WREATH!
DON'T FORGET THE PARSLEY WREATH!
IT'S A DEAL? I'LL NEVER HEAR FROM YOU AGAIN?
I PROMISE YOU THAT, BY TOUTATIS!
IT IS QUITE A GOOD TRIUMPH, AS TRIUMPHS GO... THE BOOTY ISN'T ANYTHING SPECIAL, BUT THE PRISONERS ARE PICTURESQUE...
TANTANTARA!
PARP!
TWEET TWEET!
SO THAT'S WHAT YOU MEANT WHEN YOU SAID YOU'D LEAD US TO A GREAT TRIUMPH!
...AND THE ACCLAMATIONS ARE SO DEAFENING, AND POPULAR ENTHUSIASM SO GREAT, THAT NO ONE NOTICES THAT CAESAR'S WREATH IS NOT MADE OF LAUREL...
LONG LIVE JULIUS CAESAR!
LONG LIVE CAESAR!
CAESAR!
CAESAR!
NO ONE? WELL, HARDLY ANYONE... FOR NOTHING CAN BE HIDDEN FROM THAT GREAT MAN AMONG GREAT MEN, THAT WOLF, SON OF THE ROMAN SHE-WOLF...
THAT'S FUNNY... I FEEL LIKE A PIECE OF FISH!

WELL, HOMEOPATHIX, HOW DO YOU LIKE THE TASTE OF CAESAR'S LAURELS?
YOU MAY BE RICH, BUT I BET YOU NEVER EAT ANYTHING LIKE THAT IN YOUR HOUSE!
TRUE... IT'S A BIT OVERCOOKED, AND IT WASN'T A PRIME CUT OF MEAT...
BIFF!
AND SO, IN THE GAULISH VILLAGE, UNDER A STARRY SKY, THEY CELEBRATE THE SUCCESS OF THIS EXTRAORDINARY DISH. BUT THE ADVENTURE OF ASTERIX AND OBELIX WAS TO HAVE CONSEQUENCES AS SERIOUS AS THEY WERE UNEXPECTED. FROM NOW ON, HAVING THE RECIPE FOR A REMEDY AGAINST THE EXCESSES OF DRINKING, THE ROMANS BEGAN TO INDULGE IN ORGIES OF WINE, WHICH LED TO THE DECLINE AND FALL OF THEIR EMPIRE. BE WARNED! ALCOHOL, UNLESS TAKEN IN MODERATION, IS THE FATHER OF ALL VICES... FERPECTLY TRUE!
DO YOU SING AS WELL?
THE END
UDERZO & GOSCINNY

ASTERIX IN SWITZERLAND

TEXT BY GOSCINNY

DRAWINGS BY UDERZO

TRANSLATED BY ANTHEA BELL AND DEREK HOCKRIDGE

HODDER DARGAUD
LONDON SYDNEY AUCKLAND

Asterix in Switzerland

Copyright © Dargaud Editeur 1970, Goscinny-Uderzo
English language text copyright © Brockhampton Press Ltd 1973
(now Hodder Children's Books)

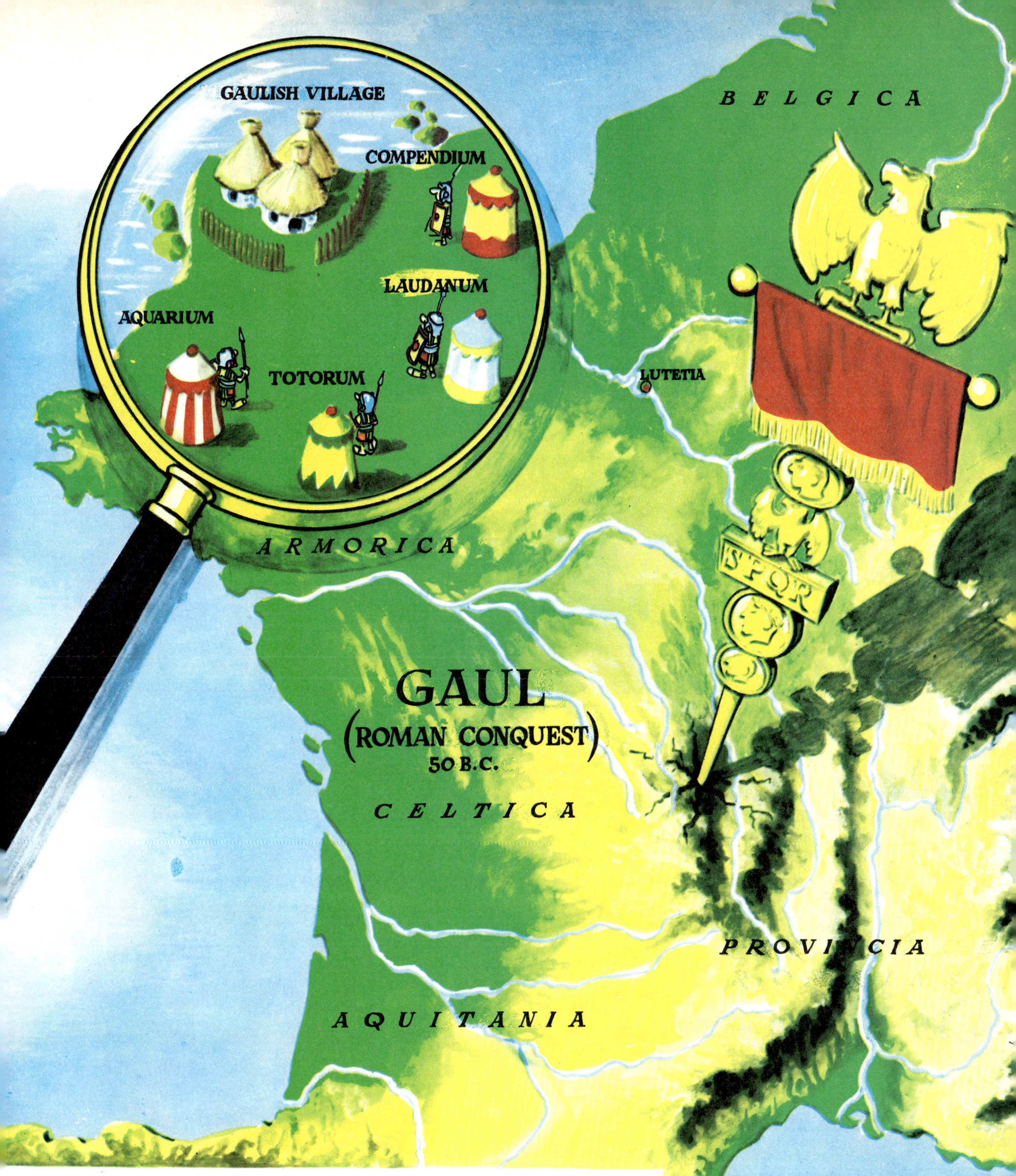

The year is 50 BC. Gaul is entirely occupied by the Romans. Well, not entirely... One small village of indomitable Gauls still holds out against the invaders. And life is not easy for the Roman legionaries who garrison the fortified camps of Totorum, Aquarium, Laudanum and Compendium...

a few of the Gauls

Asterix, the hero of these adventures. A shrewd, cunning little warrior; all perilous missions are immediately entrusted to him. Asterix gets his superhuman strength from the magic potion brewed by the druid Getafix...

Obelix, Asterix's inseparable friend. A menhir delivery-man by trade; addicted to wild boar. Obelix is always ready to drop everything and go off on a new adventure with Asterix – so long as there's wild boar to eat, and plenty of fighting.

Getafix, the venerable village druid. Gathers mistletoe and brews magic potions. His speciality is the potion which gives the drinker superhuman strength. But Getafix also has other recipes up his sleeve...

Cacofonix, the bard. Opinion is divided as to his musical gifts. Cacofonix thinks he's a genius. Everyone else thinks he's unspeakable. But so long as he doesn't speak, let alone sing, everybody likes him...

Finally, Vitalstatistix, the chief of the tribe. Majestic, brave and hot-tempered, the old warrior is respected by his men and feared by his enemies. Vitalstatistix himself has only one fear; he is afraid the sky may fall on his head tomorrow. But as he always says, 'Tomorrow never comes.'

IENIX
YOU'RE ABSOLUTELY USELESS! THE PAIR OF YOU! I NEVER WANT TO SET EYES ON YOU AGAIN!!!
?
HEY, AREN'T THOSE CHIEF VITALSTATISTIX'S SHIELD-BEARERS?
YES, HE'S GIVEN US THE SACK. HE WAS IN A GOOD MOOD THIS MORNING, TOO; HE EVEN SAID IT WAS A NICE DAY...
SO WE LEANT OVER BACKWARDS TO HAVE A LOOK AT THE SKY...
... AND WHEN WE STRAIGHTENED UP THE CHIEF WASN'T ON HIS SHIELD
HE'S BECOMING QUITE UNBEARABLE. HE'LL LOSE HIS STANDING IN THE TRIBE IF HE THROWS HIS WEIGHT ABOUT LIKE THAT
ASTERIX! OBELIX! I AM GOING TO CONFER AN HONOUR ON YOU. I APPOINT YOU MY SHIELD-BEARERS!
WHAT, US?

BUT, CHIEF VITALSTATISTIX...
NO ARGUING! TO WORK!
TEEHEEHEE! YOU'D DO BETTER IF YOU WERE WALKING ALONG A SLOPE!
IT SHOWS THE CHIEF IS BENT ON GETTING A GOOD ANGLE ON THINGS!
PROVES WHAT YOU CAN DO IF YOU'VE GOT THE INCLINATION!
PUT ME DOWN, BOYS. I HAVE A SUSPICION THAT PEOPLE ARE LAUGHING AT US!
IT WOULD WORK BETTER IF OBELIX CARRIED YOU ON HIS OWN, O CHIEF
ON HIS OWN? IN HIS FULL CAPACITY, A CHIEF MUST BE SERVED BY TWO WARRIORS. I'D FEEL LIKE A HALF-PINT CHIEF IF...
ANYWAY, I'VE GOT SOME MENHIRS TO POLISH
SOON AFTERWARDS...
WHAT ON EARTH IS OBELIX DOING?
HE'S JUST SERVING A HALF-PINT OF MILD AND BITTER
BY TOUTATIS! ARE YOU REFUSING TO SERVE ME? I'M A MILD MAN, BUT THIS MAKES ME FEEL VERY BITTER!

THE GOOD HUMOUR PREVALENT IN THE GAULISH VILLAGE IS CONSPICUOUSLY ABSENT FROM THE PALACE OF VARIUS FLAVUS, THE POWERFUL ROMAN GOVERNOR OF CONDATUM*, THOUGH HIS GUESTS ARE DOING THEIR BEST TO HAVE A GOOD TIME...
* RENNES
BY JUPITER, O SUBLIME FLAVUS, YOUR ORGIES ARE BEAUTIFULLY DECADENT. THEY MAKE US QUITE FORGET HOW FAR WE ARE FROM ROME!
GOOD TASTE, THAT'S THE WHOLE SECRET... I GET THE ROMAN IMPRESARIO FELLINUS TO LAY ON MY ORGIES
BRING ON THE DANCING GIRLS!
ZING!
BOOM!
ZING!
BOOM BOOM!
WINE! MORE WINE!
MASTER... THE PERSON YOU WERE EXPECTING IS IN YOUR ROOMS
COMING... BRING ON THE BOAR'S TRIPE FRIED IN AUROCHS DRIPPING!
YOU REALLY ARE SPOILING US, DIVINE FLAVUS!
HAVE FUN, FRIENDS! I'LL BE BACK IN A MINUTE
HAVEN'T YOU GOT YOUR GREEN BLUSHER? I WANT TO MAKE MYSELF LOOK WORSE
HI! SLAVE! THIS DISH IS CLEAN! IT'S DISGRACEFUL!
THAT'S RIGHT! WHY NOT FINGER-BOWLS, WHILE YOU'RE ABOUT IT?

AVE, CAIUS EUCALYPTUS! ARE THE TAKINGS GOOD?
VERY GOOD, O VARIUS FLAVUS! HERE'S THE GOLD FROM THE TAXES, FINES, CHARIOT PARKING METERS, ROMAN ROAD TAX, AND LICENCES TO LISTEN TO THE TOWN CRIERS!
EXCELLENT! NOW TO SHARE IT OUT...
THAT'S FOR YOU...
THAT'S FOR ME...
... AND THAT'S FOR ROME
DON'T YOU THINK YOU MAY BE GOING A BIT FAR? SOONER OR LATER ROME'S GOING TO REALISE HOW LITTLE MONEY COMES FROM THIS PROVINCE
CLINK! CLONK! CLANK!
SPQR
MY APPOINTMENT HERE IS FOR A YEAR! I HAVE ONE YEAR TO GET RICH! I'LL BE FAR AWAY BY THE TIME ROME CAN ACT! FAR AWAY AND RICH!
MY LIFE WILL BE ONE LONG ORGY!
YES, BUT WHAT IF ROME SENDS OUT AN INSPECTOR — A QUAESTOR?
BY JUNO, I'LL KNOW HOW TO DEAL WITH HIM! EITHER I'LL MAKE HIM DECADENT, AND FAST, OR I'LL GET RID OF HIM!
THAT'S ENOUGH WORK FOR ONE DAY! COME ON! DO YOU LIKE BOAR'S TRIPE FRIED IN AUROCHS DRIPPING?
WITH HONEY?

HIC!
GET YOUR HEAD OUT OF THAT AMPHORA!
I... GLUG GLUG ... CAN'T...
SHUT THAT WINDOW! YOU'RE LETTING IN THE FRESH AIR!
NO ADMITTANCE!
DON'T TALK SUCH RUBBISH. ANNOUNCE ME TO YOUR MASTER
ZING! BOOM! ZING!
QUAEST... QUAESTOR VEXATIUS SINUSITUS!
WH... WHAT A DELIGHTFUL SURPRISE!
AVE, AVE, QUAESTOR! YOU FIND US RIGHT IN THE MIDDLE OF A FAMILY REUNION... A LITTLE PARTY OF CLOSE FRIENDS... COME AND JOIN US
AVE, GOVERNOR. JULIUS CAESAR HAS SENT ME FROM ROME AS TREASURER FOR THE PROVINCES. I'M HERE TO AUDIT YOUR ACCOUNTS, NOT TO TAKE PART IN ORGIES. TELL THESE PEOPLE TO GO AWAY
OF COURSE, OF COURSE... NOW THEN, FRIENDS, THOSE OF YOU WHO CAN STILL WALK TAKE THE REST AWAY!
AND OPEN THE WINDOWS, BY THE GODS!
WHERE ARE WE GOING?
SOMEWHERE ELSE, TO CARRY ON WITH THE PARTY

IT'S LATE, AND YOU MUST BE TIRED. WE CAN START WORK TOMORROW... WOULDN'T YOU LIKE JUST A BITE TO EAT? I THINK WE STILL HAVE SOME BOAR'S TRIPE FRIED IN...
YES, I AM TIRED. IT WAS A LONG JOURNEY, AND WE WERE EVEN ATTACKED BY PIRATES ON THE CROSSING. LUCKILY THEY STARTED ARGUING WITH EACH OTHER AND SCUTTLED THEIR OWN SHIP
GET YOUR SERVANTS TO TAKE ME TO MY ROOMS AND SEND ME UP SOME VEGETABLE SOUP
CERTAINLY, CERTAINLY... I'LL SEE TO IT MYSELF
SOON AFTERWARDS...
O MASTER, AM I TO SERVE UP THE BEAR BLACK PUDDING AND THE STUFFED GIRAFFES' NECKS NOW?
NO! I WANT YOU TO MAKE A SMALL BOWL OF VEGETABLE SOUP
6A
WHATEVER WILL THEY THINK UP NEXT FOR THEIR ORGIES?
SCRAPE! SCRAPE! SCRAPE!
LATER...
HERE YOU ARE, MASTER. IT'S READY
PUT IT DOWN HERE AND GO AWAY
HEE! HEE! HEE!
CREAK!
EMPTY, BY JUPITER!
THIS ONE'S EMPTY TOO...
CREAK!
AH, AT LAST!... I MUST REMEMBER TO GET REFILLS
6B

HERE'S THE SOUP!
YOU MAKE YOURSELF PRETTY COMFORTABLE HERE... ODD, FOR THE GOVERNOR OF A PROVINCE SO POOR THAT IT CONTRIBUTES ONLY A FEW PIECES OF GOLD TO THE ROMAN TREASURY
GOOD TASTE, THAT'S THE SECRET. IT'S SURPRISING WHAT A LOT YOU CAN DO ON VERY LITTLE...
WELL, WE'LL SEE ABOUT THAT TOMORROW
GOOD NIGHT, QUAESTOR
TEEHEEHEE!
AND THAT NIGHT...
MASTER! MASTER! THE QUAESTOR'S BEEN TAKEN ILL
WHAT, ALREADY?
OOOOH! I FEEL TERRIBLE! I DON'T THINK I'LL LIVE, BY JUPITER!
IT MUST HAVE BEEN THE VEGETABLE SOUP. VERY INDIGESTIBLE. I'LL HAVE THE COOK WHIPPED
LEAVE THE COOK ALONE! SEND FOR DOCTORS INSTEAD!
GOOD IDEA! I'LL CALL IN ALL THE DOCTORS IN THE GARRISON.
AREN'T YOU AFRAID THE DOCTORS MAY SPOIL YOUR PLAN, O VARIUS FLAVUS?
I KNOW THE DOCTORS IN THIS GARRISON...
WHEN THEY GET TOGETHER, THEY'RE MORE MURDEROUS THAN A LEGION ARMED TO THE TEETH!

LATER THAT NIGHT...
THE DOCTORS ARE HERE, QUAESTOR...CAN THEY COME IN?
YES... OUCH!*
WHERE'S THE PATIENT?
IS HE THE ONE IN BED?
LEAVE HIM TO ME!
DON'T PUSH!
!
LET'S FEEL HIS PULSE!
HE'S IN CONVULSIONS
MY DEAR COLLEAGUE, I SHOULD SAY, MYSELF, THAT HE HAD PINS AND NEEDLES
YOU MUST BE JOKING, MY DEAR FELLOW! HE'S FEVERISH!
MAY I REMIND YOU THAT I WAS IN CHARGE OF THE VALETUDINARIUM AT VINDONISSA?*
WELL, I STUDIED AT THE FAMOUS MEDICAL SCHOOL IN MASSILIA!
*MILITARY HOSPITAL AT WINDISCH (SWITZERLAND)
CONSIDERING YOUR UGLY MUG, YOU OUGHT TO CONFINE YOUR ATTENTIONS TO STUDENT ORGIES!
MAYBE, BUT THE CASUALTIES IN THE VALETUDINARIUM AT VINDONISSA ARE A LOT HIGHER THAN IN ANY OF CAESAR'S CAMPAIGNS!
84
OOOOOOH!
WE MUST BLEED HIM!
HIS ARTERIES NEED AIR! WE'D BETTER BLOW SOME INTO HIM!
WHERE ARE THE CUCURBITULAE?*
YOU DON'T KNOW A THING! MIX UP SOME GROUND IVORY WITH TORTOISE AND PIGEON BLOOD! IF THE PATIENT LIVES...
*CUPPING-GLASSES
BY AESCULAPIUS, THIS IS RIDICULOUS! A MAN WOULD REALLY HAVE TO BE AT DEATH'S DOOR BEFORE HE'D CONSULT A DOCTOR LIKE YOU!
WANT A SMACK IN THE AMPHORA THEN?
EXCUSE ME!
PEACE AND QUIET, THAT'S WHAT YOU NEED, PEACE AND QUIET!
LET ME SPEAK!
83

I SHOULD LIKE YOU TO SACRIFICE TO APOLLO, THE GOD OF HEALING, ON MY BEHALF...
A SPLENDID IDEA! WE WILL OFFER APOLLO OUR CHOICEST DISHES. THAT'S SURE TO CURE THE PATIENT...
ALL THE SAME, I THINK...
AS IT HAPPENS, MY COOK HAS BEEN MAKING BEAR BLACK PUDDING AND STUFFED GIRAFFES' NECKS... I THINK THERE'S SOME BOAR'S TRIPE FRIED IN AUROCHS DRIPPING LEFT TOO
WITH HONEY?
PLOP!
O QUAESTOR SINUSITUS, DO YOU THINK THE SACRIFICE WILL BE ENOUGH TO CURE YOU?
THAT WAS JUST A PRETEXT TO GET RID OF THOSE IDIOTS. NOW, LISTEN...
IN HIS EPILEPTIC FITS, JULIUS CAESAR OFTEN MENTIONS A LITTLE GAULISH VILLAGE NOT FAR FROM HERE... THERE'S A DRUID IN THIS VILLAGE... I THINK HIS NAME IS GEOMETRIX...
GETAFIX...
THAT'S RIGHT. GO AND LOOK FOR HIM, QUICK! AND DON'T LET ANYONE SEE YOU!
NEVER FEAR, QUAESTOR! THEY'RE FAR TOO BUSY TO STOP ME LEAVING!
SURE ENOUGH...
ALL THE SAME, WE MUSTN'T FORGET TO LEAVE A LITTLE SOMETHING FOR APOLLO
HUH! THERE'LL BE PLENTY TO GO ROUND!
THAT'S RIGHT! WHO DO THESE GODS THINK THEY ARE, WITH THEIR HOLIER-THAN-THOU ATTITUDE?

NEXT MORNING, IN THE VILLAGE...
YOUR MASTER'S ILL? HE NEEDS ME? I'M ON MY WAY!
ASTERIX! OBELIX! WE'RE OFF TO CONDATUM, AT ONCE! DROP EVERYTHING!
I AM ALWAYS BOUND TO HELP SICK PEOPLE, EVEN ROMANS
I DON'T LIKE ROMANS TO BE ILL. IT MAKES THEM SOFTER THAN USUAL
YOU MAY HAVE DIFFICULTY GETTING TO SEE MY MASTER
OBELIX AND I WILL SEE TO THAT. NO ROMAN EVER STOPPED US GETTING ANYWHERE YET!
DELIGHTED TO HEAR IT!
WELL, THAT'S THE FIRST TIME I EVER MET ONE OF YOU WHO WAS!
SOON AFTERWARDS, IN THE PALACE OF GOVERNOR VARIUS FLAVUS...
ZZZZZZZZ
WHEEEEEEE
ZZZZZZZ
SPLOSH!
?
SENTRY! WHY HAVE YOU LEFT YOUR POST? AND WHAT ARE YOU DOING IN MY COLD BOAR'S TRIPE FRIED IN AUROCHS DRIPPING?
I...GLUG!... I CAME TO WARN YOU THAT THREE GAULS HAVE BROKEN INTO THE PALACE. ONE OF THEM'S A DRUID
A DRUID?
HAS ANYONE GOT A SPOT OF HONEY?

SAY LXXXXIX ROMAN...
WHAT ARE YOU DOING HERE GAULS?
I INVITED THEM, SO SHUT UP!
BUT THEY'RE ENEMY ALIENS... BETTER LEAVE IT TO APOLLO! WE OFFERED HIM A BIG SLICE OF BEAR BLACK PUDDING...
DID YOU HEAR, ROMAN? HE TOLD YOU TO SHUT UP!
I'M THE GOVERNOR IN THESE PARTS! I'LL HAVE YOU HOUNDED OUT OF THIS PALACE!
GUARDS!!!
GUARD ROOM
WHAT'SH UP?
I... I THINK IT'SH USH HE WANTSH...
JOIN UP, THEY SHAID... SHEE THE WORLD, THEY SHAID...
A FEW MOMENTS LATER...
WH... WHAT HAPPENED TO YOU?
WELL, WE HAD A LITTLE ORGY IN THE GUARDROOM, AND WE...
TEEHEE HEE!
HIC!
THERE ARE A SIGHT TOO MANY ORGIES IN THIS PALACE!!! THROW THESE GAULS OUT OF HERE!
ALL RIGHT, ALL RIGHT, BUT PLEASE DON'T SHOUT
BIFF! BIMM! BOOM! PLOFFF! SHTONK!
STOP!
MERCY!
STOP! PLEASE STOP!
HMM!
COULD YOU JUST EXAMINE MINE WHEN YOU'VE FINISHED WITH YOURS, GETAFIX? THEY DON'T SEEM AT ALL WELL

YOU'RE ILL... VERY ILL. THE ONLY THING THAT MIGHT SAVE YOU IS A POTION OF WHICH I HAPPEN TO KNOW THE SECRET
MAKE IT, O DRUID! YOU WILL NOT FIND ME UNGRATEFUL
UNFORTUNATELY, AN ESSENTIAL INGREDIENT OF THIS POTION IS THE SILVER STAR *
SILVER STAR?
* EDELWEISS
A SMALL FLOWER WHICH GROWS ONLY ON THE HIGHEST MOUNTAINS... IT'S VERY DIFFICULT TO GET HOLD OF
GOOD, GOOD! I'LL SEND SOME OF MY MEN TO LOOK FOR IT!
BUT THEY'RE NOT WELL!
EXACTLY! THE MOUNTAIN AIR WILL DO THEM GOOD!
WHERE DO YOU HAVE TO GO TO FIND THIS WONDERFUL FLOWER?
HELVETIA, FOR PREFERENCE. THE BEST SPECIMENS FOR MY POTION GROW IN HELVETIA
DRUID, I HAVE COMPLETE CONFIDENCE IN YOU! SEND YOUR MEN IN SEARCH OF THIS SILVER STAR!
BUT WHY BRING FOREIGNERS INTO IT? LET'S KEEP THIS ROMAN!
ASTERIX, OBELIX, WOULD YOU MIND GOING TO HELVETIA?
NOT AT ALL. IT'S SOME TIME SINCE WE TOOK A TRIP ABROAD
AND YOU NEVER KNOW, WE MAY FIND ROMANS IN BETTER SHAPE ON THE MOUNTAINS THERE... I'M REALLY WORRIED ABOUT THE ONES WE HAVE HERE
WILL SOMEONE PLEASE LISTEN TO ME?
I MAKE JUST ONE CONDITION: YOU MUST STAY IN OUR VILLAGE AS A HOSTAGE UNTIL MY FRIENDS RETURN
NO, NO! NEVER!
VERY WELL, DRUID

AND I WARN YOU, IF MY FRIENDS DON'T COME BACK, THE HOSTAGE WILL BE EXECUTED!
WILL HE, THOUGH?
SINCE I HAVE NO ALTERNATIVE, I WILL GIVE ORDERS FOR YOUR DEPARTURE!
BUT WE DON'T USUALLY TAKE HOSTAGES, GETAFIX...
THIS MAN SINUSITUS HAS BEEN POISONED. IF HE STAYS HERE, I WOULDN'T GIVE TWO DENARII FOR HIS CHANCES OF SURVIVING. HE'LL BE SAFE FROM HIS WOULD-BE MURDERERS IN OUR VILLAGE
BUT I CAN'T KEEP HIM ALIVE VERY LONG! YOU MUST LEAVE AT ONCE, AND HURRY! I'LL SAY GOODBYE TO THE OTHERS FOR YOU
LOOK AFTER LITTLE DOGMATIX!
MEANWHILE...
EUCALYPTUS, THERE ARE TWO REASONS WHY I DON'T WANT THOSE GAULS TO COME BACK FROM HELVETIA. FIRST, SO THEY WON'T BRING BACK THE FLOWER TO CURE THE QUAESTOR. SECOND, IF THEY DON'T COME BACK, THE GAULS WILL EXECUTE SINUSITUS!...
13A
SET OUT FOR GENAVA!* YOU WILL GIVE THIS MESSAGE TO GOVERNOR CURIUS ODUS. HE'S AN OLD FRIEND OF MINE. DON'T STOP ON THE WAY; I'LL GET THEM TO GIVE YOU A PACKED ORGY
* GENEVA
AND SO, THAT SAME NIGHT, A CHARIOT LEAVES CONDATUM FOR THE LITTLE GAULISH VILLAGE...
...A MESSENGER LEAVES FOR GENAVA...
... AND A GAULISH WARRIOR, ACCOMPANIED BY A MENHIR DELIVERY-MAN, GOES IN SEARCH OF A LITTLE FLOWER OVER THE HILLS AND FAR AWAY
13B

THE NEW CHARIOTWAYS BUILT BY THE ROMANS ALLOW OUR FRIENDS TO TRAVEL FAST
WHAT DO YOU MEAN, YOU'RE HUNGRY? WE'VE ONLY JUST LEFT!
I ALWAYS FEEL HUNGRY WHEN I'M TRAVELLING!
I'VE GOT AN EMPTY HOLE INSIDE ME, JUST HERE
II MILIA PASSVVM
LOOK, OBELIX! WE CAN STOP TO EAT THERE
SERVITUTES
YES, IT'S VERY NICE. WITH LUCK, YOU'LL SEE SOME ACCIDENTS ON THE CHARIOTWAY WHILE YOU EAT...
MEANWHILE...
I SHOULDN'T HAVE HAD THAT COLD BEAR BLACK PUDDING... IT COULD BE INDIGESTIBLE... ANYWAY, AN ORGY'S NO FUN ON YOUR OWN
14

WHILE GOVERNOR VARIUS FLAVUS'S MESSENGER RIDES DESPERATELY ON, OUR FRIENDS ARE SPENDING THE NIGHT IN A NEW KIND OF INN WHICH HAS A STABLE TO EVERY ROOM ...
CHARIOTEL
... AND IN THE PALACE OF GOVERNOR CURIUS ODUS, IN GENAVA, HELVETIA, AN ORGY IS JUST BEGINNING ...
BRING ON THE CAULDRON OF MELTED CHEESE!
EVERYONE GOT IT? IF YOU LOSE YOUR PIECE OF BREAD IN THE FONDUE, YOU PAY A FORFEIT! THE FIRST TIME IT'S FIVE OF THE BEST WITH A STICK; THE SECOND TIME YOU GET TWENTY LASHES WITH A WHIP; THE THIRD TIME YOU GET THROWN INTO THE LAKE WITH WEIGHTS TIED TO YOUR FEET!
WHAT AMUSING NOTIONS YOU DO HAVE, O DIVINE ODUS!
WE NEED THEM IN THIS STRAIT-LACED COUNTRY. I'VE TRIED HOLDING CIRCUSES, BUT THE WILD BEASTS WERE SO WELL FED THEY WOULDN'T EVEN TAKE A BITE OF THE PRISONERS!
AND AS FOR THEIR MANIA FOR CLEANLINESS!... AN ORGY IS SUPPOSED TO BE DIRTY!... STOP MOPPING THAT FLOOR, BY JUPITER!
OH DEAR! I'VE LOST MY PIECE OF BREAD!
THE STICK! THE STICK!
HERE YOU ARE! HERE YOU ARE!

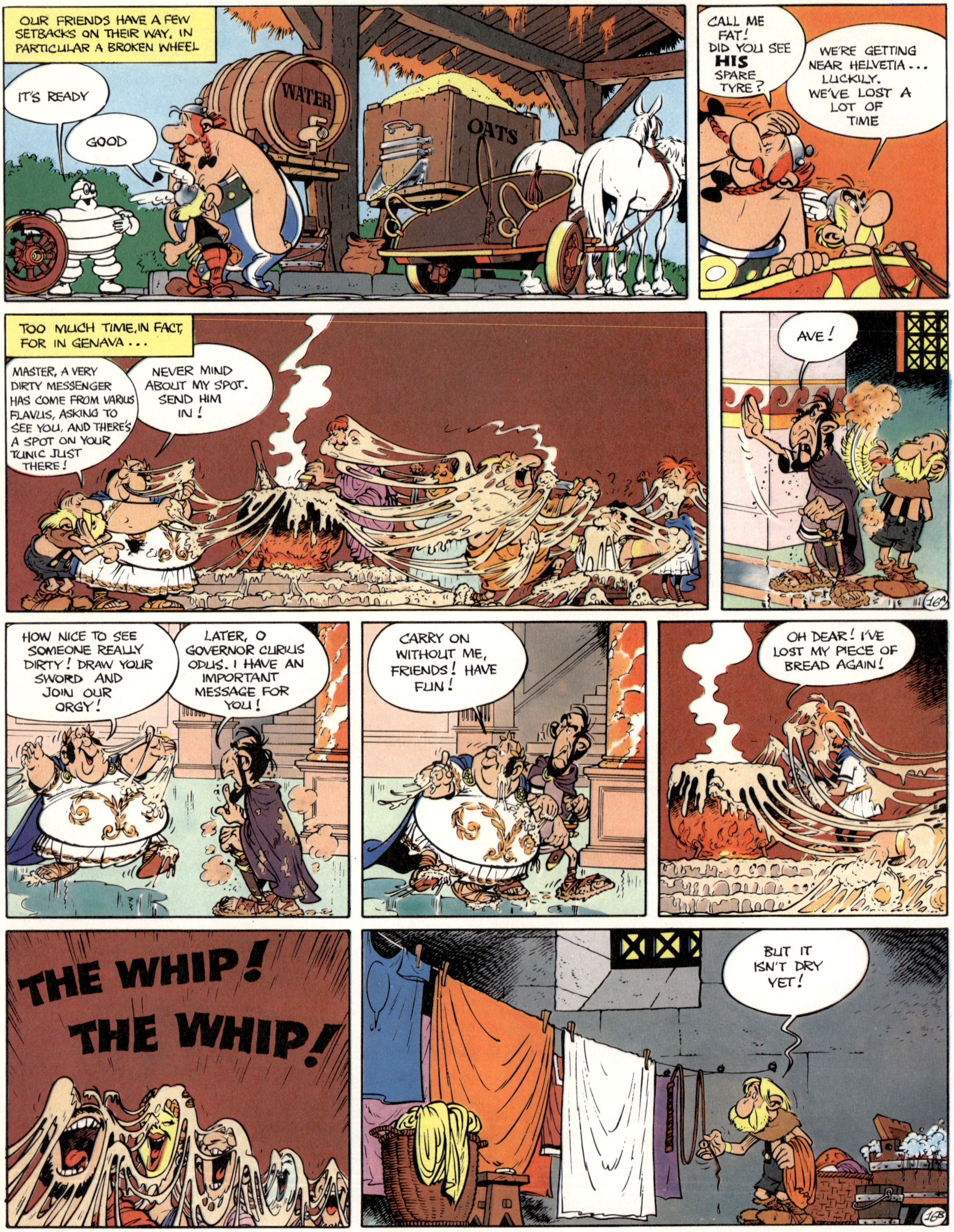

OUR FRIENDS HAVE A FEW SETBACKS ON THEIR WAY. IN PARTICULAR A BROKEN WHEEL
IT'S READY
GOOD
WATER
OATS
CALL ME FAT! DID YOU SEE HIS SPARE TYRE?
WE'RE GETTING NEAR HELVETIA... LUCKILY. WE'VE LOST A LOT OF TIME
TOO MUCH TIME, IN FACT, FOR IN GENAVA...
MASTER, A VERY DIRTY MESSENGER HAS COME FROM VARIUS FLAVUS, ASKING TO SEE YOU, AND THERE'S A SPOT ON YOUR TUNIC JUST THERE!
NEVER MIND ABOUT MY SPOT. SEND HIM IN!
AVE!
HOW NICE TO SEE SOMEONE REALLY DIRTY! DRAW YOUR SWORD AND JOIN OUR ORGY!
LATER, O GOVERNOR CURIUS ODUS. I HAVE AN IMPORTANT MESSAGE FOR YOU!
CARRY ON WITHOUT ME, FRIENDS! HAVE FUN!
OH DEAR! I'VE LOST MY PIECE OF BREAD AGAIN!
THE WHIP! THE WHIP!
BUT IT ISN'T DRY YET!

I CAN REFUSE NOTHING TO THAT OLD FRUIT FLAVUS, AND WHAT'S MORE, DISPOSING OF A QUAESTOR WILL BE A POSITIVE PLEASURE! I'LL GIVE ORDERS TO HAVE THESE GAULS STOPPED AT THE BORDER... NOW LET'S GET BACK TO THE ORGY
OH DEAR! I'VE LOST MY THIRD PIECE OF BREAD!
HARD CHEESE! INTO THE LAKE WITH WEIGHTS TIED TO HIS FEET!
WHAT BARBARIANS!
YES, THE WATER OF THE LAKE IS ALL MUDDY AT THIS TIME OF YEAR!
CURIUS O
MEANWHILE...
HERE WE ARE, OBELIX!
GAUL ROMAN EMPIRE
HELVETIA ROMAN EMPIRE TOO
HALT! THIS IS A CHECKPOINT! YOU ARE NOW LEAVING GAUL!
WHAT DO WE DO, ASTERIX?
THESE ARE JUST THE FORMALITIES, OBELIX. WE HAVE TO GO THROUGH THEM
GAUL ROMAN EMPIRE
WHAT IS THE REASON FOR YOUR VISIT TO HELVETIA?
WE'VE COME IN SEARCH OF...
WE'VE COME IN SEARCH OF MOUNTAIN AIR
DECURION! A MESSENGER FROM GOVERNOR CURIUS ODUS. HE WANTS A WORD WITH YOU. IT'S URGENT
NO, NO, ASTERIX, THAT'S NOT WHAT WE'VE COME TO...
SHUT UP, OBELIX!
PSSSPSSSPSSSPSSSPSSS
AHA!
ALL RIGHT, GAULS! YOU CAN PASS!

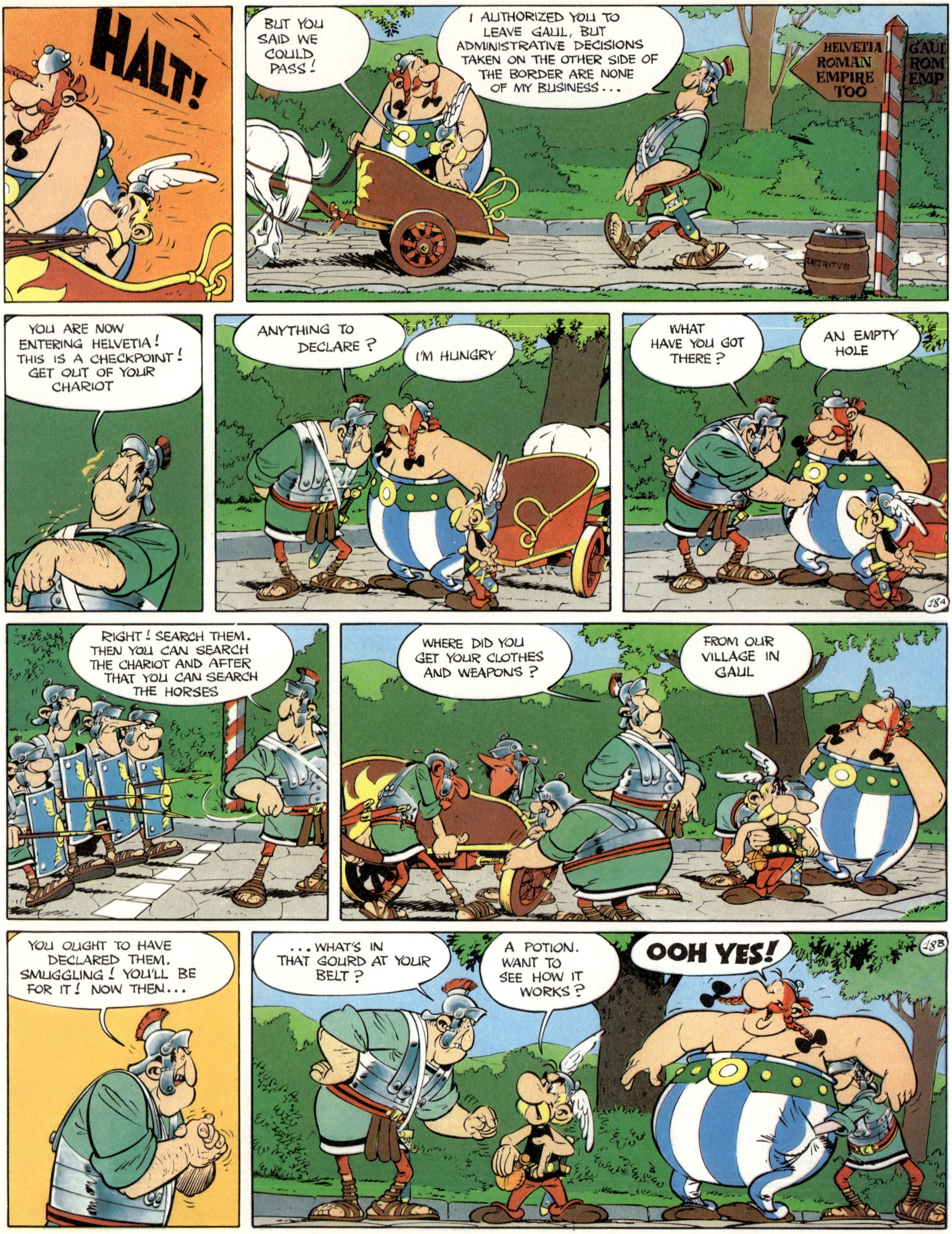
HALT!
BUT YOU SAID WE COULD PASS!
I AUTHORIZED YOU TO LEAVE GAUL, BUT ADMINISTRATIVE DECISIONS TAKEN ON THE OTHER SIDE OF THE BORDER ARE NONE OF MY BUSINESS...
HELVETIA ROMAN EMPIRE TOO
DETRITVS
YOU ARE NOW ENTERING HELVETIA! THIS IS A CHECKPOINT! GET OUT OF YOUR CHARIOT
ANYTHING TO DECLARE?
I'M HUNGRY
WHAT HAVE YOU GOT THERE?
AN EMPTY HOLE
RIGHT! SEARCH THEM. THEN YOU CAN SEARCH THE CHARIOT AND AFTER THAT YOU CAN SEARCH THE HORSES
WHERE DID YOU GET YOUR CLOTHES AND WEAPONS?
FROM OUR VILLAGE IN GAUL
YOU OUGHT TO HAVE DECLARED THEM. SMUGGLING! YOU'LL BE FOR IT! NOW THEN...
...WHAT'S IN THAT GOURD AT YOUR BELT?
A POTION. WANT TO SEE HOW IT WORKS?
OOH YES!

GLUG GLUG GLUG GLUG
THIS IS A MAGIC POTION, BREWED BY OUR DRUID, WHICH GIVES US SUPERHUMAN STRENGTH...
?
SEE ?
BIFF!
I DON'T HAVE TO TAKE ANY BECAUSE I FELL INTO THE CAULDRON WHEN I WAS A BABY
?
SEE ?
BOFF!
WELL, WHERE DID THE OTHERS GO ?
19A
I THINK THEY'VE GOT PROBLEMS BACK THERE IN HELVETIA
WELL, IT'S ABOUT THEIR TURN
GAUL
HELVETIA
?!
LET'S NOT WASTE TIME HERE, OBELIX! I THINK THE DRUID WAS RIGHT; IT WON'T BE ALL THAT SIMPLE TO GET HIM THE SILVER STAR!
DON'T TURN ROUND YET, BUT I THINK THINGS ARE QUIETENING DOWN IN HELVETIA
GET ACROSS THAT BORDER, BY JUPITER, AND JUMP TO IT! AFTER THOSE MEN! WE MUST GET THEM DEAD OR ALIVE! OUR OWN LIVES DEPEND ON IT!
HELVETIA IS NOT WHAT IT USED TO BE
MAIOR E LONGINQUO REVERENTIA
YOU CAN SAY THAT AGAIN
19B

I SAY, ASTERIX, WHERE ARE THE MOUNTAINS?
SSH, OBELIX! WE LOOK LIKE HAVING ALL THE ROMAN GARRISONS ON OUR HEELS PRETTY SOON
WELL, THEN, LET'S CLIMB A MOUNTAIN, PICK THE SILVER STAR, AND GO HOME TO GAUL
IT'S NOT AS SIMPLE AS ALL THAT. WE HAVE TO KNOW WHERE THE FLOWER GROWS
THERE'S A TOWN ON THE OTHER SIDE OF THE LAKE. WE'LL SET OFF AFTER DARK. WE'LL FIND HELP THERE
OH, DO THEY HAVE A LAKE HERE?
LATER...
LET'S SWIM ACROSS THE LAKE... WE'LL GET INTO THE TOWN MORE EASILY THAT WAY. THE GATES ARE SURE TO BE GUARDED
I CAN'T SEE A THING, ASTERIX
GOOD, OBELIX! THAT MEANS THE ROMANS WON'T BE ABLE TO STOP US
ALL RIGHT?
ALL RIGHT
ALL RIGHT
WHO ARE YOU, THEN?
OBELIX
MALODORUS CASEUS
I'M GLAD I MET YOU. I MANAGED TO GET RID OF THE WEIGHTS ON MY FEET, BUT I'M ABSOLUTELY CHEESED OFF WITH THIS LAKE. HELP ME BACK TO THE BANK, PLEASE
IS IT THAT WAY? WE'RE STRANGERS HERE OURSELVES
YES. DID YOU LOSE YOUR PIECES OF BREAD IN THE FONDUE TOO? LACUS LEMANUS IS FULL OF BUTTERFINGERS
MAYBE THE AIR IS HEALTHY, BUT IT DOESN'T SEEM TO SUIT THE ROMANS

COULD YOU TELL US THE WAY TO A HOTEL, ROMAN ?
THERE ARE HOTELS ALL ROUND THE LAKE. LOOK, THERE'S ONE RIGHT OPPOSITE
AND WHAT ARE YOU GOING TO DO ?
GET SOME DRY CLOTHES ON AND GO BACK TO THE ORGY. WHAT FUN !
LAKESIDE HOTEL
WHAT'S A FONDUE, ASTERIX ?
I EXPECT IT'S SOME KIND OF LOCAL ORGY
...YES, I HAVE GOT A ROOM FREE, EVEN THOUGH THEY'RE HOLDING THE ICTC- THE INTERNATIONAL CONFERENCE OF TRIBAL CHIEFTAINS - IN GENAVA JUST NOW
!
THERE WAS A BARBARIAN DELEGATION WHICH DIDN'T WANT THEIR ROOM. THEY SAID IT WAS TOO CLEAN
YOU MUST BE STRANGERS HERE... I'D BETTER TELL YOU, YOU SHOULD HAVE COME OVER THE BRIDGE. JULIUS CAESAR DESTROYED IT, BUT IT'S BEEN REBUILT NOW
MEANWHILE, IN THE GOVERNOR'S PALACE...
YOU BUNGLING IDIOTS! I MUST HAVE THOSE GAULS!

ALERT ALL THE GARRISONS! THE GARRISONS OF AVENTICUM, VINDONISSA, AUGUSTA RAURICA, OCTODURUM, SOLODURUM!* SEARCH GENAVA! GET MOVING!
I'M BACK, O DIVINE ODUS!
* AVENCHES, WINDISCH, AUGST, MARTIGNY, SOLEURE
I HAVEN'T GOT TIME TO LISTEN TO YOUR BURBLINGS NOW!
ALL RIGHT, ALL RIGHT
STILL, A FUNNY THING HAPPENED TO ME IN THE LAKE. I MET TWO MEN WHO HELPED ME OUT, AND...
TWO MEN?
MY PIECE OF BREAD! YOU MADE ME DROP MY PIECE OF BREAD IN THE CAULDRON!
NEVER MIND YOUR PIECE OF BREAD! WHERE ARE THEY?
OH, YOU MEAN THE TWO MEN? THEY WENT TO THE HOTEL BY THE BRIDGE
GUARDS! GUAAAARDS!
WHAT ABOUT THE STICK THEN? YOU'RE NOT PLAYING FAIR IF I DON'T GET THE STICK!
AT THAT MOMENT...
XII^A
HERE'S YOUR ROOM!
THIS HOURGLASS KEEPS VERY GOOD TIME. HELVETIAN MADE! BUT YOU HAVE TO WATCH IT. WHENEVER I SHOUT 'CUCKOO' IT'S TIME FOR ALL THE HOTEL GUESTS TO TURN THEIR HOURGLASSES OVER
I'LL TAKE YOUR SHOES AND CLEAN THEM. SLEEP WELL

TUT! TUT! TUT!
WE'RE FULL
WE'RE NOT LOOKING FOR ACCOMMODATION. HAVE YOU GOT ANY DAMP GAULS STAYING HERE?
NO. I'VE GOT SOME SICAMBRI, AEDUI, TRIBOCI, A CHARIOTLOAD OF IBERIANS, A FEW BRITONS AND SEQUANI, ALL QUITE DRY
?!.
WHAT ABOUT THOSE MUDDY FOOTPRINTS?
THEY'RE MINE. I OFTEN GO FOR A STROLL AT NIGHT BY THE SIDE OF THE LAKE... THE AIR'S SO GOOD ROUND HERE
ARE THOSE YOUR SHOES?
YES, I'VE GOT SEVERAL PAIRS... LOOK...
ALL RIGHT, ALL RIGHT, I BELIEVE YOU!
SPLAT!
WE'RE GOING TO SEARCH THE OTHER HOTELS. IF YOU SEE ANY GAULS, LET US KNOW. THEY'RE DANGEROUS TROUBLEMAKERS
I CERTAINLY WILL
SPLAT!
SPLAT!
I'VE MESSED UP MY OWN FLOOR! I'VE MADE MUDDY FOOTPRINTS ON MY OWN PREMISES! I MIGHT HAVE PUT MY FOOT IN IT! ALL BECAUSE OF THOSE BLASTED ROMANS!
CLONK!

WAKE UP! THE ROMANS ARE AFTER YOU! FOLLOW ME! YOU MUST HIDE!
!?
XII A
ALL CLEAR! LET'S GO!
OH!
EXCUSE ME! I'LL BE BACK IN A MINUTE!
?!
CUCKOO!
Their punctuality is starting to get me down!
POC!
WHERE ARE YOU TAKING US?
SOMEWHERE SAFE, FOR THE MOMENT. AFTER THAT WE'LL SEE
THE BANK IS SHUT AT THIS TIME OF NIGHT!
ZURIX BANK
KNOCK! KNOCK!
ZURIX! OPEN UP, IT'S ME, PETITSUIX!
DO YOU KNOW WHAT TIME IT IS?

THE ROMANS ARE AFTER THESE TWO MEN. THEY'RE SEARCHING THE WHOLE TOWN. WE MUST SAVE THEM!
YES, OF COURSE. YOU HAVE OUR SYMPATHY. WE HAVE OFTEN FOUGHT AGAINST THE ROMANS, AND JULIUS CAESAR CONSIDERS US FORMIDABLE ENEMIES... BUT WHERE CAN WE HIDE YOU?
I HAD THOUGHT OF ONE OF YOUR SAFES, IN THE VAULT...
YOU'D HAVE TO OPEN AN ACCOUNT
WHAT, TO HIDE IN A SAFE?
WHAT YOU PUT IN THE SAFE IS NO CONCERN OF MINE. DISCRETION IS OUR WATCHWORD! YOU'LL JUST BE TWO ANONYMOUS NUMBERS TO ME. WILL YOU TAKE A SAFE EACH, OR DO YOU WANT A JOINT ACCOUNT?
IF YOU HAVE A BIG ENOUGH SAFE, WE'D RATHER BE TOGETHER
THAT'LL BE QUITE IN ORDER. SIGN, PLEASE. THERE, THERE AND THERE
THIS WAY, PLEASE
HERE'S YOUR SAFE
CREEAK!
I'LL COME BACK TOMORROW. WE'LL KEEP YOU IN TOUCH
THANKS FOR EVERYTHING, PETITSUIX!
WAIT A MOMENT! THERE ARE NO REGULATIONS COVERING THE OPENING OF A SAFE FROM THE INSIDE. IF YOU WANT PETITSUIX TO COME AND OPEN IT, YOU MUST GIVE HIM A POWER OF ATTORNEY!

GOOD NIGHT!
SLEEP TIGHT!
I MUST HURRY BACK TO THE HOTEL, OR I'LL BE ONE CUCKOO LATE
BROOOMMM!
YAWN...! I'M GOING BACK TO BED
BOF!
ASTERIX, WE CAME HERE TO CLIMB MOUNTAINS, AND HERE WE ARE UNDERGROUND!
YOU'RE SO RIGHT, OBELIX!
WHAT'S MORE, I'M HUNGRY, ASTERIX. I DON'T LIKE BEING HOLED UP HERE WITH A HOLE INSIDE ME!
ON THE WHOLE, I AGREE. I'M HUNGRY TOO. THEY FORGOT TO GIVE US ANYTHING TO EAT
I DON'T KNOW WHETHER WE'RE ALLOWED TO OPEN THE SAFE FROM THE INSIDE...
WHY NOT ASTERIX? IT'S OUR SAFE!
TCHONK!
ZURIX!
HMMM?
WE'VE COME BACK UP BECAUSE WE'RE HUNGRY
HOW ON EARTH...? VERY WELL! GO BACK DOWN. I'LL BRING YOU A LITTLE SOMETHING
YOU CAN USE THIS LAMP FOR LIGHT AND TO MELT THE CHEESE
EEEEK! HOW TERRIBLE! A SAFE WITHOUT A DOOR!
?

YOU CAN'T STAY IN A SAFE WITHOUT A DOOR... YOU'LL HAVE TO OPEN ANOTHER ACCOUNT
OPEN UP, IN THE NAME OF CAESAR!
THE ROMANS!!! GET INTO THIS SAFE, QUICKLY!
VII
CLONG! CLING!
WHOSE SAFE IS IT?
I DON'T KNOW AND I DON'T WANT TO KNOW. GET IN, QUICK!
I THINK I CAN GUESS YOUR CUSTOMER'S NATIONALITY...
JUMP IN, AND MAKE IT SNAPPY!!!
27A
ARE YOU GOING TO OPEN UP, BY JUPITER!?
POF!
COMING, JUST COMING!
CUT UP THE CHEESE, OBELIX!
ASTERIX, I'M JUST GOING TO ASK ZURIX IF HE'S GOT ANY CHEESE WITHOUT HOLES IN IT
SHUT UP AND EAT UP, OBELIX!
I DON'T KNOW... WE CAME HERE LOOKING FOR MOUNTAINS AND WE END UP IN A HOLE EATING HOLES!
SHHH!
27B

VERY SORRY TO DISTURB YOU AT THIS TIME OF NIGHT, BUT WE'VE HAD ORDERS TO SEARCH THE WHOLE TOWN FOR TWO OUTLAWS
THERE ARE ONLY SAFES DOWN HERE, AND THEY'RE AS SAFE AS THE BANK OF BRITAIN
I KNOW ALL ABOUT THAT, AND I'D BE THE LAST ONE TO BLAME YOU. RIGHT, WE'RE OFF
WHAT THE...?
WHAT ABOUT THAT?
ER... WELL... THIEVES GOT IN AND TOOK EVERYTHING OUT OF THIS ONE...
WHAT?
IS THAT WHAT YOU CALL AS SAFE AS THE BANK OF BRITAIN? I'VE GOT A SAFE HERE MYSELF, YOU KNOW!
ER... NOT THAT THERE'S A LOT IN IT, OF COURSE... JUST A FEW SOUVENIRS FROM EGYPT... SENTIMENTAL VALUE ONLY. ANYWAY, I'M NOT HERE TO GIVE YOU MY CURRICULUM VITAE...
NOT 'ARF YOU'RE NOT!
I'M BUSY TONIGHT, BUT TOMORROW MORNING I'M COMING IN TO CLOSE MY ACCOUNT! KEEP A CLOSE EYE ON THIS ONE. WHAT'S INSIDE IS VERY PRECIOUS TO ME
BOOHOOHOO!
HEAR THAT, OBELIX? SOMEONE REALLY DOES SEEM TO BE DOWN IN THE DUMPS
ARE YOU SURE THERE ARE ANY MOUNTAINS IN THIS DUMP?
SHUT UP! SILENCE! DISCRETION IS OUR WATCHWORD!
BANG! BANG! BANG!

SCRATCH! SCRATCH!
CUCKOO!
SHUT UP!
I SAY, WHAT A FEARFUL BORE!
CUCKOO! WAKE UP, CHÉRI, HE SAID CUCKOO!
AND YOU KNOW WHAT I SAY TO HIM...?
IF ONLY WE COULD TURN THESE HOURGLASSES OVER SEVERAL TIMES IN ADVANCE!
LAKESIDE HOTEL
HALF A CUCKOO LATER...
GOOD MORNING, ZURIX. I'VE COME FOR THE GAULS
GET THEM OUT OF HERE! THEY'VE BROUGHT DISHONOUR ON MY NAME! THEY MADE ME LIE ABOUT THE SECURITY OF MY ESTABLISHMENT!
I'VE HAD JUST ABOUT ENOUGH OF THESE GAULS!
CALM DOWN, ZURIX. THEY MADE ME DIRTY MY HOTEL
CLICK!
IT'S ENOUGH TO MAKE YOU WANT TO BECOME NEUTRAL
I'VE BROUGHT YOU DISGUISES. WITH THESE, YOU WON'T BE SPOTTED IN THE CROWD
THAT'S A DISGUISE??
CARRYING THOSE WEAPONS, YOU'LL LOOK LIKE HELVETIANS GOING TO THEIR ANNUAL CAMP. EVERY YEAR WE HAVE TO DO OUR MILITARY SERVICE FOR A NONES AND A CALENDS
ZURIX BAN
SLAM!
ALONE AT LAST! HOW GHASTLY, HAVING TO MIX WITH ALL THOSE FOREIGNERS. MY HORN RUNNETH OVER...

LOOK WELL FED AND RELAXED. NO ONE WILL NOTICE YOU
WELL FED! HOLES DON'T FILL IN A HOLE!
LOOK, LEGIONARIES MANNING A ROAD BLOCK!
HUH! WE'RE DISGUISED, WE'RE QUITE SAFE!
YOUR EMPTY HOLE IS VERY DISTINCTIVE, OBELIX!
THE GOLDEN HOURGLASS
SURE ENOUGH...
THERE THEY ARE! THOSE ARE THE ONES WHO PULLED ME OUT OF THE LAKE THE OTHER NIGHT!
HEY! DON'T FORGET YOU OWE ME FIVE OF THE BEST!
THEY WON'T GET FAR! ALL THE EXITS ARE BLOCKED!
ROMANS AHEAD!
LET'S GO AND HIDE IN THE UNITED TRIBES BUILDING!
INTERNATIONAL CONFERENCE OF TRIBAL CHIEFS CLXVIIITH SESSION

... AND I MUST SAY THAT I THINK WE CAN CO-EXIST WITH THE ROMANS. ALL WE NEED IS A LITTLE GOODWILL ON BOTH SIDES, AND RESPECT FOR INDIVIDUAL LIBERTY...
LET'S SPLIT UP. SIT DOWN AND IMITATE THE OTHERS!
OF COURSE, WE SHALL HAVE TO MAKE GREAT EFFORTS...
PRETEND TO BE ASLEEP
... BUT THE ROMANS HAVE ALREADY GIVEN AMPLE EVIDENCE OF THEIR DESIRE FOR PEACE...
?!
ZZZZZZZ!
PAX ROMANA! THAT COULD BE THE FORMULA FOR FUTURE PEACE, AND IF WE FORGET OLD HATREDS AND RESENTMENTS...
...I SEE BEFORE US A PERIOD OF UNTROUBLED CALM...
I SEE THE LITTLE TOUGH ONE!
FOLLOW ME!
COME ALONG, OBELIX!
...AND THAT IS WHY I SAY TO YOU...
OBELIX!
ZZZZZ!
... THAT PEACE IS POSSIBLE...
CUCKOO!
...AND MUST BE POSSIBLE. THANK YOU FOR YOUR KIND ATTENTION

THE DELEGATE FROM THE TRIBE OF THE CARDUCHI WILL SPEAK NEXT...
MR. CHAIRMAN, FELLOW DELEGATES, I SHALL BE BRIEF...
S. P. Q. R.
THE LAKE! IN WE GO!
I REALLY DIDN'T THINK MOUNTAINS WOULD BE LIKE THIS!
RIGHT! TAKE A RUNNING JUMP!
WITH OUR BREASTPLATES?
OUR HELMETS?
OUR CALIGAE?
I DON'T MIND GETTING WET, BUT I'M NOT SURE IF IT'S THREE HOURS SINCE WE FINISHED OUR DINNER...?
GET UNDRESSED! KEEP YOUR WEAPONS! JUMP TO IT! NUNC EST BIBENDUM!
FROM AN ODE OF HORACE
YOU DON'T SAY! IF I WAS AS WELL VERSED IN SWIMMING AS POETRY, I SHOULDN'T BE WORRIED!
WHAT ARE YOU DOING, YOU IDIOT?
I'M FLOATING, OF COURSE! THAT'S ALL I CAN DO! I TRAINED FOR THE INFANTRY, DIDN'T I?
THEY'RE AFTER US!...
LOOK! THERE'S A BOAT! LET'S GO ROUND THE OTHER SIDE!

WHERE'VE THEY GONE? THEY'VE DISAPPEARED!
THEY MUST REALLY BE GETTING INTO DEEP WATER!
FOLLOW THAT BOAT!
HE'S A RIGHT WET THAT ONE!
YOU'RE OBVIOUSLY NOT FROM ROUND HERE, OR YOU'D KNOW THE BRIDGE CAESAR DESTROYED HAS BEEN REBUILT
WE KNOW THAT. THANKS FOR THE RESCUE. WE WERE ALL AT SEA IN THERE!
OLELEIIIIIIIIIIIIII! YODLEIOOOOOOOO!
THAT'S A NATIONAL SONG. YOU'RE IN LUCK. YOU CAN HEAR OUR GLEE CLUB
WE'VE GOT A BARD AT HOME WHO SINGS A BIT LIKE THAT
OBELIX! COME BACK UP HERE IMMEDIATELY!

WHERE'S THAT BIG BOAT GOING, FISHERMAN?
IT'S TAKING SOME OLD SOLDIERS TO THE OTHER SIDE FOR A REGIMENTAL REUNION. THEY HAVE AN OUTING TO THE MOUNTAINS ONCE A YEAR
LET'S GO AND TELL GOVERNOR CURIUS ODUS! FOLLOW ME!
WE REALLY SHALL HAVE TO PUT UP A NOTICE ABOUT THAT BRIDGE
WE'VE GOT THEM NOW!
YES, WE'VE GOT THEM NOW! I WANT ALL AVAILABLE TROOPS SENT TO THAT REUNION! I WANT THOSE GAULS DEAD OR ALIVE!
BONG
MEANWHILE...
I'M SURE THESE JOLLY HELVETIANS WILL HELP US FIND THE FLOWER TO CURE THAT ROMAN HOSTAGE IN OUR VILLAGE...
PON!
HERE WE ARE. THERE ARE OUR FRIENDS
BOOOOOOOOOOOOOOOOOOOOOOOO
YODLE!!!!!!!!!!!!!!!!!!!!!
WHAT A BEAUTIFUL COUNTRY! SO GAY AND PEACEFUL!
YES, WE ALL LIVE IN HARMONY HERE!

I MUST LEAVE YOU HERE. I'VE GOT TO GET BACK TO MY HOTEL. I'M ALREADY SEVERAL CUCKOOS LATE. GOOD LUCK
THANKS FOR EVERYTHING, PETITSUIX
WE'RE LOOKING FOR A FLOWER, A SILVER STAR. COULD YOU HELP US TO FIND IT, PLEASE?
CERTAINLY! WE KNOW OUR WAY ABOUT THE MOUNTAINS. BUT FIRST FOR SOME SPORTS!
YOU CAN EAT YOUR APPLE LATER, SONNY. IT'S TIME FOR YOUR SWISS RÔLE NOW. HANG UP THE TARGET!
WE MUST SPEED UP THE WORKS A BIT!
I'BE CAUGHT A COLD FROB THAT WRETCHED LAKE!
AFTER YOU... VISITORS SHOOT FIRST
VERY WELL! AFTERWARDS WE'LL GO AND FIND THE FLOWER
SNIFF!
A... AAA... AAAAA...
TISHOO!
TCHOC!
OBELIX! YOU NEARLY CAUSED AN ACCIDENT!
I KNOW, BUT IT CLEARS MY HEAD
GOOD SHOT! A BULLSEYE!
A VERY GOOD SHOT, AND YET SOMEHOW I FEEL A BIT LET DOWN...
ME TOO. CAN'T THINK WHY
SCROTCH!

RIGHT! SHALL WE GO AND GET THE FLOWER NOW?
FIRST WE EAT AND DRINK, THEN WE SING, THEN WE'LL GO AND PICK FLOWERS!
COME ALONG! THE CHEESE IS NEARLY MELTED!
COULDN'T THEY MELT A FEW WILD BOAR FOR A CHANGE?
LET'S GET A MOVE ON! THE SOONER WE'VE EATEN, DRUNK AND SUNG, THE SOONER WE'LL GO AND LOOK FOR THE FLOWER. WE MUST MAKE THE MOST OF THE START WE HAVE ON THE ROMANS
YOU'LL SEE HOW I'M GOING TO SPEED UP THE WORKS, BY TOUTATIS!
?
WHAT THE...?
HEY, STRANGER, THAT'S NOT THE WAY TO...
RIGHT! NOW LET'S DRINK!
HAVING SEEN THE WAY YOU EAT, I DON'T THINK YOU'LL NEED A GLASS
SUITS ME!
SCROTCH! SCROTCH!
GLUGGLUGGLUGGLUGGL
OBELIX! NOOO!
AND NOW FOR THE SHING...HIC!...SHINGING!
OYYELELEIT... HIC!... LILUUU
BONK!
BROOOOOM!
OBELIX!
THAT'S JUST LIKE YOU GAULS! YOU DO EVERYTHING TOO QUICKLY. IT TAKES US HOURS TO DO WHAT YOUR FRIEND HAS JUST DONE IN A FEW SECONDS!

OBELIX! OBELIX!
THERE ARE HUNDREDS OF ROMANS CROSSING THE LAKE!
I MUST GO AND FIND THE SILVER STAR BEFORE THEY GET HERE!
WE'LL HELP YOU!
SOME OF YOU WILL HAVE TO STAY HERE TO HOLD BACK THE ROMANS! GO AND FIND THE CAULDRON!
HOLD THEM BACK? THERE ARE SO MANY OF THEM!
GLUG! GLUG! GLUG!
?!
THERE'S ENOUGH MAGIC POTION LEFT TO GIVE YOU THE STRENGTH TO STOP THEM
MAGIC POTION?
COME ON! SHOW ME WHERE THE FLOWER IS!
IT'S JUST THAT WE HAVE A RATHER LARGE PROBLEM!
IT'S YOUR FRIEND. I DON'T KNOW WHETHER HE'S SOBER ENOUGH TO CLIMB A MOUNTAIN. YOU CAN'T LEAVE HIM THERE. IT LOOKS MESSY AND UNTIDY
I'VE GOT IT! BRING A LONG ROPE. WE'LL TIE OURSELVES TOGETHER AND PULL OBELIX ALONG. WITH YOUR HELP AND THE MAGIC POTION, WE'LL MANAGE IT.
AND SO IT WAS THAT A TECHNIQUE WAS BORN WHICH IS STILL USED TO THIS DAY...
THIS IS A GOOD IDEA...
YES, BUT I'D HAVE THOUGHT THE ROPE WENT ROUND YOUR NECK...
BRING THE CHEESE! IT'LL JUST HAVE TIME TO MELT BEFORE THE ROMANS ARRIVE!

HERE COME THE ROMANS!
LET'S TREAT THEM TO A LITTLE WAR SONG!
NOT BAD, THIS MAGIC FONDUE!
OLEELEEIIII!
THEY'VE GOT ELEPHANTS!
DON'T BE AN IDIOT! THEY'RE SINGING
WHEN I WAS POSTED TO GAUL, I KNEW A BARD WHO SANG A BIT LIKE THAT!
BY ORDER OF GOVERNOR CURIUS ODUS, REPRESENTATIVE OF JULIUS CAESAR, LET US PASS
YOUR QUARRELS ARE NO CONCERN OF OURS. WE WANT TO REMAIN NEUTRAL, BUT...
CHARGE!
YODLEEEEEEIIIIIIIIIIIIIIIII!
PLAF!
TCHRRRAC!
HIT US, YES, BUT YOU MIGHT LET US DO THE SHOUTING!
BANG!

TCHAC!
CRUMP!
FIRST YOU HIT ME AND THEN YOU BANDAGE ME UP!
IT'S OUR VOCATION. WE LOOK AFTER ALL COMBATANTS, WHATEVER THEIR NATIONALITY...
AND WHILE THE BATTLE STILL RAGES...
LOOK OVER THERE! THE OUTLAWS ARE CLIMBING A MOUNTAIN! LET'S GET AFTER THEM WHILE THE OTHERS ARE BUSY HERE!
PAF!
BING!
WE GO SWIMMING IN THE LAKE, WE GO CLIMBING MOUNTAINS...
WHAT D'YOU EXPECT? WE'RE NOT ON HOLIDAY, YOU KNOW!
I'VE DONE IT! I'VE CAUGHT ONE!

HELP ME! QUICK!
WE'RE COMING!
I'M GOING TO PULL YOU UP!
EEEEH!
PULL HIM DOWN HERE!
I'M TRYING TO!
HOLD TIGHT! DON'T LOSE SIGHT OF THEM! WE'LL GO ROUND THE MOUNTAIN AND CATCH THEM ON THE OTHER SIDE!
HEY! DON'T LET ME DOWN!
HMMM?
!!!
THERE, THERE! GO BACK TO SLEEP! IT'S ALL RIGHT!
ZZZZZZZ!
40

THREE HOURS LATER...
GAUL! LOOK TO YOUR RIGHT!
THE SILVER STAR!
I CAN'T REACH IT! I NEED ANOTHER SWORD!
ANYBODY GOT A SWORD?
ANYBODY GOT A SWORD?
ANYBODY GOT A SWORD?
HMMM?
I'VE GOT ONE. TAKE IT, AND STOP SHOUTING. YOU COULD EASILY START SOMETHING OFF
THANK YOU!
PASS IT UP!
I'VE GOT IT, OBELIX! WE'VE DONE IT!!
BYE, INFANS* BUNTING, PATER'S GONE A-HUNTING...
41A
* BABY LATIN
LET'S GO ON CLIMBING! WE'RE NEAR THE SUMMIT!
SOON AFTERWARDS...
A ROMAN !?
YES! A ROMAN! SO WHAT!! I'VE HELD YOUR FRIEND'S HAND ALL THE WAY UP THIS DANGEROUS CLIMB... YOU'RE NOT GOING TO MAKE TROUBLE FOR ME NOW?
41B

YOU CAN GET DOWN THIS WAY. IT LEADS STRAIGHT BACK TO YOUR OWN COUNTRY
THE DIFFICULTY IS THAT OBELIX IS STILL OUT COLD. I'LL HAVE TO TAKE HIM IN TOW
GOODBYE, HELVETIANS! I SHALL NEVER FORGET WHAT YOU DID FOR US, AND I'LL TELL OBELIX ALL ABOUT IT!
42A
EEEEH!
THERE THEY ARE!
HALT, GAUL! IN THE NAME OF GOVERNOR CURIUS ODUS, CAESAR'S REPRESENTATIVE, HALT!
WATCH OUT!
FLOTCH!
42B

YOU ALL RIGHT, CENTURION?
I'M ALL RIGHT. I JUST KEEP WISHING I WAS BACK IN EGYPT
BONK!
THE SILVER STAR, OBELIX! WE'VE FOUND IT! LET'S GET BACK TO THE VILLAGE!
ARE WE IN THE DRINK AGAIN?
A FEW DAYS LATER...
AND HOW IS THE UNFORTUNATE QUAESTOR SINUSITUS, O DRUID?
I'VE MANAGED TO KEEP HIM GOING, O GOVERNOR VARIUS FLAVUS
WHAT A PITY THAT YOUR MEN AREN'T BACK. YOU'LL HAVE TO EXECUTE HIM. AFTER ALL, HOSTAGES ARE HOSTAGES.
IT'S READY!
EXCELLENT! JUST ADD A FEW DROPS OF MAGIC POTION, AND GIVE HIM THE MIXTURE TO DRINK
WHAT'S READY?

PRINTED IN BELGIUM BY proost INTERNATIONAL BOOK PRODUCTION

THE MANSIONS OF THE GODS

TEXT BY GOSCINNY

DRAWINGS BY UDERZO

TRANSLATED BY ANTHEA BELL AND DEREK HOCKRIDGE

HODDER DARGAUD
LONDON SYDNEY AUCKLAND

The Mansions of the Gods

Copyright © Dargaud Editeur 1971, Goscinny-Uderzo
English language text copyright © Brockhampton Press Ltd 1973
(now Hodder Children's Books)

The year is 50 BC. Gaul is entirely occupied by the Romans. Well, not entirely... One small village of indomitable Gauls still holds out against the invaders. And life is not easy for the Roman legionaries who garrison the fortified camps of Totorum, Aquarium, Laudanum and Compendium...

HIDDEN IN THE GREAT ARMORICAN FOREST SWARMING WITH JUICY WILD BOAR, THE LITTLE VILLAGE THAT WE KNOW SO WELL IS BASKING HAPPILY IN THE WARM SPRING SUNSHINE. YES, THE LITTLE VILLAGE IS QUIETLY CONFIDENT ABOUT THE FUTURE...

... AND IT IS MAKING A BIG MISTAKE, BECAUSE THE FUTURE MIGHT BE THIS!
WILL YOU EXPLAIN THE MEANING OF THIS TO US, O CAESAR?

I WILL NOW GIVE YOU A BRIEF COMMENTARY. THE GAULS HAVING BEEN DEFEATED, THEIR CHIEF VERCINGETORIX LAID HIS ARMS AT THE FEET OF THE GLORIOUS GENERAL...
...WHO OCCUPIED ALL GAUL. ALL? NO! ONE SMALL VILLAGE INHABITED BY INDOMITABLE BARBARIANS DARED, AND STILL DARES, TO RESIST HIM!
WHO'S HE TALKING ABOUT?
HIMSELF. HE ALWAYS TALKS ABOUT HIMSELF IN THE THIRD PERSON
HE'S GREAT!
WHO?
ER...YOU!
OH, HIM!
THESE GAULS, WITH THE AID OF A MAGIC POTION WHICH GIVES THEM SUPERHUMAN STRENGTH, AND PROTECTED BY A FOREST WHICH PROVIDES THEM WITH FOOD, REJECT THE ADVANTAGES OF ROMAN CIVILIZATION...
WHICH I HAVE DECIDED TO FORCE THEM TO ACCEPT! THE FOREST WILL BE DESTROYED TO MAKE WAY FOR A NATURAL PARK!
TCHAC!
AND THEN BLOCKS OF FLATS FULL OF ROMAN TENANTS WILL SURROUND THE VILLAGE, WHICH WILL BECOME A MERE NATIVE RESERVATION. THESE GAULS MAY BE CRAZY* BUT THEY'LL HAVE TO ADAPT TO OUR WAYS THEN!
*HENCE THE OLD GAULISH EXPRESSION 'A MENTAL RESERVATION'

SO I HAVE CALLED IN ONE OF OUR MOST TALENTED YOUNG ARCHITECTS TO STUDY THIS PROJECT. I REFER TO SQUARONTHEHYPOTENUS...
NOT ONLY HAS SQUARONTHEHYPOTENUS BUILT MANY INSULAE* SOME OF WHICH HAVE NOT FALLEN DOWN...
* BLOCKS OF FLATS
... HE IS ALSO THE INVENTOR OF THE DRIVE-IN AMPHITHEATRE...
... OF POTION-TABERNAE* WHERE YOU CAN BUY ANYTHING...
SLAVES
STATUES
GLADIATORS
ORGY EQUIPMENT
BALM ~ OINTMENTS
* TABERNAE: STORES
... AND OF THE LATEST THING IN BATHS.
BATHTIQUE
AND WHAT ARE YOU GOING TO CALL THIS NEW DEVELOPMENT WHICH IS TO CIVILIZE THE GAULS?
SQUARONTHEHYPOTENUS WANTED TO CALL IT ROME NEW TOWN, BUT THERE IS ONLY ONE ROME...
SO I HAVE DECIDED TO CALL IT 'THE MANSIONS OF THE GODS'... THAT WILL HELP TO PULL IN THE CUSTOMERS
3

AT THE MOMENT, PEACE REIGNS ON THE FUTURE SITE OF THE MANSIONS OF THE GODS, AND ONLY THE BOARS SEEM TO HAVE ANY REASON TO WORRY
THERE'S SOMEONE COMING! LET'S HIDE IN THIS THICKET!
BONG!
WELL, I THINK THEY OUGHT TO DO THE HIDING! IT'S OUR FOREST, AFTER ALL!
... AND TEN FEET, THAT MAKES SIX HUNDRED AND TWO FEET, THREE HANDS...
???
WE'LL START THE NEXT SET OF MEASUREMENTS FROM THIS TREE
?
DOGMATIX! HEEL!
GRRRRRRAOOO
OUCH!
CALL YOUR DOG OFF!
ALL RIGHT, BUT DON'T GO INTERFERING WITH TREES IN FRONT OF DOGMATIX. HE DOESN'T LIKE IT
COME ALONG, DOGMATIX, YOU'LL SPOIL YOUR APPETITE
YOU KNOW, YOU SHOULDN'T VENTURE INTO THIS FOREST; IF ANYONE MET YOU YOU MIGHT HAVE AN UNFORTUNATE EXPERIENCE

THE BOARS ARE RATHER RETIRING TODAY!
THEY GO INTO HIDING WHEN THEY SEE A CROWD
THESE FORESTS AREN'T PROPERLY KEPT UP. WE OUGHT TO BE SNIFFING OUT ROMANS
WE'RE HERE TO SNIFF OUT BOARS, OBELIX
LOOK, ASTERIX! DOGMATIX IS COMING ON! THERE'S SOMETHING MOVING IN THAT THICKET!
LEAVE IT TO ME!
EEEEEK!
?!
CAN'T YOU LET ME GO ABOUT MY BUSINESS IN PEACE?
YOU HAVEN'T ANY BUSINESS HERE!
WHAT'S MORE, YOU'RE FRIGHTENING THE BOARS AWAY!
BIFF!
SOON AFTERWARDS...
WELL, IT'S QUITE TRUE! I DON'T LIKE PEOPLE TO FRIGHTEN THE BOARS! POOR THINGS, THEY'RE SCARED OF STRANGERS... WE'RE DIFFERENT; THEY'RE USED TO US
I'LL HAVE TO HAVE A WORD WITH OUR CHIEF. IT'S NOT NORMAL FOR ROMANS TO BRAVE THE DANGERS OF THE FOREST, ESPECIALLY WHEN THE DANGERS ARE US!
ROMANS IN THE FOREST ?!?

WE'LL HAVE TO KEEP AN EYE ON THOSE ROMANS! AFTER ALL, THEY CAN'T GO TAKING LIBERTIES WITH OUR FOREST, BY TOUTATIS!
MEASURING... THEY WERE MEASURING... YOU DON'T GO MEASURING BITS OF THE FOREST JUST FOR FUN... WHAT ARE THEY UP TO?
WE'LL KEEP AN EYE ON THEM, O DRUID GETAFIX!
AND AS SOON AS WE SEE THEM UP TO ANYTHING AGAIN, WE'LL DEAL WITH IT!
PAF!
IN THE SICK-BAY OF THE FORTIFIED CAMP OF AQUARIUM...
I WARNED YOU, SQUARONTHEHYPOTENUS! THOSE GAULS ARE BARBARIANS, AND THEY DON'T LIKE PEOPLE WANDERING AROUND THEIR FOREST
IT'S NOT THEIR FOREST, CENTURION SOMNIFERUS! IT'S THE FUTURE SITE OF THE MANSIONS OF THE GODS! BARBARIANS AND FORESTS ARE OUT! FINISHED! DONE WITH!
CIVILIZATION IS IN! WE'RE ABOUT TO START THE WORK OF DEFORESTATION!
YOU'LL HAVE TO DO SOME DEGALLICIZATION FIRST
I'M COUNTING ON YOU FOR THAT! CAESAR'S ORDERS! YOUR TROOPS ARE TO GUARD THE BUILDING SITE!
DO KEEP STILL, PLEASE!
ALL RIGHT, ALL RIGHT, BUT WE'LL WORK AT NIGHT, UNOBTRUSIVELY. THERE'S LESS CHANCE OF MEETING GAULS IN THE FOREST AT NIGHT
JUST AS YOU LIKE, BUT SPEAKING FOR MYSELF, I'M NOT SCARED OF GAULS!
HAVE YOU FINISHED, DOCTOR?
I AM VERY MUCH AFRAID THAT I'VE ONLY JUST BEGUN...

THAT VERY NIGHT, TOGETHER WITH THEIR OVERSEERS AND AN ESCORT OF LEGIONARIES, A COLUMN OF IBERIAN, LUSITANIAN, NUMIDIAN, BELGIAN AND GOTHIC SLAVES IS MAKING ITS WAY TOWARDS THE FOREST...
RIGHT! HERE WE ARE! START ROOTING UP THE TREES! WE...
SSSH! FOR THE GODS' SAKE, NO NOISE. GET THE WORK DONE IN SILENCE. I DON'T WANT A SQUEAK OUT OF YOU, I DON'T WANT TO HEAR THE CRACK OF A SINGLE WHIP. WE MUSTN'T PUT THE GAULS ON THEIR GUARD
TO WORK
AYYAAAAYYAA YYAAAAY
WHO WAS THAT?
THAT'S THE IBERIAN SLAVES. THEY CAN'T WORK WITHOUT SINGING
ALL RIGHT! THE IBERIANS ARE LET OFF WORK
BUT...
OLE!
BELGIANS NEVER, NEVER, NEVER WILL BE SLAVES...
THAT'S THE BELGIANS
WE'LL DO WITHOUT THE BELGIANS
'SCUSE ME... I'M LUSITANIAN *
WELL, WHAT ABOUT IT?
* PORTUGUESE
I DON'T KNOW ANY SONGS, BUT I COULD GIVE YOU A RECITATION IF YOU LIKE

Silent night, holy night, all is calm...
THAT'S THE GOTHS SINGING. THEY'RE DREADFUL WHEN THEY ALL SING TOGETHER
MAKE THEM SHUT UP!
WHAT WITH? YOU DON'T WANT TO HEAR THE CRACK OF A SINGLE WHIP!
EXCUSE ME, HOMBRES, BUT US AND THE BELGIANS, WE'RE TRYING TO GET TO SLEEP OVER THERE. WOULD YOU MIND MAKING A LITTLE LESS NOISE?
EVERYBODY QUITE FINISHED? ALL OF YOU GET DOWN TO WORK! YOU WORK UNTIL DAWN OR YOU'LL BE SKINNED ALIVE!
8A
CREEEAK!
POF! POF! POF!
COCK-A-DOODL
DAWN! WE'RE OFF!
WHAT DO YOU MEAN, DAWN?
COCK-A-DOODLE-DOOOOO
COME ON! WE'RE OFF!
BUT IT'S THE MIDDLE OF THE NIGHT!
AND IN THE GAULISH VILLAGE...
COCK-A-DOODLE-DOO? GOODNESS ME, I HAD NO IDEA IT WAS SO LATE
COCK-A-DOODLE-DOO
COCK-A-DOODLE-DO
WHAT, ALREADY?
THIS IS IT! WE MIGHT HAVE KNOWN IT! THE SKY'S FALLEN ON OUR HEADS!
A-DOODLE-DO
8B

FULLIAUTOMATIX
DING
DING
FRESH FISH! IT'S LUVERLY!
WHAT ARE THESE STRANGE GOINGS-ON, O DRUID? THE COCK'S CROWING AND THE SUN HASN'T RISEN YET!
NO IDEA, ASTERIX... WHEN THE DAWN COMES, YOU GO AND SCOUT AROUND IN THE FOREST. THERE MUST BE SOMETHING GOING ON!
YOU GO TO BED, OBELIX. WE'LL HAVE WORK TO DO WHEN DAWN COMES
BUT I'VE GOT A MENHIR TO DELIVER BEFORE BREAKFAST...
AND WHEN THE SUN FINALLY CONDESCENDS TO RISE ...
WHAT ARE WE LOOKING FOR, ASTERIX?
I DON'T KNOW YET, OBELIX
HOWWWL!
POOR LITTLE DOGMATIX! THE SIGHT OF THAT FALLEN TREE MADE HIM COME OVER ALL QUEER!
YOU WAIT! I'LL FIX THAT!
CHTONK!
THERE, THERE, DOGMATIX. NOTHING HAPPENED, YOU CAN SEE FOR YOURSELF!
LET'S GO AND WARN THE DRUID. WE SEEM TO BE GETTING BROKEN NIGHTS IN THESE PARTS

ARE YOU ABSOLUTELY SET ON GOING BACK TONIGHT?
YOU BET I AM! WE'RE GOING TO DEMOLISH THIS FOREST, AND THEN THE MANSIONS OF THE GODS WILL BECOME A REALITY! BESIDES, THE GAULS AREN'T DANGEROUS. THEY DIDN'T TURN A HAIR AT ALL THE ROW WE WERE KICKING UP!
THEY HAVE MAGICAL POWERS. THE TREES OF THE FOREST ARE IN LEAGUE WITH THEM
BEATI PAUPERES SPIRITU!
TAP TAP TAP
THAT VERY NIGHT...
I WARN YOU, I'M NOT PUTTING UP WITH ANY FUNNY BUSINESS. START ROOTING UP THE TREES ROUND THE ONE WE ROOTED UP YESTERDAY
O SQUARONTHEHYPOTENUS, THE TREE WE ROOTED UP YESTERDAY HAS TAKEN ROOT AGAIN!
!
CO... CO... COME AGAIN?
CO...CO... COCK-A-DOODLE-DO!
FRESH FISH! IT'S LUVERLY!
GET BACK TO BED, YOU IDIOT!
FULLIAUTOMATIX
YOU'LL SEE WHO'S AN IDIOT!

WHO STARTED THIS FIGHT?
THE COCK! THESE SLEEPLESS NIGHTS ARE GETTING RATHER TIRING
FULLIAUTO
ASTERIX, WE'RE GOING TO THE FOREST TOMORROW NIGHT
IN THE CAMP OF AQUARIUM
MY LEGIONARIES CAN'T FIGHT MAGIC! I REFUSE TO HELP YOU!
ALL RIGHT, THEN, I'LL DO WITHOUT YOUR LEGION-ARIES!
THAT NIGHT ...
WE'RE GOING TO DRAG THE TREES AWAY TO STOP THEM TAKING ROOT AGAIN ONCE THEY'RE DOWN
CRAAACK!
IT'S A GOOD THING WE DIDN'T BRING DOGMATIX; HE WOULDN'T HAVE LIKED THIS
SEE THAT, O DRUID? THEY'RE DRAGGING THE TREES AWAY
YES, I SEE. WE'RE GOING TO HAVE SOME FUN TOMORROW. LET'S GET BACK
AND FOR THE FIRST TIME FOR SEVERAL NIGHTS, THE VILLAGE IS ABLE TO SLEEP IN PEACE
CLUCK?

IT'S DAYLIGHT, SOMNIFERUS! COME AND SEE THE WORK WE GOT THROUGH DURING THE NIGHT!
HMM?
SOON WE'LL BE ABLE TO BUILD THE FIRST BLOCK OF FLATS IN THE MANSIONS OF THE GODS
SCRATCH! SCRATCH!
THIS IS ALL TOO EASY. DON'T COUNT YOUR CHICKENS BEFORE THEY'RE HATCHED... GNOTHE SEAUTON!
AND WHAT MIGHT THAT MEAN?
NO IDEA; IT'S GREEK TO ME
SCRATCH! SCRATCH!
MEANWHILE...
WHAT ARE WE GOING TO DO, O DRUID?
YOU'RE GOING TO DROP AN ACORN INTO EACH OF THOSE HOLES...
12A
THEY'RE COMMON OR GARDEN ACORNS TREATED WITH ONE OF MY LITTLE POTIONS
LIKE THIS?
WELL, YOU MIGHT HAVE DONE IT IN A MORE DIGNIFIED MANNER, BUT THAT'S THE IDEA
FLOOOOP!
FANTASTIC!
WHY? IT'S ONLY AN OAK TREE LIKE THE REST
BUT DIDN'T YOU SEE HOW FAST IT GREW?
WELL, I'VE NEVER SEEN AN OAK TREE GROWING BEFORE, SO I DON'T KNOW HOW FAST THEY DO USUALLY GROW
POC!
12B

THE TREES HAVE ALL GROWN AGAIN
THE ROMANS AREN'T GOING TO BE TOO PLEASED!
COME AND HAVE DINNER WITH ME TO CELEBRATE!
WOOF! WOOF!
SIT DOWN. IT'LL SOON BE READY
GOODY! WILD BOAR!
OH, LOOK, I'VE STILL GOT ONE OF THOSE ACORNS LEFT!
NO! OBELIX, DON'T THROW IT AWAY!
AND NOW YOU CAN UPROOT THIS ONE FOR ME!
DOGMATIX WOULDN'T LIKE THAT... WE'D BETTER MOVE HOUSE. I SAY, YOU'RE RIGHT, OAK TREES DO GROW FAST!
NEXT NIGHT, IN THE FOREST...
RIGHT, MAKE THE CLEARING BIGGER, AND YOU'LL GET DOUBLE RATIONS OF...
THERE ISN'T ANY CLEARING LEFT!
13

WHAT DO YOU MEAN, THERE ISN'T ANY CLEARING LEFT?
SEE FOR YOURSELF
I... I CAN'T MAKE IT OUT... BUT WE MUST GO ON WORKING... NOT A WORD TO THE GARRISON!
NEXT MORNING...
I MUST ADMIT, THE WORK'S GOING WELL, SQUARONTHEHYPOTENUS
I'M SURPRISED THE GAULS ARE BEING SO PATIENT... I CAN ONLY SUPPOSE THEY REALIZE THEY'VE MET THEIR MATCH IN YOU... THOUGH JUST TO LOOK AT YOU...
BUT THE WORK DONE OVERNIGHT IS UNDONE AGAIN DURING THE DAY...
JUST WATCH THIS DOGMATIX! YOU'LL ENJOY IT!
FLOOP! FLOOP! FLOOP! FLOOP!
AND NEXT NIGHT...
I CAN'T LOOK. IS... IS THE CLEARING STILL THERE?
I KNEW IT! WELL, NEVER MIND. PRESS ON!
HOMBRE, I GET THE FEELING WE'RE NOT DOING ANYTHING VERY USEFUL... NOT THAT WE'RE BEING PAID FOR IT, MIND YOU!

AFTER SEVERAL NIGHTS' STRENUOUS WORK...
IN THE FACE OF THE EVIDENCE, I HAVE TO ADMIT YOU WERE RIGHT. YOU'VE DONE IT! LET'S BURY THE HATCHET. I'LL HELP YOU...
YOU'LL BE ABLE TO TELL CAESAR HOW USEFUL I WAS... LET'S GO AND HAVE A LOOK!
HAVE A LOOK AT WHAT?
THE BUILDING SITE. THERE MUST BE A VAST CLEARING BY NOW
BUT... AREN'T YOU AFRAID OF THE GAULS, IN BROAD DAYLIGHT?
HUH! YOU GET PLENTY OF TIME TO SEE THEM COMING, IN OPEN COUNTRY
WELL? WHERE IS THIS CLEARING?
THERE ISN'T ANY CLEARING!
NO CLEARING? BUT THE TREE TRUNKS? WHERE DID THEY COME FROM?
CLICK!
?!
HEEEEEERE! BOOHOOOOO!
BUT I'M GOING ON! EVEN IF I HAVE TO WORK THE SLAVES TO DEATH, I'M GOING ON!
DID YOU HEAR THAT? WE CAN'T HAVE THE SLAVES PAYING FOR THE STUPIDITY OF THESE ROMANS... I HAVE AN IDEA!
AREN'T YOU EVER AFRAID YOU MAY RUN OUT OF IDEAS?

LATER
WHY DID OUR DRUID GIVE YOU AN AMPHORA FULL OF MAGIC POTION ?
YOU'LL SOON SEE, AND NO, YOU CAN'T HAVE ANY
THE SLAVES ARE SHUT UP IN THIS PART OF THE CAMP: IT'S SURROUNDED BY GUARDS
IT'LL TAKE TOO LONG TO GO AFTER THEM ONE BY ONE. LEAVE THIS TO ME !
CALL YOUR MATES
G-GUARDS! HELP ME !
NO, NO, NOT LIKE THAT !
GUARDS! HELP HIM!
SOON AFTERWARDS...
WHICH OF YOU IS THE LEADER, SLAVE ?
FLATURTHA, THE NUMIDIAN
ARE YOU HAPPY IN YOUR WORK, O FLATURTHA ?
WELL, THERE'S NOT MUCH FUTURE IN SLAVERY
THE ROMANS ARE GOING TO WORK YOU TO DEATH. YOU MUST REBEL!
IT'S EASY TO SAY THAT, BUT THERE ARE THE LEGIONARIES, THE OVERSEERS... THEY HAVE WHIPS AND WEAPONS. THEY'RE STRONGER THAN US
THIS IS WHAT YOU NEED
?

THAT'S IT. THEY'VE GONE
RIGHT. LET'S GET BACK TO OUR POSTS. NO POINT IN MAKING THIS LITTLE INCIDENT KNOWN. NOTHING HAPPENED ANYWAY!
OF COURSE IT DIDN'T!
LATER...
SOUP'S UP, SLAVES!
COME ALONG, YOU LOT! THIS SOUP WILL GIVE YOU STRENGTH... PLENTY OF STRENGTH!
CLACK!
NOW THEN, SLAVES, OFF TO WORK!
NO. WE'RE GOING ON STRIKE. WE'RE TIRED OF UPROOTING TREES THAT KEEP GROWING AGAIN
WHAT WAS THAT? WANT A TASTE OF MY WHIP?
PLAF!
POOR CHAP...HOW WAS HE TO KNOW A NUMIDIAN WOULDN'T NECESSARILY BE A BLACKLEG?
LET'S GET THEM TO WORK!
BONG!
SOON AFTERWARDS...
GUARDS! HELP ME!
PAF!
BING!
PLAONNG!
OH NO! I'M NOT FALLING FOR THAT ONE AGAIN!

THE SLAVES ARE RISING!
THAT WAS ALL WE NEEDED!
AH, YES, BUT I KNOW ALL ABOUT THIS SORT OF THING! I'LL BRING THEM TO HEEL, BY JUPITER!
RAISE THE ALARM! THE SLAVES ARE REVOLTING!
PAFFF!
BONG
TCHAC!
AND REVOLTING IS THE WORD!
18A
WELL, ARE YOU BRINGING THEM TO HEEL OR AREN'T YOU?
WAIT A MINUTE... I'M JUST WONDERING WHETHER...
SOON AFTERWARDS...
YOU LOT WERE ON GUARD OUTSIDE THE SLAVES' CAMP TODAY... YOU DIDN'T HAPPEN TO SEE ANYONE GO IN, DID YOU?
ER... NO...
ABSOLUTELY POSITIVE?
NOW I COME TO THINK OF IT... THERE WAS THIS BIG FAT BLOKE...
I THINK HE HAD A LITTLE BLOKE WITH HIM... BUT SO SMALL THAT...
BESIDES, WE HARDLY EXCHANGED A WORD
COULDN'T YOU HAVE TOLD ME THAT ASTERIX AND OBELIX HAD BEEN IN OUR CAMP!?!
SO THAT'S IT! I KNEW I'D SEEN THEM SOMEWHERE BEFORE...
18B

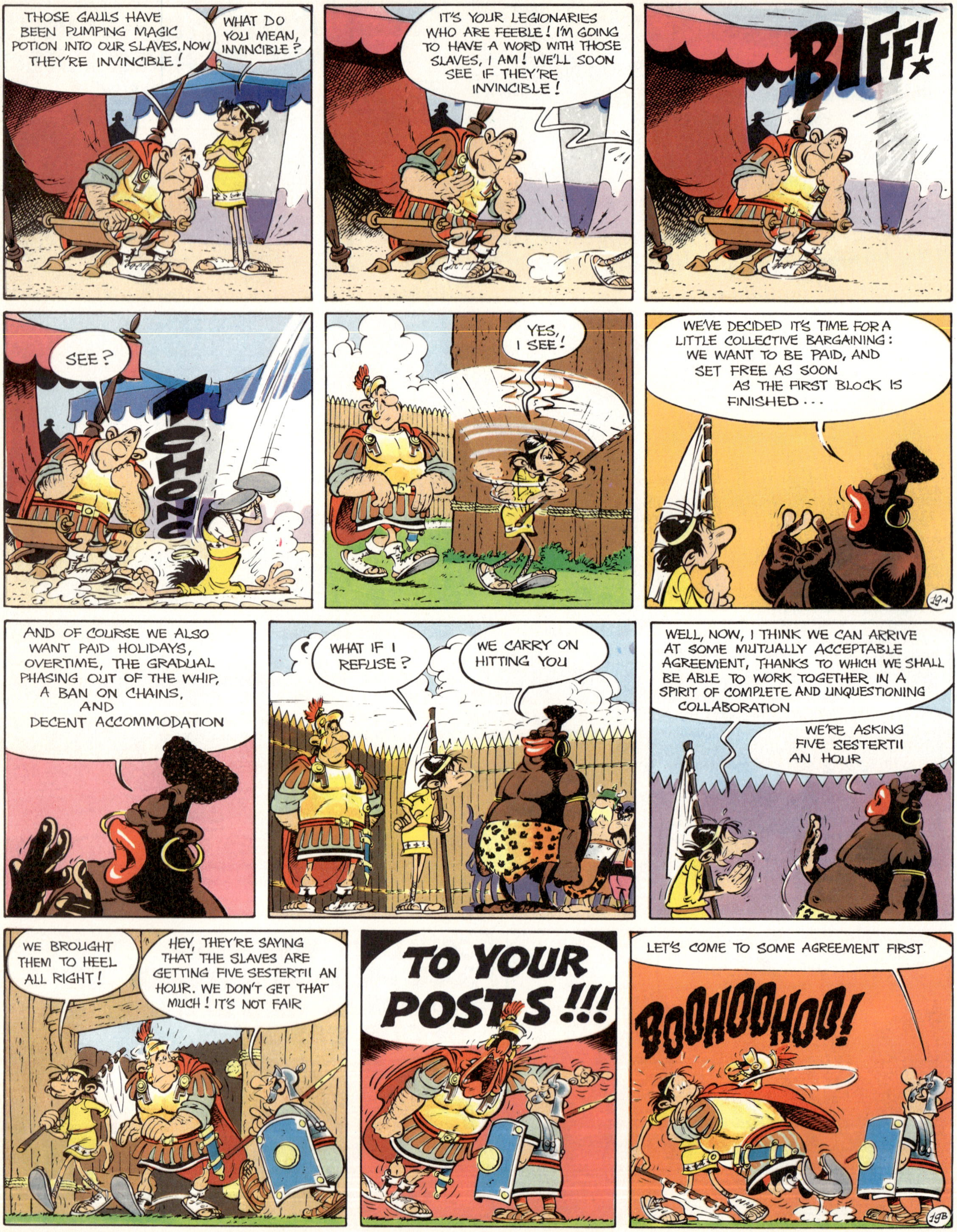
THOSE GAULS HAVE BEEN PUMPING MAGIC POTION INTO OUR SLAVES. NOW THEY'RE INVINCIBLE!
WHAT DO YOU MEAN, INVINCIBLE?
IT'S YOUR LEGIONARIES WHO ARE FEEBLE! I'M GOING TO HAVE A WORD WITH THOSE SLAVES, I AM! WE'LL SOON SEE IF THEY'RE INVINCIBLE!
BIFF!
SEE?
TCHONG
YES, I SEE!
WE'VE DECIDED IT'S TIME FOR A LITTLE COLLECTIVE BARGAINING: WE WANT TO BE PAID, AND SET FREE AS SOON AS THE FIRST BLOCK IS FINISHED...
AND OF COURSE WE ALSO WANT PAID HOLIDAYS, OVERTIME, THE GRADUAL PHASING OUT OF THE WHIP, A BAN ON CHAINS, AND DECENT ACCOMMODATION
WHAT IF I REFUSE?
WE CARRY ON HITTING YOU
WELL, NOW, I THINK WE CAN ARRIVE AT SOME MUTUALLY ACCEPTABLE AGREEMENT, THANKS TO WHICH WE SHALL BE ABLE TO WORK TOGETHER IN A SPIRIT OF COMPLETE AND UNQUESTIONING COLLABORATION
WE'RE ASKING FIVE SESTERTII AN HOUR
WE BROUGHT THEM TO HEEL ALL RIGHT!
HEY, THEY'RE SAYING THAT THE SLAVES ARE GETTING FIVE SESTERTII AN HOUR. WE DON'T GET THAT MUCH! IT'S NOT FAIR
TO YOUR POSTS!!!
LET'S COME TO SOME AGREEMENT FIRST
BOOHOOHOO!

WHILE SOMNIFERUS IS DEALING WITH HIS OWN LITTLE PROBLEMS, WORK HAS BEGUN AGAIN ON THE BUILDING SITE, NOW THAT THE AGREEMENT AND THE MAGIC POTION HAVE PROVED EFFECTIVE...
ALLEZ...
OOOP!
CRACK!
IT'S UNHEARD-OF! THE SLAVES HAVE BEEN WORKING BETTER SINCE WE STARTED PAYING THEM!
YES, IT MEANS MORE INITIAL OUTLAY, BUT BIGGER PROFITS!
AND THINK OF THE SAVING ON WHIPS!
I DON'T UNDERSTAND, ASTERIX! I THOUGHT THEY WERE GOING TO REBEL AGAINST THE ROMANS AND STOP WORK...
EEEK! THIS TREE'S MOVING!
CRAAAACK!
FLOOTCH!
FLATURTHA! WHY ARE YOU PULLING UP THESE TREES?
NO VISITORS ON THE BUILDING SITE. PUSH OFF!
LOOK HERE, NUMIDIAN...
OVERSEERS! NO SLACKING! I FEEL TIRED AND HUNGRY. I'D LIKE A QUICK WHIP!
20

THESE SLAVES ARE CRAZY!
HUH! LET'S LEAVE THEM TO WEAR THEMSELVES OUT. TOMORROW WE'LL MAKE THE TREES GROW AGAIN AS USUAL
WHAT A BORE, MOVING NEST ALL THE TIME!
NEXT MORNING, IN THE CAMP OF AQUARIUM...
RIGHT, IT'S PAY DAY... AND WE AND OUR MATES THINK THAT NIGHT WORK OUGHT TO COUNT AS OVERTIME
BEFORE I PAY YOU I WANT TO MAKE SURE THE WORK'S BEEN DONE TO MY SATISFACTION
HOW ABOUT THAT, THEN?
21A
I'M NOT PAYING YOU TO BRING ME TREES; I'M PAYING YOU TO CLEAR THE FOREST AND BUILD FLATS. LET'S GO AND HAVE A LOOK AT THE BUILDING SITE
SOON AFTERWARDS...
WELL, THE FOREST IS STILL HERE!
BUT YOU KNOW THE TREES WE PULLED UP CAME FROM HERE
THERE ISN'T ANY PROOF. AND REMEMBER THAT YOU WON'T BE FREED UNTIL THE WORK'S FINISHED. IT'S NOT COMING ALONG VERY WELL, IS IT?
YOUR TROUBLE IS YOU CAN'T SEE THE WOOD FOR THE TREES
....
THE PROBLEM'S CLEARING
21B

CENTURION! YOUR MEN ARE NOT DOING THEIR DUTY! THEY'LL HAVE TO GUARD THE SITE BY DAY, TO STOP PEOPLE MAKING THE TREES GROW AGAIN AFTER WE PULL THEM UP BY NIGHT!
MY MEN ARE ON STRIKE, BUT NEGOTIATIONS HAVE NOT BROKEN DOWN. TODAY WE TACKLE THE QUESTION OF EVENING PASSES. THE DELEGATES WANT THEM EXTENDED BY AN HOUR
MEANWHILE...
I WANT TO SEE YOUR CHIEF, GAUL
HE'S IN HIS HUT NUMIDIAN
YOU'RE KEEPING US FROM BEING FREED BY NOT ALLOWING US TO FINISH THE WORK
22A
BUT WHEN YOU GO UPROOTING TREES YOU HURT DOGMATIX AND THE BOARS...
... AND THE BIRDS...
YES, WE CAN'T HAVE FOWL PLAY. IT'S THE ROMANS WE WANT TO GET THE BIRD
THE BIRDS ARE FREE AS AIR, AND SO ARE THE BOARS AND YOUR DOG!
YOU'RE RIGHT, NUMIDIAN
NOT ONLY WILL WE STOP KEEPING YOU FROM FINISHING THE WORK, BUT I'LL GIVE YOU SOME MAGIC POTION TO HELP YOU GET IT DONE FASTER. COME ON!
DON'T WORRY; WE'RE GOING TO HAVE A BIT OF FUN WITH THE ROMANS. WE'LL TEACH THEM ANOTHER LESSON AND HELP THESE POOR SLAVES AT THE SAME TIME
22B
CLANG!

SQUARONTHEHYPOTENUS, THE ARCHITECT, HAS EVERY REASON TO BE PLEASED. THE WORK GETS DONE AT SPECTACULAR SPEED... NOW THEY'RE PAYING OVERTIME...
OH, COME ON, OBELIX! GETAFIX KNOWS WHAT HE'S DOING
THE SUPPLY OF BOARS IS DRYING UP!
SNIFFF!
ON THE OTHER HAND, WE'RE GOING TO HAVE HEAPS OF NEW ROMANS
I HOPE YOU'RE RIGHT, ASTERIX, I JUST HOPE TO TOUTATIS YOU'RE RIGHT!
CENTURION SOMNIFERUS IS SATISFIED AS WELL. A PERMANENT COUNCIL HAS BEEN SET UP AND THE POSSIBILITY OF THE TWO SIDES REACHING AN AGREEMENT AT SOME FUTURE DATE CANNOT BE RULED OUT
SOMNIFERUS, I'M OFF TO ROME TO TELL CAESAR HOW WELL THE PROJECT IS GETTING ON
AS SOON AS THE FIRST BLOCK OF FLATS IS FINISHED AND THE ROMANS HAVE MOVED IN, WE SHALL BE ABLE TO SAY THAT THE MANSIONS OF THE GODS HAVE DEFEATED THE BARBARIANS
MEANWHILE THEY'VE CHANGED A GREAT MANY THINGS ALREADY...
LISTEN TO THE NEW COOKHOUSE CALL. IT'S THE RESULT OF A NEW AGREEMENT BETWEEN THE OFFICERS AND THE MEN...

THE ARCHITECT SQUARONTHEHYPOTENUS, BACK FROM GAUL, CRAVES AN AUDIENCE OF CAESAR!
SHOW HIM IN!
AVE, CAESAR! THE FIRST BUILDING IN THE MANSIONS OF THE GODS WILL SOON BE FINISHED!
IF WE SUCCEED IN GETTING ROMANS TO LIVE IN THE VICINITY OF THOSE GAULS, I CAN SAY NOT ONLY VENI AND VIDI, BUT REALLY VICI AS WELL!
I'VE PREPARED A PUBLICITY CAMPAIGN TO FIND TENANTS FOR THE MANSIONS OF THE GODS
THE CAMPAIGN IN QUESTION IS WELL THOUGHT OUT, AND BEGINS WITH A GALA PERFORMANCE AT ROME'S CIRCUS MAXIMUS...
GALA PERFORMANCE
A GRAND RAFFLE WILL BE HELD AT THE END OF THE GLADIATORS' FIGHTS
THE WINNER WILL RECEIVE A FLAT IN THE MANSIONS OF THE GODS
RETAIN THE NUMBERED TICKET YOU RECEIVED AT THE TURNSTILE
THE MANSIONS OF THE GODS? WHAT IN THE NAME OF THE ELYSIAN FIELDS ARE THOSE?
PERHAPS WE'LL FIND OUT FROM THIS BROCHURE THEY HANDED US
24

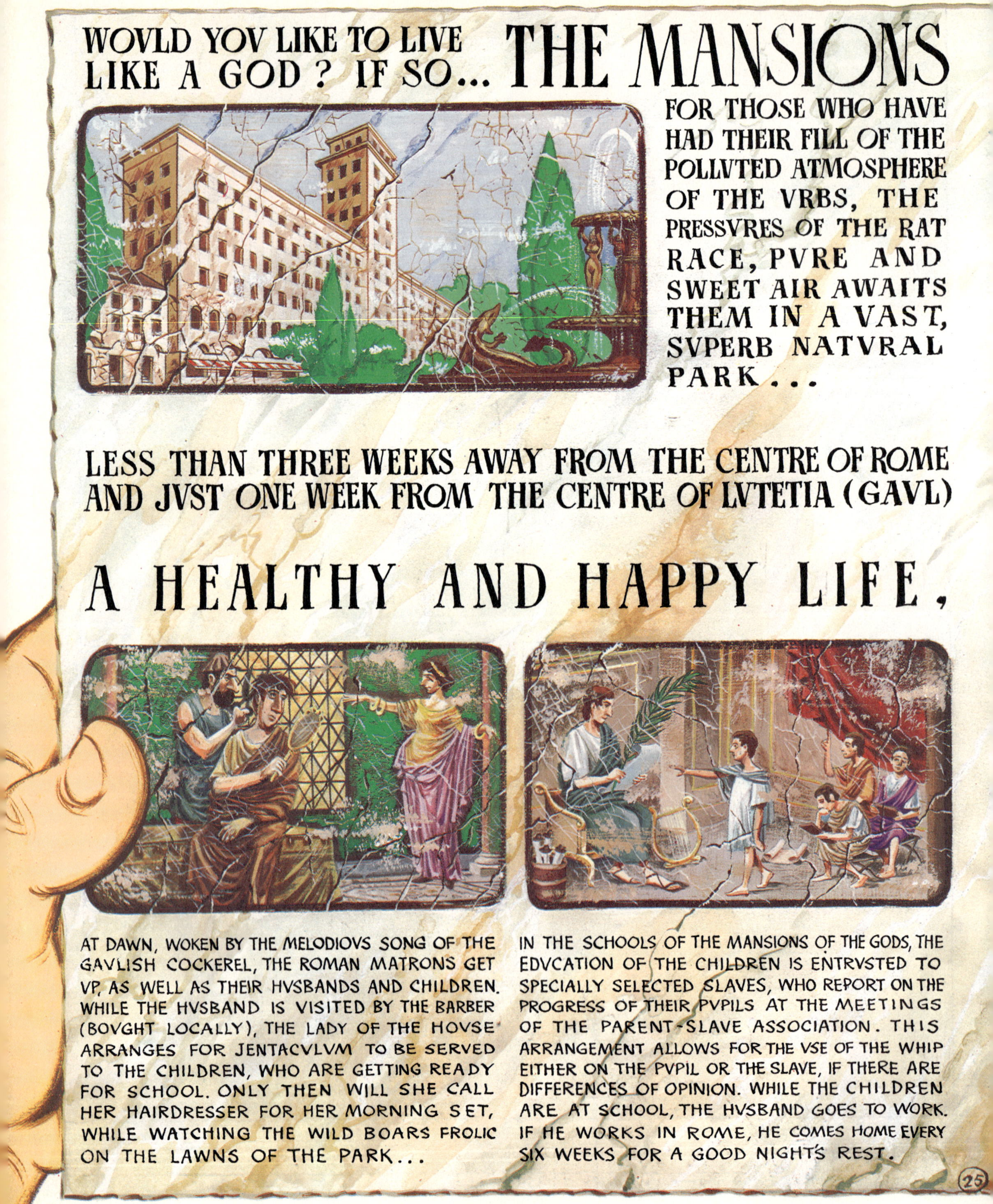
WOVLD YOV LIKE TO LIVE LIKE A GOD ? IF SO... THE MANSIONS
FOR THOSE WHO HAVE HAD THEIR FILL OF THE POLLVTED ATMOSPHERE OF THE VRBS, THE PRESSVRES OF THE RAT RACE, PVRE AND SWEET AIR AWAITS THEM IN A VAST, SVPERB NATVRAL PARK...
LESS THAN THREE WEEKS AWAY FROM THE CENTRE OF ROME AND JVST ONE WEEK FROM THE CENTRE OF LVTETIA (GAVL)
A HEALTHY AND HAPPY LIFE.
AT DAWN, WOKEN BY THE MELODIOVS SONG OF THE GAVLISH COCKEREL, THE ROMAN MATRONS GET VP, AS WELL AS THEIR HVSBANDS AND CHILDREN. WHILE THE HVSBAND IS VISITED BY THE BARBER (BOVGHT LOCALLY), THE LADY OF THE HOVSE ARRANGES FOR JENTACVLVM TO BE SERVED TO THE CHILDREN, WHO ARE GETTING READY FOR SCHOOL. ONLY THEN WILL SHE CALL HER HAIRDRESSER FOR HER MORNING SET, WHILE WATCHING THE WILD BOARS FROLIC ON THE LAWNS OF THE PARK...
IN THE SCHOOLS OF THE MANSIONS OF THE GODS, THE EDVCATION OF THE CHILDREN IS ENTRVSTED TO SPECIALLY SELECTED SLAVES, WHO REPORT ON THE PROGRESS OF THEIR PVPILS AT THE MEETINGS OF THE PARENT-SLAVE ASSOCIATION. THIS ARRANGEMENT ALLOWS FOR THE VSE OF THE WHIP EITHER ON THE PVPIL OR THE SLAVE, IF THERE ARE DIFFERENCES OF OPINION. WHILE THE CHILDREN ARE AT SCHOOL, THE HVSBAND GOES TO WORK. IF HE WORKS IN ROME, HE COMES HOME EVERY SIX WEEKS FOR A GOOD NIGHT'S REST.
25

OF THE GODS ARE FOR YOV!

GENERAL PLAN OF THE MANSIONS OF THE GODS
ARCHITECT: SQUARONTHEHYPOTENUS

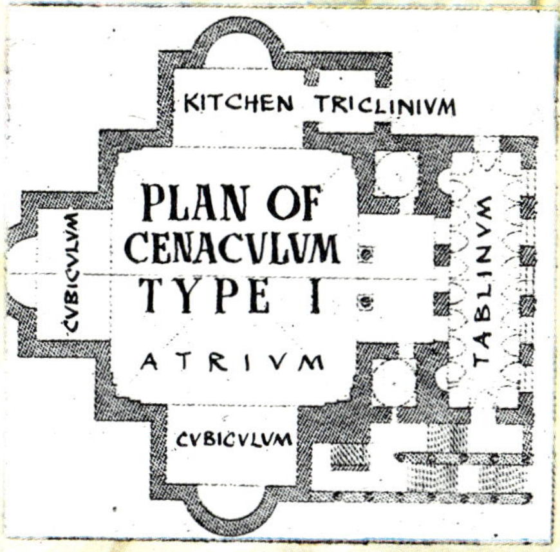

SHOPPING PRECINCT TO BE CONSTRVCTED

BATHS AND SPORTS HALL TO BE CONSTRVCTED

GAVLISEVM TO BE CONSTRVCTED

WORTHY OF A GOD!

ONCE HER HVSBAND AND CHILDREN HAVE GONE, THE MATRON VISITS HER FRIENDS FOR XISES. AFTERWARDS SHE MAY GO TO THE SHOPPING PRECINCT (TO BE CONSTRVCTED) WHERE SHE CAN FIND ALL SHE NEEDS, FROM FOOD AND CLOTHES TO JEWELLERY AND SLAVES. SHE IS HAVING A DINNER PARTY, AND SHE'S ONE SLAVE SHORT? SHE GOES STRAIGHT TO THE SELF-SERVICE SLAVE MARKET! SOON THE FAMILY WILL BE HOME. IT IS TIME TO PREPARE THE CENA.

WHEN THE HVSBAND COMES HOME FROM WORK HE CAN VISIT THE BATHS AND THE SPORTS HALL WITH HIS FRIENDS, OR GO FOR A ROMANTIC STROLL WITH HIS WIFE ALONG THE SHADY FOOTPATHS OF THE PARK (WHERE THE WILD BOARS FROLIC). IN THE EVENING, HE CAN GO TO THE GAVLISEVM (TO BE CONSTRVCTED), OR SIMPLY HAVE A FEW FRIENDS IN FOR AN ORGY. ALL HE HAS TO DO THEN IS GO TO BED AND AWAIT THE DAWNING OF A MAGNIFICENT NEW DAY, THE SORT OF DAY YOV CAN FIND ONLY IN THE MANSIONS OF THE GODS!

26

THAT'S ALL VERY WELL, BUT I SEEM TO REMEMBER THAT THERE ARE PARTS OF GAUL WHICH ARE NOT VERY RESTFUL...
OH, IT'S IN GAUL, IS IT?
THE LAST PAIR OF GLADIATORS HAVE FINISHED MASSACRING EACH OTHER, AND SHOWBUSINUS THE FAMOUS MASTER OF CEREMONIES, COMES TO THE CENTRE OF THE ARENA
AND NOW THE GREAT MOMENT HAS ARRIVED! YOU'RE ALL WONDERFUL, AND AFTER THESE WONDERFUL GLADIATORS WHO HAVE KILLED ONE ANOTHER FOR YOU...GIVE THEM A BIG HAND, FOLKS, THE SURVIVORS AS WELL AS THE OTHER ONES...
THANK YOU... WE'RE GOING TO PICK THE FORTUNATE WINNER OF ONE OF THE CENACULA IN THE MANSIONS OF THE GODS... WE HAVE HERE A WONDERFUL VESTAL VIRGIN - GIVE HER A BIG HAND, FOLKS! SHE WILL DRAW THE WINNING NUMBER
CLAP CLAPCLAP CLAPCLAPCLAP CLAP
CIV! WHO HAS GOT CIV?
CIV
IT'S YOU!
SHHHHHHH!
CIV
HERE HE IS! OVER HERE!
CIV
AH, I SEE WE HAVE A WONDERFUL WINNER! COME DOWN INTO THE ARENA, PLEASE!
GIVE HIM A BIG HAND, FOLKS!
WHAT IF I REFUSE TO GO TO GAUL?
YOU'LL STAY IN THE ARENA AND WE'LL LET IN THE LIONS
IN THAT CASE, I ACCEPT
DID YOU HEAR THAT?
HE ACCEPTS! GIVE THIS WONDERFUL WINNER A BIG HAND, FOLKS!!!

I'VE HEARD THE FIRST TENANTS ARE ARRIVING FROM ROME TODAY
AND GETAFIX TOLD US NOT TO BASH THEM ABOUT...
I'M VERY WORRIED ABOUT THESE ROMANS, GETAFIX
THEY MAY BE WONDERFUL...
I KNOW WHAT LINE I'M TAKING: I SHALL IGNORE THEM!
SO SHALL I!
I CAN'T THINK WHAT'S STOPPING ME KNOCKING THEIR BLASTED FLATS DOWN!
TAKE IT EASY! AT LEAST THE SLAVES HAVE BEEN FREED. THAT'S ONE GOOD THING!
SURE ENOUGH...
WHAT ARE WE GOING TO DO NOW WE'RE FREE?
NOW OUR SHIP'S COME HOME, WE'LL FLOAT A COMPANY, ME HEARTIES!
CLING! CLING!
WELCOME TO THE MANSIONS OF THE GODS!

THE SHOPPING PRECINCT IS NOT QUITE FINISHED. YOU CAN BUY FOOD IN THE NEARBY MILITARY CAMPS. WE'VE MADE ALL THE NECESSARY ARRANGEMENTS
WHY SHOULD WE GO TO THOSE CAMPS WHEN THERE'S A CHARMING NATIVE VILLAGE CLOSE BY ?
SO THERE IS ! WHAT A GOOD IDEA ! WE'LL GO TOMORROW
?!?
FRESH FISH ! IT'S LUVERLY !
UNHYGIENIX
FISHMONGER
THEY DO LOOK FRESH ... HOW MUCH IS THAT ONE ?
ER ... ONE SESTERTIUS
TO THINK THEY'D ASK FIVE SESTERTII FOR THE SAME FISH IN ROME ! I'LL HAVE THREE !
I'LL HAVE THREE TOO !
WELL DONE ! OH, VERY WELL DONE !
WHAT D'YOU MEAN ? YOU DIDN'T EXPECT ME NOT TO SERVE THEM JUST BECAUSE THEY'RE ROMANS !
DO YOU REALIZE THAT IF YOU WERE IN ROME YOU WOULD HAVE CHARGED FIVE SESTERTII EACH FOR THOSE FISH ?!!
!?!
SOON AFTERWARDS...
... AND I BOUGHT THIS SWORD AT A CHARMING LITTLE SHOP BELONGING TO FULLIAUTOMATIX - A GENUINE ANTIQUE, HE MADE IT HIMSELF !

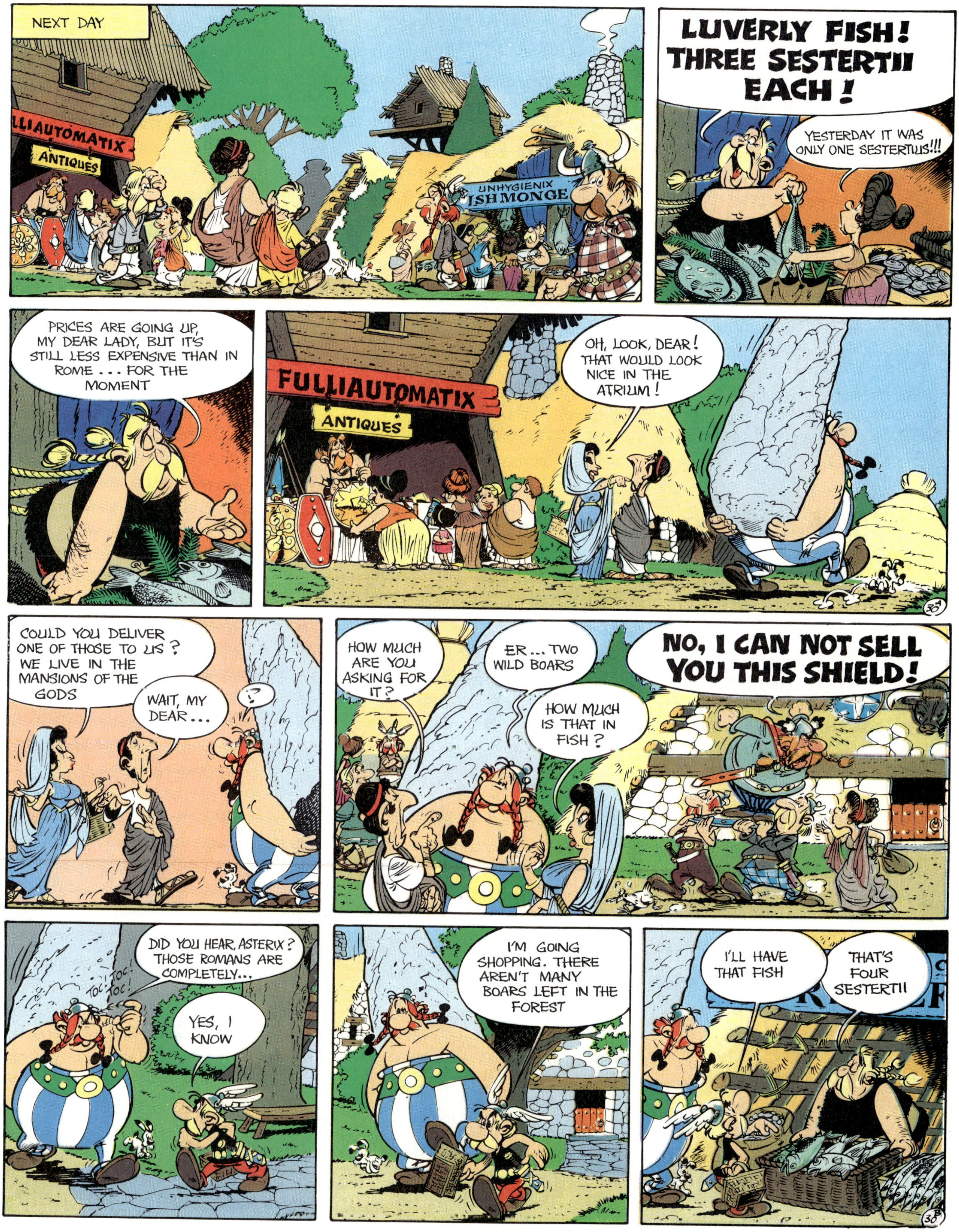
NEXT DAY
FULLIAUTOMATIX
ANTIQUES
UNHYGIENIX
FISHMONGER
LUVERLY FISH! THREE SESTERTII EACH!
YESTERDAY IT WAS ONLY ONE SESTERTIUS!!!
PRICES ARE GOING UP, MY DEAR LADY, BUT IT'S STILL LESS EXPENSIVE THAN IN ROME . . . FOR THE MOMENT
FULLIAUTOMATIX
ANTIQUES
OH, LOOK, DEAR! THAT WOULD LOOK NICE IN THE ATRIUM!
COULD YOU DELIVER ONE OF THOSE TO US? WE LIVE IN THE MANSIONS OF THE GODS
WAIT, MY DEAR . . .
?
HOW MUCH ARE YOU ASKING FOR IT?
ER . . . TWO WILD BOARS
HOW MUCH IS THAT IN FISH?
NO, I CAN NOT SELL YOU THIS SHIELD!
TOC! TOC! TOC!
DID YOU HEAR, ASTERIX? THOSE ROMANS ARE COMPLETELY . . .
YES, I KNOW
I'M GOING SHOPPING. THERE AREN'T MANY BOARS LEFT IN THE FOREST
I'LL HAVE THAT FISH
THAT'S FOUR SESTERTII

FOUR SESTERTII FOR A FISH?
I'M SORRY, ASTERIX. PRICES ARE GOING UP
THAT'S DAYLIGHT ROBBERY!
ROBBERY? GO TO ROME AND SEE HOW MUCH FISH COSTS THERE!
ALL RIGHT, THERE YOU ARE
HOW MUCH IS YOUR FISH IN MENHIRS?
I DON'T KNOW THE WILD BOAR EXCHANGE RATE
I'LL TAKE YOUR FISH, BUT YOUR ATTITUDE AMAZES ME!
OH, WE CAN DO WITHOUT GAULS, WE CAN! THE ROMAN TRADE IS ENOUGH FOR US
SPLATCH!
I DON'T WANT TO POKE MY NOSE INTO SOMETHING WHICH DOESN'T CONCERN ME, ASTERIX, BUT YOU WERE UNWISE TO...
SCHPLONK!
PAF!
YOUR ATTITUDE AMAZES ME, FULLIAUTOMATIX!
I DON'T LIKE THE WAY THINGS ARE GOING GETAFIX. YOU DIDN'T FORESEE ALL THIS, DID YOU?
NO, I DIDN'T EXPECT THIS. SOME ROMANS HAVE EVEN BEEN IN HERE TO BUY MY CAULDRON!
THE ROMANS HAVE GONE HOME NOW. LET'S TAKE ADVANTAGE OF IT TO HAVE A MEETING AND DECIDE WHAT TO DO

FRIENDS! THE ROMANS HAVE DESTROYED THE FOREST, AND IN THE END THEY WILL DESTROY US ALL. I'M JUST WONDERING WHETHER WE SHOULDN'T GET RID OF THEM!
FROM THE POINT OF VIEW OF THE FISH TRADE, ROMANS MEAN PROGRESS
I WAS A BLACKSMITH, AND THANKS TO THEM, I'M NOW AN ANTIQUE DEALER!
YOU ARE THE OLDEST MEMBER OF THE VILLAGE, GERIATRIX. HOW DO YOU FEEL ABOUT HAVING ROMANS IN OUR FOREST?
WELL... ER...
HE THINKS IT'S A GOOD THING THAT THEY'RE HERE! THEY WILL HELP US TO EMERGE FROM THE BARBARIAN AGE
YOU MUST ADMIT IT'S MORE ELEGANT THAN OUR USUAL TATTERS!
MY LITTLE GERIATRIX AND I HAVE DECIDED TO CHANGE OUR LIFESTYLE; WE'RE GOING TO OPEN SHOPS
SHOPS? WHAT SHOPS?
I SHALL HAVE AN ANTIQUE SHOP, AND DEAR GERIATRIX A FISHMONGER'S
ANTIQUES, ALL RIGHT, BUT A FISHMONGER'S? ARE YOU OUT OF YOUR MIND?
ANTIQUES? IF GERIATRIX IS GOING TO SELL ANTIQUES YOU WON'T BE ABLE TO MAKE OUT WHICH IS WHICH
HOW ABOUT MY STICK? CAN YOU MAKE OUT MY STICK?
TAKE NO NOTICE OF THEM, GERIATRIX MY LOVE!
THERE ARE GOING TO BE TOO MANY FISHMONGERS ROUND HERE. I'M OPENING MINE TOMORROW!
AND I'M OPENING MINE!
THAT'S WHAT YOU THINK!
I DON'T WANT ANY FISHMONGERS NEAR MY ANTIQUE SHOP!

NEXT MORNING
GETAFIX, LOOK HOW OUR VILLAGE HAS CHANGED! AND THAT'S NOT ALL...
FISHMONGER
ANTIQUES
ANTIQUES
FISHMONGER
ANTIQUES
DEAR ME, NO...
...THE WONDERFUL SPIRIT OF CO-OPERATION WE USED TO HAVE HAS DISAPPEARED
NOW I'M CERTAIN, ASTERIX. ALL THIS IS PART OF JULIUS CAESAR'S PLAN TO GET RID OF US!
I'LL SELL MY FISH CHEAPER THAN YOURS!
CAN YOU SEE MY FISH? CAN YOU SEE IT?
WHO WANTS TO FEEL MY ANTIQUE?
CAESAR IS USING THE ROMANS WHO LIVE IN THE MANSIONS OF THE GODS, BUT THEY DON'T REALIZE WHAT IS HAPPENING
WE MUST GET RID OF THEM... I'VE GOT AN IDEA
33A
NEXT MORNING
A VACANT FLAT IN THE MANSIONS? AFRAID NOT, EVERYTHING'S TAKEN - IT'S A GREAT SUCCESS!
SOON WE'RE GOING TO CUT DOWN THE REMAINDER OF THE FOREST AND BUILD SOME NEW FLATS. WE COULD RESERVE YOU ONE OF THOSE...
TEEHEE! IF THE GAULS ARE STARTING TO LEAVE THE VILLAGE, THE LAST CENTRE OF RESISTANCE AGAINST THE ROMAN OCCUPATION WILL HAVE DISAPPEARED. CAESAR WILL BE DELIGHTED!
THAT SAME AFTERNOON, IN THE VILLAGE...
ANTIQU
FISHM
GRRRRRRRRRR!
AAAAH!
OBELIX! CALM DOWN, OBELIX, TAKE IT EASY!
GRRRRRR!
33B

BY JUPITER! WHAT'S GOT INTO HIM?
TAKE NO NOTICE, HE DOESN'T LIKE THE LOOK OF YOU, THAT'S ALL. WE BARBARIANS ARE LIKE THAT, WE ACT ON INSTINCT
GRRRRR!
THAT GAUL IS CRAZY!
GRRRRRRR
JUST A LITTLE, YES. BUT AS LONG AS I'M HERE THERE'S NO NEED TO WORRY
ISHMONGER
ANTIQUE
LET'S GET BACK HOME!
YES, LET'S!
OH, LOOK AT THE PRETTY FLOWERS! HOLD MY BAG, I'M GOING TO PICK A LITTLE BUNCH
ALL RIGHT, BUT GET ON WITH IT
GRRRRRRRRRR!
YOU CAN COME DOWN. I'M HERE!
GRRRRR
D-D-DON'T LET GO OF HIM!
DON'T BE AFRAID; HE'S NOT REALLY VICIOUS, YOU KNOW. HE JUST LIKES TO PLAY GAMES
GRRRRRRR
PLAY GAMES?
A FINE GAME THAT WAS!
HOW DO YOU MANAGE TO SEEM SO FEROCIOUS, OBELIX?
I'VE BEEN WATCHING DOGMATIX WHEN HE'S IN A BAD TEMPER!

I'VE JUST ABOUT HAD ENOUGH OF LIVING AMONG THESE SAVAGES!
THERE, THERE, DEAR! AREN'T THESE FLOWERS BEAUTIFUL?
THEY DIDN'T MENTION THOSE BARBARIANS IN THE BROCHURE!
THEY SEEM QUITE NICE, HOWEVER. THE PRICE OF FISH IS GOING DOWN EVERY DAY. NOW THEY'RE OFFERING A FREE GIFT OF AN ANTIQUE WITH EVERY FISH...
...AND A FREE GIFT OF A FISH WITH EVERY ANTIQUE. COME ON, LET'S EAT!
THERE'S SARDINES IN SUGAR, MACKEREL'S EYES IN JELLY, AND ANCHOVY JAM, JUST LIKE WE HAD IN ROME
AH... ROME, SWEET ROME...
KNOCK! KNOCK! KNOCK!
TH... THERE'S SOMEONE AT THE DOOR!
EVERY TIME WE LIE DOWN TO THE TABLE, IT'S THE SAME! GO AND SEE WHO IT IS, QUICK, DEAR. THE STEWED OCTOPUS WILL GET COLD
I'M SORRY TO DISTURB YOU, BUT YOU HAVEN'T SEEN MY FRIEND, HAVE YOU?
WHAT? ISN'T HE WITH YOU?
HE GOT AWAY... HE WANTED TO SEE YOU. IF HE COMES, GIVE HIM SOME RAW MEAT. THAT CALMS HIM DOWN... SOMETIMES
CLV
WHO WAS IT?
GUESS! ANYWAY, TOMORROW WE'RE LEAVING!

DAYBREAK, THE FOLLOWING MORNING...
WHAT'S THIS? YOU'RE GOING BACK TO ROME, JUST LIKE THAT?
I WON THIS FLAT IN A GAME AND NOW I'M GIVING IT BACK. AND WHAT A GAME THAT WAS!
I'VE HEARD YOU MIGHT HAVE A FLAT VACANT?
HMM?
NEWS TRAVELS FAST! WELL, IT JUST SO HAPPENS WE DO. YOU CAN HAVE IT IF YOU LIKE
OH, IT ISN'T FOR ME
IT'S FOR OUR BARD CACOFONIX
THERE YOU ARE. STAIRCASE A, LAST FLOOR, NUMBER CLV- DO YOU WANT ME TO SHOW YOU THE WAY?
DON'T BOTHER; I KNOW IT
DO YOU LIKE IT?
YES, IT'S VERY NICE... BUT WHY ARE YOU AND OBELIX TREATING ME TO THIS FLAT?
SO YOU CAN SING IN PEACE. YOU HAVE OFTEN CALLED US BARBARIANS, AND YOU WERE RIGHT. HERE, IN THE MANSIONS OF THE GODS YOU WILL HAVE CIVILIZED NEIGHBOURS
IN THAT CASE, I ACCEPT! AT LAST I CAN PRACTISE MY ART SURROUNDED BY REFINED PEOPLE!
THAT'S WHAT WE SAID TO EACH OTHER: NOTHING BUT THE BEST FOR OUR BARD!
THOSE POOR ROMANS... I'M SORRY FOR THEM
WE REALLY ARE LAYING IT ON A BIT THICK!

AH, HOW PEACEFUL... WE ARE FAR FROM THE PLEASURES OF ROME, BUT HOW QUIET IT IS ...
GOOD NIGHT
GOOD NIGHT
TZOIING! TZOIING!
CAN YOU HEAR A FUNNY LITTLE NOISE?
IT'S PROBABLY A WILD BOAR FROLICKING ON THE LAWN
RIGHT. HERE GOES!
ON THE FIRST DAY OF SOLSTICE MY TRUE LOVE SENT TO ME...
TZOIN! TZOIN!
A WILD BOAR IN AN OAK TREE...
ON THE SECOND DAY OF SOLSTICE MY TRUE LOVE SENT TO ME, TWO STANDING STONES AND A WILD BOAR IN AN OAK TREE. ON THE THIRD DAY...
THE GAULS ARE ATTACKING!
THE GODS ARE ANGRY!
THE BUILDING'S COLLAPSING!
I PREFER THE STREET CRIES OF ROME!
QUOUSQUE TANDEM? QUOUSQUE TANDEM?
START PACKING! TOMORROW WE'RE OFF!

SURE ENOUGH, NEXT MORNING...
WHAT? YOU'RE ALL LEAVING THE FLATS? JUST BECAUSE OF A GAUL WHO SINGS LOUD AND FLAT?
PEOPLE WHO SING LIKE THAT ARE CAPABLE OF ANYTHING! WE'VE HAD ENOUGH OF BARBARIANS! WE'RE GOING BACK TO ROME!
THE WHOLE BUILDING HAS EMPTIED ITSELF AT ONE GO! ONLY ONE TENANT IS LEFT – A GAUL...
A GAUL? WHICH GAUL?
A BARD... CACOFONOGRAFIX, I THINK HE'S CALLED...
CACOFONIX, THE BARD? YOU'VE BEEN HAD BY THE GAULS! HE'S A MENACE. YOU'LL NEVER SEE YOUR TENANTS AGAIN!
38A
I DON'T ADMIT DEFEAT! IF CAESAR KNOWS THE BUILDING IS EMPTY, HE'LL ABANDON THE PLAN!
BUT YOU'VE NO MORE TENANTS...
PAF!
THE GARRISON OF AQUARIUM! YOUR GARRISON CAN TAKE UP QUARTERS IN THE MANSIONS OF THE GODS. THERE ARE THE TENANTS!
THE LEGIONARIES WON'T OBEY ME ANY MORE... THEY'RE STILL ON STRIKE
IF YOU SUCCEED IN WINNING YOUR MEN OVER, I'LL SHARE MY FEES WITH YOU!
IN THAT CASE, I'LL TRY
SOON AFTERWARDS...
I'VE CALLED THIS MEETING TO TELL YOU THAT I AGREE TO ALL YOUR DEMANDS... BUT THERE'S ONE PROBLEM LEFT...
THE PROBLEM OF ACCOMMODATION. YOU HAVEN'T YET BROUGHT IT UP, BUT I IMAGINE YOU WILL NO LONGER BE CONTENT TO SLEEP UNDER CANVAS...
38B

QUITE RIGHT! IT'S DISGRACEFUL! WE REFUSE TO LIVE IN A CAMP ANY LONGER!
TAKE IT OR LEAVE IT!
I AGREE, I AGREE... I HAVE REQUISITIONED THE MANSIONS OF THE GODS. YOU CAN MOVE IN IMMEDIATELY
GOOD. THAT DID THE TRICK... BUT YOU'LL HAVE TO GET THE BARD OUT OF THE BUILDING, OTHERWISE MY LEGIONARIES WILL GO ON STRIKE AGAIN
YOU BET YOUR LIFE I'LL GET HIM OUT!
LATER...
AH, SO YOU'RE BACK, ARE YOU? THEY SAY IT WAS YOUR FAULT THAT THE ROMANS LEFT! LOOK WHAT YOU'VE DONE TO OUR VILLAGE!
SALE
FOR SALE
SALE
ANTIQUES
FINAL CLEARANCE
FISHMONGER
FOR SALE
FOR SALE
FINAL CLEARANC
SALE
THERE ARE BARBARIANS EVERYWHERE. I HAVE BEEN THROWN OUT OF THE BUILDING; THEY'VE REQUISITIONED IT FOR THE ARMY
WHAT?
I SAID, THERE ARE BARBARIANS EVERYWHERE, AND...
?
THE LEGIONARIES HAVE THROWN OUT ONE OF OUR MEN. ARE WE GOING TO STAND FOR THAT?!
NEVER!
NEVER!

THE N.C.O.'S WILL HAVE THE LUXURY FLATS ON THE LOWER FLOORS... THE OTHER RANKS WILL LIVE ON THE UPPER FLOORS...
I'VE STATIONED SENTRIES ON THE ROOF... THEY WILL ACT AS AERIALS TO WARN US OF ANY DANGER
MEALS WILL BE SERVED IN THE ENTRY ATRIUM. EVERY LEGIONARY ON DUTY WILL COME WITH HIS COMRADES TO FETCH HIS RATIONS TO EAT IN HIS PRIVATE TRICLINIUM...
OF COURSE, WE SHALL HAVE TO HAVE MEETINGS OF THE TENANTS' ASSOCIATION. I DON'T CARE VERY MUCH FOR THE DECORATION IN THE ATRIUM...
WHAT'S THE MATTER WITH THE DECORATION? I THINK IT'S VERY NICE...
WHAT ABOUT LETTERS? WILL THEY BE DELIVERED, OR SHALL WE HAVE TO GO AND COLLECT THEM?
AND THE LAWN? WHO'LL LOOK AFTER THAT?
SOME TIME LATER...
MY LEGIONARIES NEED A GOOD BATTLE. THEY'RE GOING SOFT...
THAT'S YOUR PROBLEM. MINE IS JUST THE REVERSE: TO SEE THERE AREN'T ANY MORE QUARRELS
TANTARAA
TANTAN TARAAAA
THAT'S THE SENTRIES ON THE ROOF!
TARAAAAAA
LET'S HAVE SOME HUSH!
MUSIC ISN'T ALLOWED!
WE MUST PUT THAT ON THE AGENDA FOR THE NEXT MEETING OF THE TENANTS' ASSOCIATION!
WHAT THE...
LOOK, CENTURION! LOOK!

HAS EVERYONE HAD HIS MAGIC POTION?
NO
STOP! STOP! THIS IS PRIVATE PROPERTY!
AND WHAT IS MORE, PLEASE KEEP OFF THE GRASS!
IN THE FIRST PLACE, I'M NOT ON THE GRASS, AND IN THE SECOND PLACE, YOU ROMANS HAVE THROWN ONE OF OUR MEN OUT, SO WE ARE GOING TO THROW YOU OUT!
CHARGE! REPULSE INTRUDERS!!
RIGHTO!
HEY? HEY! FIGHTING IN A BLOCK OF FLATS IS NOT ALLOWED!!!
SPLIT UP! I'LL TAKE STAIRCASE A. ASTERIX AND THE OTHERS WILL TAKE STAIRCASE B!

MAY WE COME IN?
I'M IN MY BATH! I'M IN MY BATH!
THE LAST THREE FLOORS ARE MINE!
KNOCK AFTER GOING IN, BY TOUTATIS!
SHUT UP, OBELIX! YOU'LL HAVE WHAT'S LEFT!
WHY ARE YOU WAITING TO GO DOWN, BY JUPITER?
I'VE ALREADY HAD MINE! I'VE ALREADY HAD MINE!
TELL THAT DOG TO LET GO OF ME! DOGS ARE NOT ALLOWED IN THE BUILDING!
THE CHANGING OF THE GUARD'S IN TWO HOURS' TIME; THOSE ARE OUR ORDERS
OUCH! WATCH OUT, BY BELISAMA!
SORRY, O CHIEF! THE CEILING'S RATHER LOW HERE!
I'M NOT HERE! I TELL YOU I'M NOT HERE!
I SHALL HAVE SOMETHING TO SAY AT THE NEXT MEETING OF THE TENANTS' ASSOCIATION!
LISTEN, WE DON'T LIVE HERE, YOU UNDERSTAND... WE'RE JUST VISITING FRIENDS WHO ARE HAVING A FANCY DRESS BALL, THAT'S WHY WE'RE ALL DISGUISED AS LEGIONARIES... NOW, IN THE OTHER FLATS... ARE YOU LISTENING WHEN I SPEAK TO YOU?
GET THEM ROUND THE BACK, AT THE SERVICE ENTRANCE, BY BELENOS!
42

SOUND THE RETREAT!
SOON AFTERWARDS...
HOW NICE IT WILL BE TO BE BACK IN CAMP...
YES, LIFE UNDER CANVAS IS SO MUCH HEALTHIER!
COME ON, OUT OF YOUR BATH!
NOT BEFORE WE'RE BACK HOME!
SO THERE YOU ARE! GET OUT OF HERE AND NEVER DARKEN OUR CAMP SITE AGAIN! THE MANSIONS OF THE GODS ARE DONE FOR!
YOU'RE RIGHT; I NEVER WANT TO HEAR ANOTHER WORD ABOUT THOSE BARBARIANS. LET CAESAR DEAL WITH THEM AS BEST HE CAN... ANYWAY, I'VE GOT A CONTRACT TO BUILD SOME PYRAMIDS IN EGYPT...
IT WILL BE A PLEASANT CHANGE. BUILDINGS IN THE MIDDLE OF THE DESERT, WITH NICE QUIET TENANTS...
COME ON, BOYS! BACK TO THE VILLAGE!
IT WAS INTERESTING, THAT BUILDING. I TOOK THE OPPORTUNITY TO HAVE A GOOD LOOK ROUND... VERY INTERESTING
I DON'T LIKE TO SAY SO, BUT THESE MODERN BUILDINGS ARE RATHER FLIMSY...
WHAT ARE WE GOING TO DO NOW, GETAFIX?
WE'LL GET THE TREES TO GROW AGAIN

AT NIGHTFALL, THE FOREST HAS TAKEN OVER ONCE AGAIN. ONLY A FEW ROMAN REMAINS SHOW THAT THE MANSIONS OF THE GODS EVER STOOD THERE ...
O DRUID GETAFIX, DO YOU THINK WE CAN ALWAYS STOP THE COURSE OF EVENTS AS WE HAVE JUST DONE?
OF COURSE NOT, ASTERIX ...
BUT WE STILL HAVE TIME, PLENTY OF TIME!
WHAT DO YOU MEAN, TIME?
WE HAVEN'T GOT ANY TIME TO WASTE! THE WILD BOARS ARE READY; WE'RE ONLY WAITING FOR YOU!
AND NOT FAR FROM THE ROMAN RUINS, IN A NATURAL CLEARING IN THE FOREST, FREQUENTED BY WILD BOARS AND BIRDS, OUR FRIENDS THE GAULS, GATHERED TOGETHER FOR ONE OF THEIR TRADITIONAL FEASTS, CELEBRATE ANOTHER VICTORY, A VICTORY OVER THE ROMANS AND OVER THE INEXORABLE PASSAGE OF TIME ...
THE END
UDERZO.
GOSCINNY

PRINTED IN BELGIUM BY
proost
INTERNATIONAL BOOK PRODUCTION

OBELIX AND CO.

TEXT BY GOSCINNY
DRAWINGS BY UDERZO

TRANSLATED BY ANTHEA BELL AND DEREK HOCKRIDGE

HODDER DARGAUD
LONDON SYDNEY AUCKLAND

Obelix and Co.

ISBN 0 340 22709 5 (cased)
ISBN 0 340 25307 X (limp)

Copyright © Dargaud Editeur 1976, Goscinny-Uderzo
English language text copyright © Hodder and Stoughton Ltd 1978
(now Hodder Children's Books)

First published in Great Britain 1978 (cased)
This impression 110 109 108 107 106 105

First published in Great Britain 1980 (limp)
This impression 110 109 108 107

All rights reserved. No part of this publication may be reproduced or transmitted in any form or by any means, electronically or mechanically, including photocopying, recording, or any information storage and retrieval system, without either prior permission in writing from the publisher or a licence permitting restricted copying. In the United Kingdom such licences are issued by the Copyright Licensing Agency, 90 Tottenham Court Road, London W1P 9HE.

Published by Hodder Dargaud Ltd,
338 Euston Road, London NW1 3BH

Printed in Belgium by Proost International Book Production

The year is 50 BC. Gaul is entirely occupied by the Romans. Well, not entirely... One small village of indomitable Gauls still holds out against the invaders. And life is not easy for the Roman legionaries who garrison the fortified camps of Totorum, Aquarium, Laudanum and Compendium...

a few of the Gauls

Asterix, the hero of these adventures. A shrewd, cunning little warrior; all perilous missions are immediately entrusted to him. Asterix gets his superhuman strength from the magic potion brewed by the druid Getafix...

Obelix, Asterix's inseparable friend. A menhir delivery-man by trade; addicted to wild boar. Obelix is always ready to drop everything and go off on a new adventure with Asterix – so long as there's wild boar to eat, and plenty of fighting.

Getafix, the venerable village druid. Gathers mistletoe and brews magic potions. His speciality is the potion which gives the drinker superhuman strength. But Getafix also has other recipes up his sleeve...

Cacofonix, the bard. Opinion is divided as to his musical gifts. Cacofonix thinks he's a genius. Everyone else thinks he's unspeakable. But so long as he doesn't speak, let alone sing, everybody likes him...

Finally, Vitalstatistix, the chief of the tribe. Majestic, brave and hot-tempered, the old warrior is respected by his men and feared by his enemies. Vitalstatistix himself has only one fear; he is afraid the sky may fall on his head tomorrow. But as he always says, 'Tomorrow never comes.'

DISCIPLINE IS FAIRLY LAX IN THE FORTIFIED ROMAN CAMP OF TOTORUM...
IT'S OUR RELIEF, BOYS! IT'S OUR RELIEF!
OPEN THE GATES! OPEN THE GATES!
HEY, CENTURION SCROFULUS! IT'S THEM ALL RIGHT!
I AM CENTURION IGNORAMUS! AVE!
HI! I'M CENTURION SCROFULUS ... AVE! WHAT A RELIEF!
NOT IN UNIFORM, CENTURION SCROFULUS?
WE HARDLY EVER GO OUT, SO WE DON'T BOTHER TO DRESS UP.
SCRATCH SCRATCH
FORWARD MARCH!

I LIKE A NICE MARCH PAST, I DO!
EH?
A WORD OF ADVICE... TAKE IT EASY AND WAIT FOR YOUR RELIEF. AND IGNORE ANY PROVOCATION FROM THE LOCAL GAULS. THEY'RE CRAZY. THEY'RE ALSO INVINCIBLE.
I HAVE EVERY INTENTION OF BRINGING THOSE VERY GAULS TO HEEL! THAT WILL PLEASE JULIUS CAESAR... AND I DON'T WANT TO STAY A CENTURION MY WHOLE LIFE LONG!
SOUNDS LIKE YOUR WHOLE LIFE WON'T BE LONG... WELL, GET MOVING, LADS!
2A
2B

THIS IS GREAT! THIS IS GREAT!
THIS IS...
WHAT'S GREAT, ASTERIX?
HM?... OH, NOTHING... TEEHEEHEE!
WATCH OUT! HERE HE COMES!
TEEHEEHEE!
TEEHEEHEE!
TEEHEEHEE!
TEEHEEHEE!
TEEHEEHEE!
TEEHEEHEE!
TEEHEEHEE!
TEEHEEHEE!
TEEHEEHEE!
TEEHEEHEE!
WHAT'S BITTEN THEM?
TEEHEEHEE!

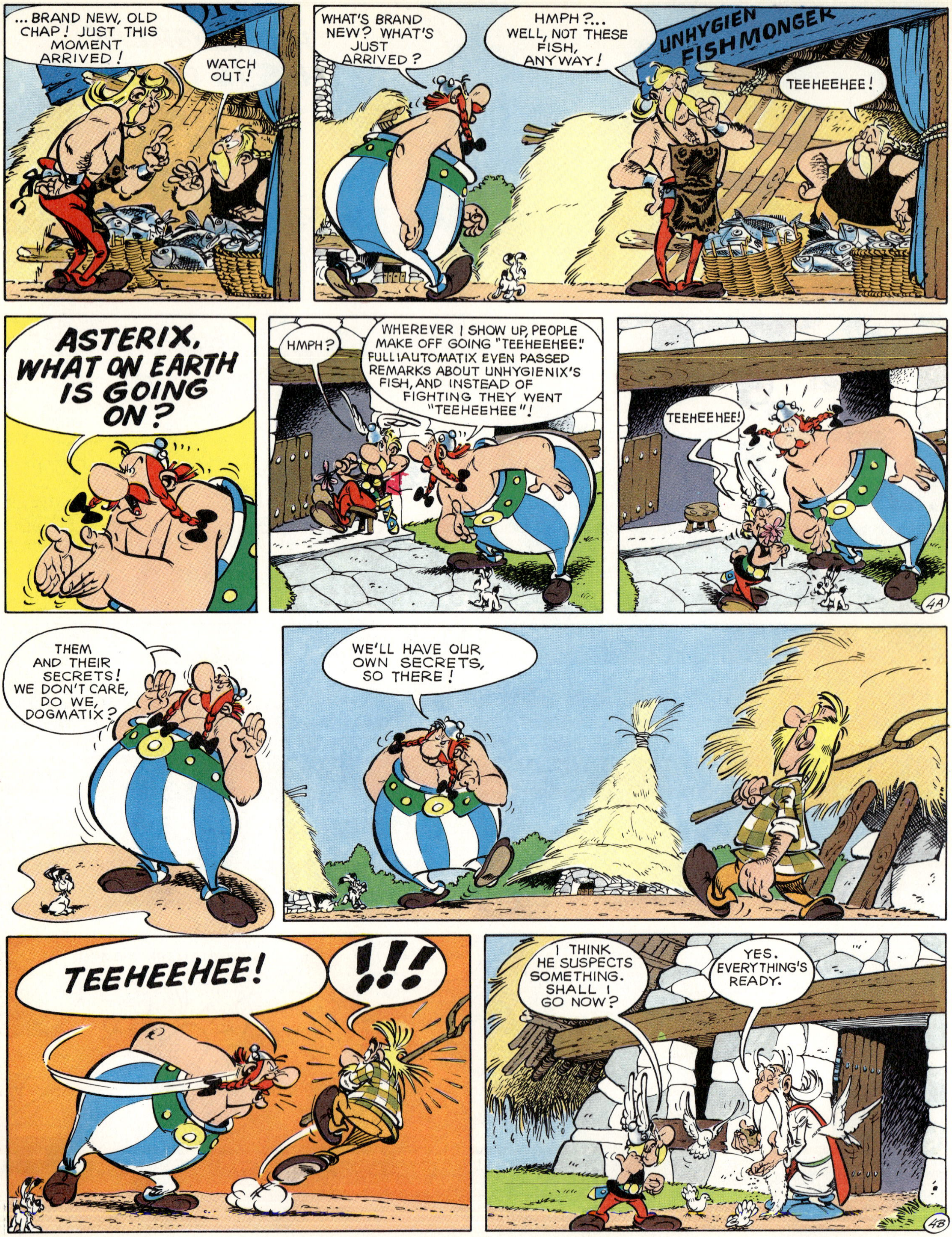
...BRAND NEW, OLD CHAP! JUST THIS MOMENT ARRIVED!
WATCH OUT!
WHAT'S BRAND NEW? WHAT'S JUST ARRIVED?
HMPH?... WELL, NOT THESE FISH, ANYWAY!
UNHYGIEN FISHMONGER
TEEHEEHEE!
ASTERIX, WHAT ON EARTH IS GOING ON?
HMPH?
WHEREVER I SHOW UP, PEOPLE MAKE OFF GOING "TEEHEEHEE." FULLIAUTOMATIX EVEN PASSED REMARKS ABOUT UNHYGIENIX'S FISH, AND INSTEAD OF FIGHTING THEY WENT "TEEHEEHEE"!
TEEHEEHEE!
4A
THEM AND THEIR SECRETS! WE DON'T CARE, DO WE, DOGMATIX?
WE'LL HAVE OUR OWN SECRETS, SO THERE!
TEEHEEHEE!
!!!
I THINK HE SUSPECTS SOMETHING. SHALL I GO NOW?
YES. EVERYTHING'S READY.
4B

MEN, WE ARE HERE TO STOP THE LOCAL INHABITANTS FLOUTING THE AUTHORITY OF ROME!
S P Q R
WE SHALL BRING THAT LITTLE GAULISH VILLAGE TO HEEL, AND WE'RE NOT STANDING FOR ANY NONSENSE!
FRIENDS, ROMANS, COUNTRYMEN, WE SHALL COVER OURSELVES WITH GLORY!
THERE'S A GAUL AT THE CAMP GATES, CENTURION, SIR!
AHA! MAYBE THEY SENSED THAT THINGS WERE GOING TO CHANGE... OPEN THE GATES!
WELL, GAUL? COME TO SURRENDER?
YAAAAAAAAAH!
MEN, CATCH THAT MIDGET! WE'LL MAKE AN EXAMPLE OF HIM!

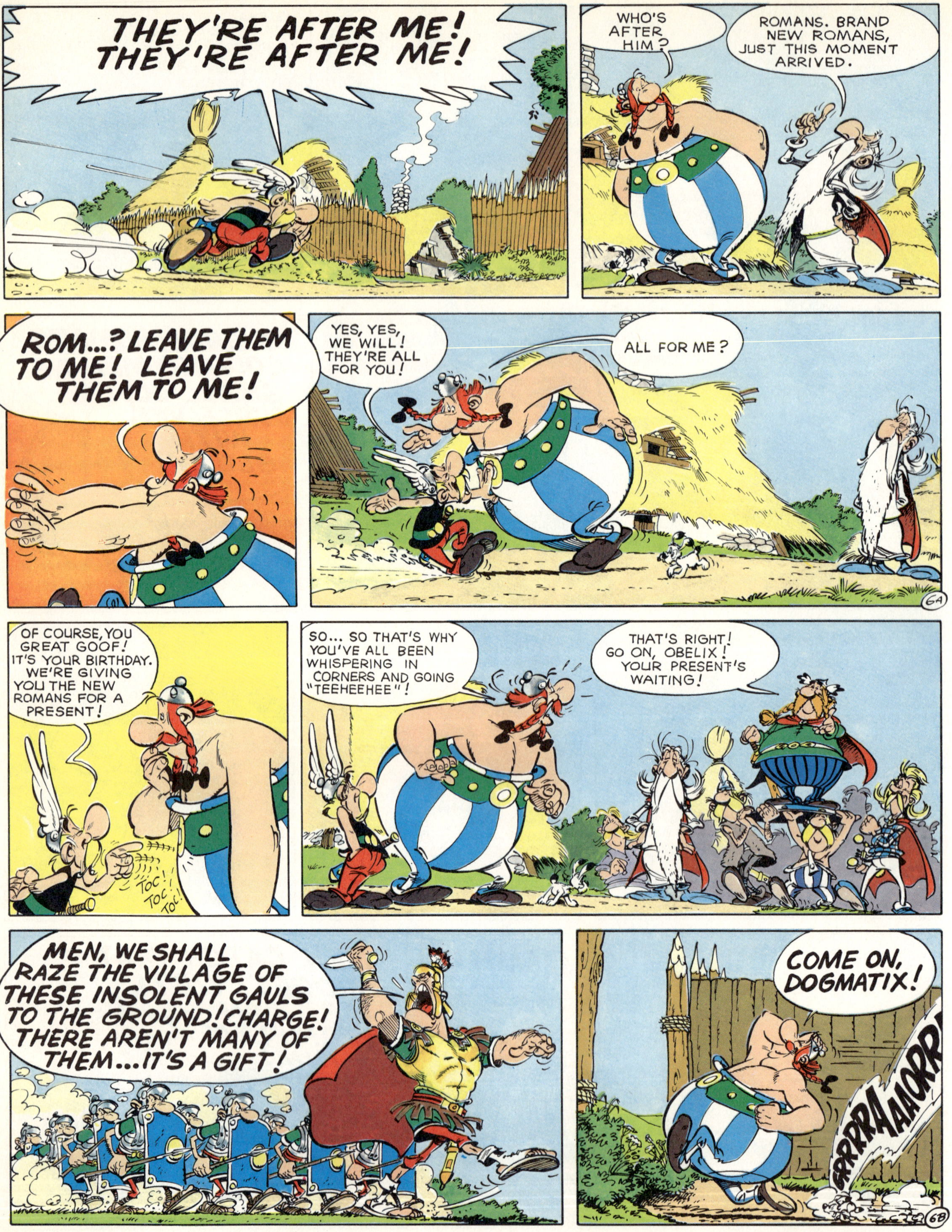
THEY'RE AFTER ME! THEY'RE AFTER ME!
WHO'S AFTER HIM?
ROMANS. BRAND NEW ROMANS, JUST THIS MOMENT ARRIVED.
ROM...? LEAVE THEM TO ME! LEAVE THEM TO ME!
YES, YES, WE WILL! THEY'RE ALL FOR YOU!
ALL FOR ME?
OF COURSE, YOU GREAT GOOF! IT'S YOUR BIRTHDAY. WE'RE GIVING YOU THE NEW ROMANS FOR A PRESENT!
TOC! TOC! TOC!
SO... SO THAT'S WHY YOU'VE ALL BEEN WHISPERING IN CORNERS AND GOING "TEEHEEHEE"!
THAT'S RIGHT! GO ON, OBELIX! YOUR PRESENT'S WAITING!
MEN, WE SHALL RAZE THE VILLAGE OF THESE INSOLENT GAULS TO THE GROUND! CHARGE! THERE AREN'T MANY OF THEM...IT'S A GIFT!
COME ON, DOGMATIX!
GRRRRAAAORR

HAPPY BIRTHDAY TO YOU, HAPPY BIRTHDAY TO YOU...
SUCH A LOVELY PRESENT... SO ELEGANT AND TASTEFUL... SO... SO THOUGHTFUL OF YOU... I REALLY DON'T KNOW WHAT TO...
NOW, NOW, OBELIX, DON'T CRY! YOU'RE OVER SENSITIVE! COME ALONG, THERE'S A FEAST WAITING, WITH LOTS OF WILD BOAR!
HAPPY BIRTHDAY... HAPPY BIRTHDAY...
HE DIDN'T EVEN BLOW OUT THE CANDLES!
WELL, NOW WHAT, CENTURION?
NOW WE GO BACK TO CAMP, SEND WORD TO JULIUS CAESAR... AND WAIT FOR OUR RELIEF!

IN ROME...
ONE MAN! ONE SOLITARY GAUL MANAGED TO DEFEAT AND DEMORALISE MY CRACK TROOPS!
THIS IS TOO MUCH! THESE GAULS MAKE ME LOOK RIDICULOUS. WE CAN'T GO ON LIKE THIS, BY JUPITER! WELL? I'M WAITING FOR SUGGESTIONS!
WE COULD SEND THE ENTIRE ARMY...
YES, BUT WE MUSTN'T LEAVE OUR FRONTIERS UNGUARDED.
SUPPOSE WE SET UP A COMMISSION TO STUDY THE PROBLEM?
GOOD IDEA! WITH SUB-COMMITTEES TO CONSIDER THE VARIOUS ASPECTS...
LET'S HAVE A WORKING LUNCH TO DISCUSS IT...
TAPTAPTAP! TAPTAP!
THEY ARE STRONG, SO WE MUST WEAKEN THEM. THEY HAVE NOTHING TO DO BUT FIGHT, SO WE MUST KEEP THEM BUSY SOME OTHER WAY...
COME HERE, CAIUS PREPOSTERUS. JUST HOW WOULD YOU SET ABOUT WEAKENING THE GAULS, WITH THEIR MAGICAL STRENGTH?
GO ON! LET'S SEE WHAT THEY TAUGHT YOU AT THE LATIN SCHOOL OF ECONOMICS...
EASY, O CAESAR. GOLD, THE PROFIT MOTIVE...
...WILL ENFEEBLE THEM AND KEEP THEM BUSY. WE MUST CORRUPT THEM.
YOU THINK THAT WILL DO THE TRICK?
LOOK AROUND YOU, O CAESAR!

NONSENSE!
THAT YOUNG KNOW-ALL HAS NO EXPERIENCE!
DON'T LISTEN TO HIM, O CAESAR. WHAT WE NEED IS A THINK TANK...
WE MUST OPPOSE FORCE WITH FORCE! REMEMBER OUR CAMPAIGNS, CAESAR? WE MADE THE WHOLE WORLD BOW BEFORE OUR LEGIONS!
I REMEMBER ALL RIGHT, LARCENUS. YOU WERE A BRAVE, ATHLETIC YOUNG TRIBUNE, YOU BROUGHT BACK A FORTUNE FROM OUR CAMPAIGNS... AND NOW LOOK AT YOU!
SEE WHAT ALL YOUR GOLD, YOUR VILLAS, YOUR ORGIES HAVE MADE OF YOU! YOU'RE DECADENT!
YOU, A THINK TANK? ALL YOU THINK OF IS TANKING UP!
HMPH? LUNCHTIME?
YOU REALLY THINK YOU CAN TURN THOSE CRAZY GAULS INTO SOMETHING LIKE THEM?
YES, CAESAR!
MARK MY WORDS, THEY'LL SOON HAVE TOO MUCH ON THEIR MINDS TO GO FIGHTING!
BUT I'LL NEED GOLD ... LOTS OF GOLD!
YOU SHALL HAVE UNLIMITED CREDIT! GET TO WORK PREPOSTEROUS!

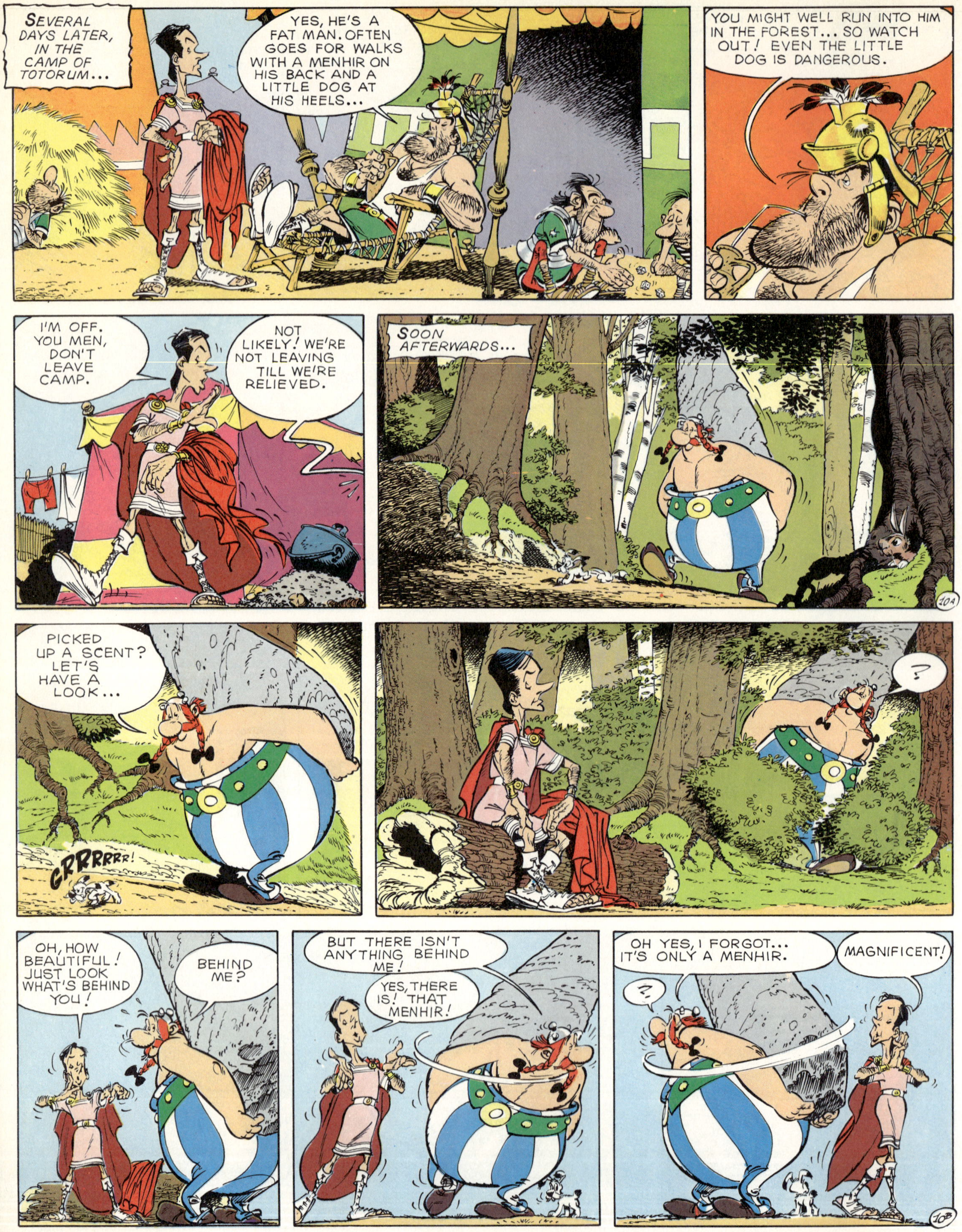
SEVERAL DAYS LATER, IN THE CAMP OF TOTORUM...
YES, HE'S A FAT MAN. OFTEN GOES FOR WALKS WITH A MENHIR ON HIS BACK AND A LITTLE DOG AT HIS HEELS...
YOU MIGHT WELL RUN INTO HIM IN THE FOREST... SO WATCH OUT! EVEN THE LITTLE DOG IS DANGEROUS.
I'M OFF. YOU MEN, DON'T LEAVE CAMP.
NOT LIKELY! WE'RE NOT LEAVING TILL WE'RE RELIEVED.
SOON AFTERWARDS...
PICKED UP A SCENT? LET'S HAVE A LOOK...
GRRRRRR!
?
OH, HOW BEAUTIFUL! JUST LOOK WHAT'S BEHIND YOU!
BEHIND ME?
BUT THERE ISN'T ANYTHING BEHIND ME!
YES, THERE IS! THAT MENHIR!
OH YES, I FORGOT... IT'S ONLY A MENHIR.
MAGNIFICENT!
?

WHERE DID YOU FIND IT?
I DIDN'T FIND IT, I MADE IT. I MAKE MENHIRS AND THEN I DELIVER THEM.
DO YOU DELIVER MANY?
NO, ONCE PEOPLE HAVE ONE MENHIR THEY DON'T WANT ANY MORE. MENHIRS DON'T WEAR OUT VERY FAST.
HOW MUCH IS IT?
OH, I DON'T KNOW ... I USUALLY SWAP THEM FOR SOMETHING
I'LL BUY IT! TWO HUNDRED SESTERTII!
SESTERTII?
YES! HAVING MONEY IS A GOOD THING. YOU CAN BUY ALL SORTS OF THINGS TO EAT... YOU'LL BE THE RICHEST MAN IN THE VILLAGE, AND THAT MEANS YOU'LL BE THE MOST INFLUENTIAL.
HERE YOU ARE.
IT'S A BIT HEAVY FOR ME... DELIVER IT TO THE CAMP OF TOTORUM.
THE CAMP OF TOTORUM?!?
NOOOOO! I'M NOT A LEGIONARY, I'M ONLY STAYING THERE! I'M A MENHIR BUYER... HERE, LET ME EXPLAIN.
GRRRAAOOR!
A MENHIR BUYER AND A MENHIR DELIVERY MAN ARE JUST MADE TO DO BUSINESS...
LOOK AT THAT!
THE RELIEF?
NO! THE BIG FAT BRUTE!

WHERE ARE THEY ALL ?
NEVER MIND. LEAVE YOUR MENHIR HERE, AND HERE'S YOUR 200 SESTERTII.
THESE ROMANS ARE CRAZY!
AND I'LL BUY ALL THE MENHIRS YOU CAN DELIVER!
12A
WHAT IS IT ?
THE END OF ALL OUR TROUBLES!
I WAS WAITING FOR YOU, OBELIX. COMING TO HUNT BOAR ?
NO.
AREN'T YOU WELL ?
WOOF! WOOF!
I'M PERFECTLY WELL! I'VE GOT WORK TO DO, I HAVE! I DON'T HAVE TIME TO FOOL AROUND!
GO AND PLAY WITH ASTERIX, DOGMATIX. I'M BUSY.
??
!
12B

NEXT DAY...
LOOK AT THAT!
THE RELIEF?
NO! THE BIG! FAT BRUTE!
TAKE COVER, ALL!
ISN'T THERE EVER ANYONE HERE?
WHAT A BEAUTY! IT'S EVEN BETTER THAN THE FIRST ONE!
HERE'S FOUR HUNDRED SESTERTII.
NO. TWO HUNDRED.
PRICES ARE GOING UP.
WHERE TO?
NO, NO... IT'S BECAUSE OF SUPPLY AND DEMAND... THE STATE OF THE MARKET... WELL, IT'S ALL RATHER COMPLICATED, BUT IT LEADS TO GALLOPING INFLATION.
AND DON'T FORGET, I'LL BUY ALL THE MENHIRS YOU CAN MAKE.
SNIFF! SNIFF!
ASTERIX!
YES?
I'M HUNGRY. DO YOU THINK...
WHEN YOU'RE NOT SO BUSY YOU CAN GO HUNTING BOAR AGAIN. THE FOREST'S FULL OF THEM.
SCRUNCH!
GRRRRR!

OH, HOW BEAUTIFUL, ANALGESIX! JUST LOOK WHAT'S BEHIND YOU!
?
IT'S ONLY A BOAR!
I KNOW IT'S A BOAR, YOU FOOL. LET ME HAVE IT!
ARE YOU CRAZY?
TAP! TAP! TAP!
HERE. YOU CAN USE THIS TO BUY THINGS, AND THEN YOU'LL BE THE SECOND RICHEST MAN IN THE VILLAGE.
AND I'LL BUY ALL YOU CAN DELIVER.
???
TOMORROW I'LL PAY YOU TWO HANDFULS OF COINS, BECAUSE PRICES ARE TROTTING THROUGH THE MARKET PLACE AND GETTING BLOWN UP IN THE AIR, AND IT'S ALL RATHER COMPLICATED.
!!!
DINNER TIME, ANALGESIX!
I CAN'T STOP! I'VE GOT WORK TO DO!
?!

IT'S THE MENHIR DELIVERY MAN!
EIGHT HUNDRED SESTERTII.
YOU MEAN MORE PRICES HAVE BEEN CANTERING THROUGH THE MARKET PLACE SINCE YESTERDAY?
EH?... OH, YES, BUT THERE'S A SLIGHT PROBLEM. YOU'RE ONLY BRINGING ME ONE MENHIR AT A TIME, AND I NEED LOTS OF MENHIRS...
I CAN'T MAKE THEM ANY FASTER. I CAN ONLY MAKE ONE A DAY BECAUSE I FELL INTO THE CAULDRON OF MAGIC POTION AS A BABY...
WHAT A PITY...
IF YOU CAN'T INCREASE THE EFFICIENCY OF YOUR PRODUCTIVITY INFRASTRUCTURE, THE MARKET WILL FALL.
UH?
IF YOU NOT ABLE MAKE BIG HEAP MENHIRS, ME NOT ABLE PAY HEAP BIG SESTERTII. YOU SAVVY?
ASTERIX, COULD YOU HELP ME MAKE MENHIRS?
?
YOU SEE, IF THE INFRASTRUCTURE DOESN'T GALLOP FASTER THERE'LL BE HEAPS OF SESTERTII FALLING IN THE MARKET.
UH?
YOU SAVVY?
TAP! TAP! TAP!

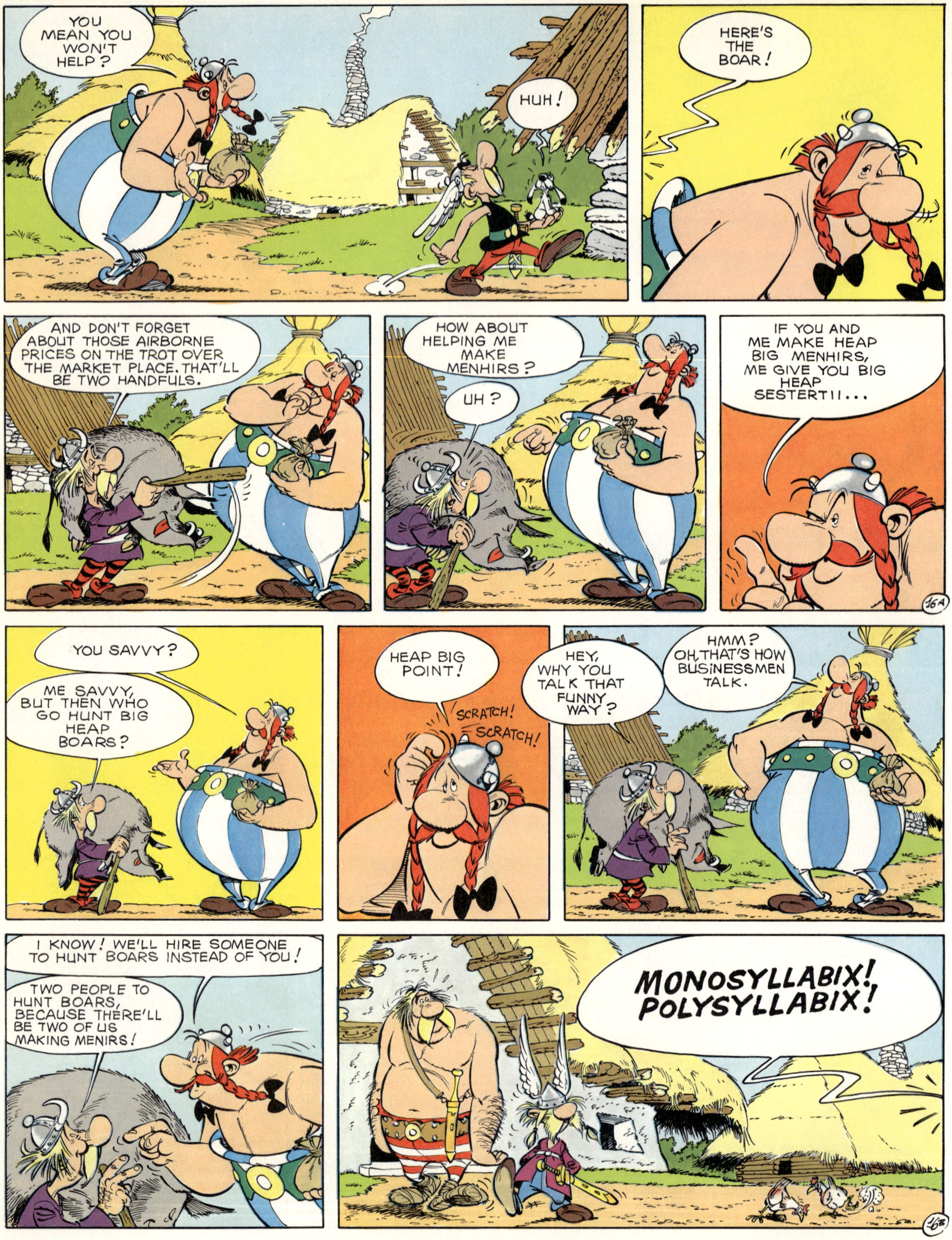

YOU MEAN YOU WON'T HELP?
HUH!
HERE'S THE BOAR!
AND DON'T FORGET ABOUT THOSE AIRBORNE PRICES ON THE TROT OVER THE MARKET PLACE. THAT'LL BE TWO HANDFULS.
HOW ABOUT HELPING ME MAKE MENHIRS?
UH?
IF YOU AND ME MAKE HEAP BIG MENHIRS, ME GIVE YOU BIG HEAP SESTERTII...
YOU SAVVY?
ME SAVVY, BUT THEN WHO GO HUNT BIG HEAP BOARS?
HEAP BIG POINT!
SCRATCH! SCRATCH!
HEY, WHY YOU TALK THAT FUNNY WAY?
HMM? OH, THAT'S HOW BUSINESSMEN TALK.
I KNOW! WE'LL HIRE SOMEONE TO HUNT BOARS INSTEAD OF YOU!
TWO PEOPLE TO HUNT BOARS, BECAUSE THERE'LL BE TWO OF US MAKING MENIRS!
MONOSYLLABIX! POLYSYLLABIX!

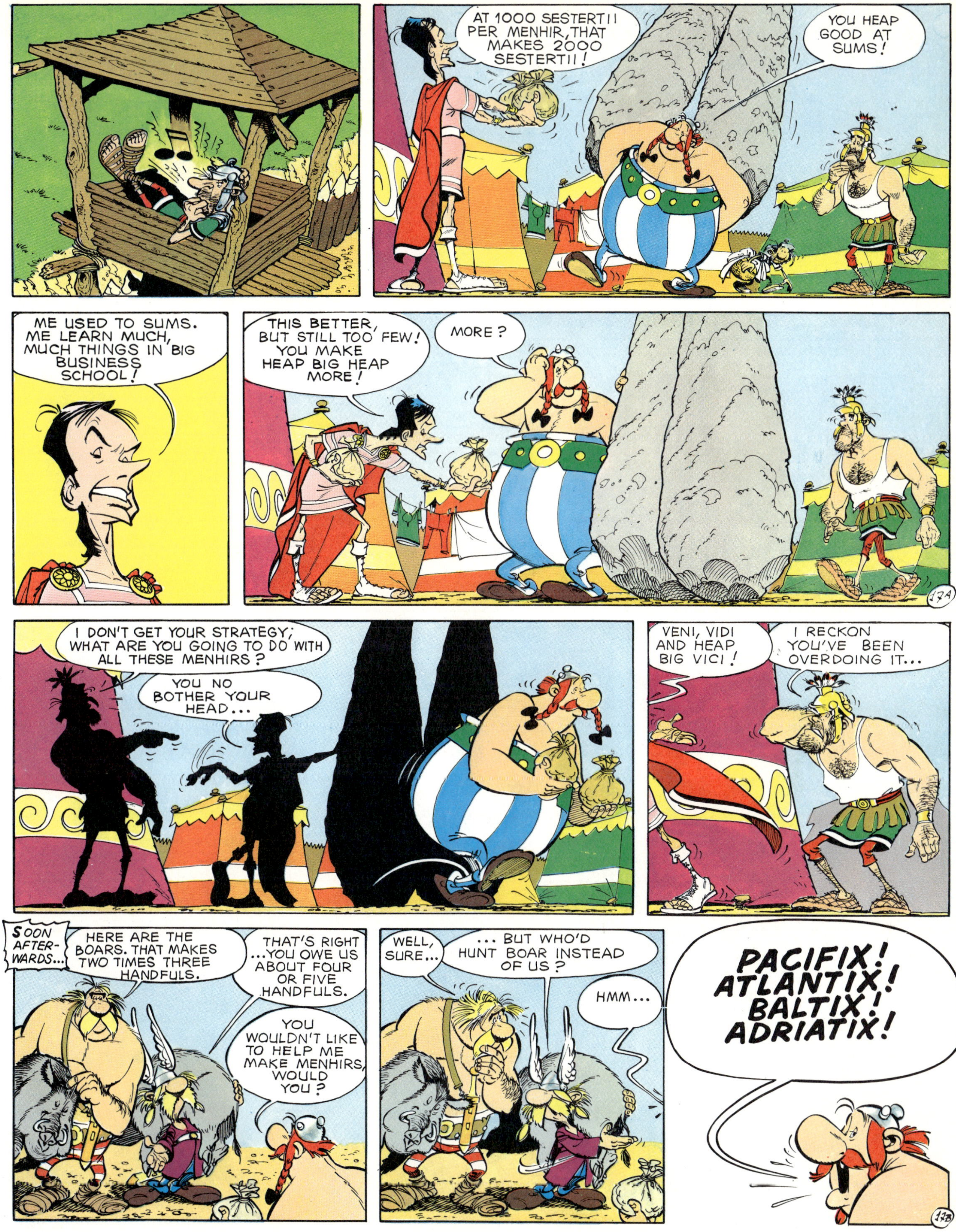
AT 1000 SESTERTII PER MENHIR, THAT MAKES 2000 SESTERTII!
YOU HEAP GOOD AT SUMS!
ME USED TO SUMS. ME LEARN MUCH, MUCH THINGS IN BIG BUSINESS SCHOOL!
THIS BETTER, BUT STILL TOO FEW! YOU MAKE HEAP BIG HEAP MORE!
MORE?
I DON'T GET YOUR STRATEGY; WHAT ARE YOU GOING TO DO WITH ALL THESE MENHIRS?
YOU NO BOTHER YOUR HEAD...
VENI, VIDI AND HEAP BIG VICI!
I RECKON YOU'VE BEEN OVERDOING IT...
SOON AFTERWARDS...
HERE ARE THE BOARS. THAT MAKES TWO TIMES THREE HANDFULS.
THAT'S RIGHT ...YOU OWE US ABOUT FOUR OR FIVE HANDFULS.
YOU WOULDN'T LIKE TO HELP ME MAKE MENHIRS, WOULD YOU?
WELL, SURE...
... BUT WHO'D HUNT BOAR INSTEAD OF US?
HMM...
PACIFIX! ATLANTIX! BALTIX! ADRIATIX!

YOU MUSTN'T WORRY ABOUT OBELIX. I KNOW HE'S ACTING STRANGELY AT THE MOMENT, BUT IT WILL PASS.
YOU KNOW WHAT WE'RE GOING TO DO? WE'RE GOING TO HUNT A NICE BOAR AND INVITE OBELIX TO DINNER!
AND HERE'S THE VERY THING! COME ON!
HANDS OFF! THAT'S MINE!
?
WHAT DO YOU MEAN, YOURS? BOARS ARE COMMON PROPERTY, SAME AS ROMANS!
ROMANS, YES, BUT NOT BOARS!
WE'RE HUNTING BOARS FOR OBELIX.
HIM PAY HEAP BIG HANDFULS FOR BOARS.
THAT'S RIGHT! WE'RE WORKING, AND YOU'RE DISTURBING US... SO GET LOST!
GLUG! GLUG! GLUG!
NO! NO! YOU CAN'T DO...
THAT!
SLONK!

WHAT HAPPENED, BY TOUTATIS?
?
BIG HEAP SKY FALL ON OUR HEADS!
LET'S HAVE A WORD WITH OBELIX!
OBELIX QUARRY CAUTION MENHIRS TURNING
19A
ARE YOU NUTS, OR WHAT?
CERTAINLY NOT... THE MENHIR BUSINESS HAS NEVER HAD IT SO GOOD. I'M GETTING TO BE THE MOST INFLUENTIAL MAN IN THE VILLAGE.
OBELIX QUARRY CAUTION MENHIRS TURNING
BUT WOULDN'T YOU RATHER HUNT BOAR AND HAVE FUN WITH YOUR FRIENDS, LIKE YOU USED TO?
OF COURSE. WHEN I'VE SOLD HEAPS OF MENHIRS I'LL BE ABLE TO HUNT BOAR AGAIN...
COME ON, DOGMATIX! THE MOST INFLUENTIAL MAN IN THE VILLAGE! HUH!
COME AND WORK FOR ME, ASTERIX, AND IN A FEW YEARS WE'LL BE...
OUCH!
DOGMATIX BIT ME!
19B

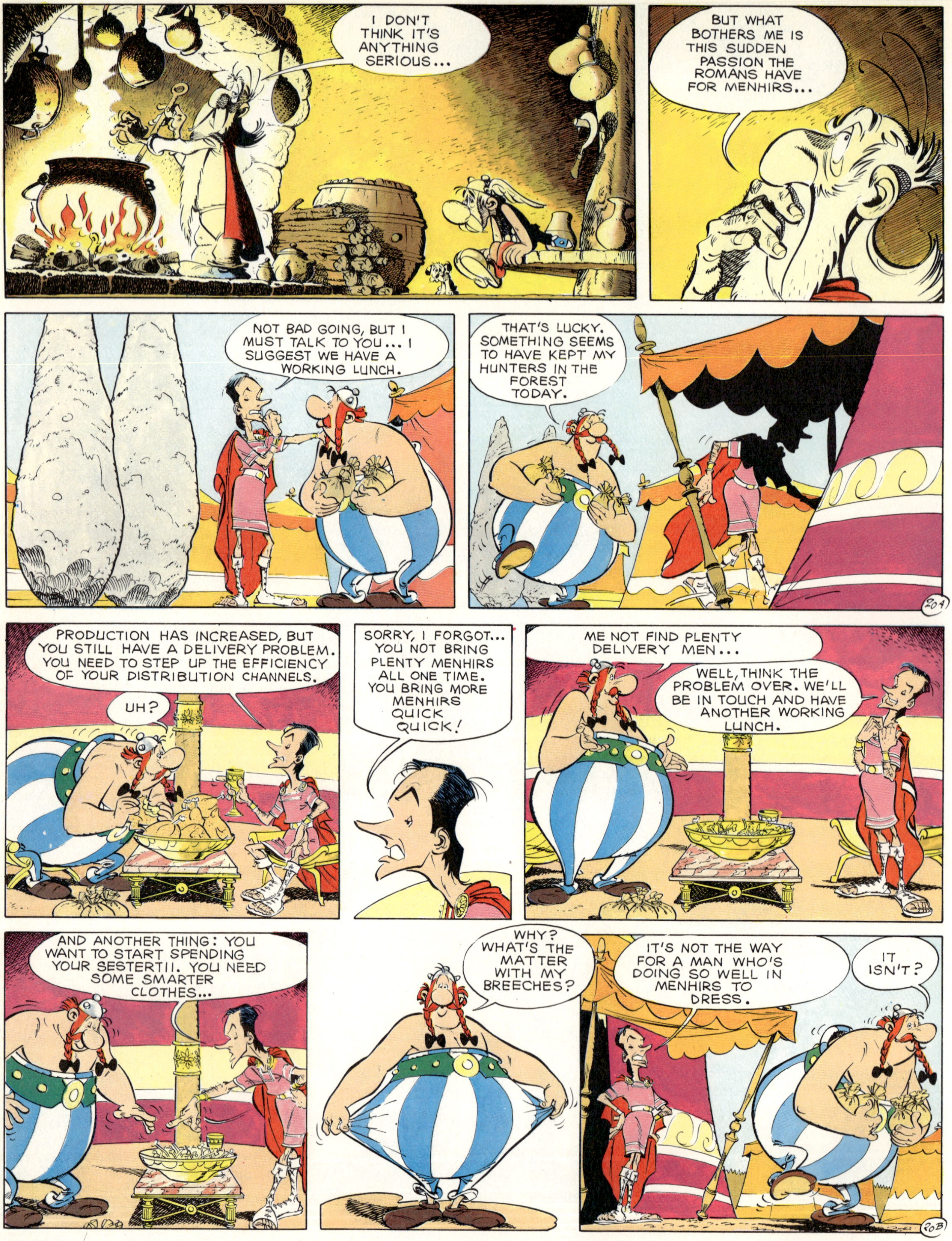
I DON'T THINK IT'S ANYTHING SERIOUS...
BUT WHAT BOTHERS ME IS THIS SUDDEN PASSION THE ROMANS HAVE FOR MENHIRS...
NOT BAD GOING, BUT I MUST TALK TO YOU... I SUGGEST WE HAVE A WORKING LUNCH.
THAT'S LUCKY. SOMETHING SEEMS TO HAVE KEPT MY HUNTERS IN THE FOREST TODAY.
PRODUCTION HAS INCREASED, BUT YOU STILL HAVE A DELIVERY PROBLEM. YOU NEED TO STEP UP THE EFFICIENCY OF YOUR DISTRIBUTION CHANNELS.
UH?
SORRY, I FORGOT... YOU NOT BRING PLENTY MENHIRS ALL ONE TIME. YOU BRING MORE MENHIRS QUICK QUICK!
ME NOT FIND PLENTY DELIVERY MEN...
WELL, THINK THE PROBLEM OVER. WE'LL BE IN TOUCH AND HAVE ANOTHER WORKING LUNCH.
AND ANOTHER THING: YOU WANT TO START SPENDING YOUR SESTERTII. YOU NEED SOME SMARTER CLOTHES...
WHY? WHAT'S THE MATTER WITH MY BREECHES?
IT'S NOT THE WAY FOR A MAN WHO'S DOING SO WELL IN MENHIRS TO DRESS.
IT ISN'T?

GERIATRIX, DARLING! WOOLIX THE PEDLAR IS HERE!
STOP ARGUING! THE PEDLAR'S HERE, AND JUST FOR ONCE YOU CAN DROP ME OFF ON THE SHIELD!
BUT PEDIMENTA DARLING, IT'S MY OFFICIAL SHIELD!
ROLL UP, ROLL UP! I'VE GOT SILK FROM LUGDUNUM,* VELVET FROM SAMAROBRIVA,* HOUR GLASSES FROM HELVETIA*...
THE WONDER OF WOOLIX
*LYONS
*AMIENS
*SWITZERLAND
THE VERY LATEST THING FROM LUTETIA... QUITE INEXPENSIVE.
CAN I, GERIATRIX DEAR?
YES, YES, MY LOVE!
WELL, WHAT DO YOU THINK?
YES, IT'S VERY SLIMMING.
CAN I PAY IN FISH?
ALL RIGHT. THIS ISN'T THE TIME AND PLAICE TO CARP!
I'LL BUY THE LOT!
?!
?!
?!
?!
?!
?!
?!
?!

THE WONDER OF WOOLIX
YOU...YOU MEAN YOU WANT TO BUY MY ENTIRE STOCK?
YOUR STOCK, YOUR CART AND YOUR OXEN!
UH?
ME GIVE HEAP BIG MONEY. YOU SAVVY?
YES, ME SAVVY... I MEAN... BUT IF I SELL MY CART AND OXEN HOW CAN I SUPPORT MY FAMILY? I'M THE ONLY BOARWINNER.
I WILL EMPLOY YOU. I SUGGEST WE HAVE A WORKING LUNCH.
UH?
YOU COME EAT HEAP BIG LUNCH. ME EXPLAIN IT ALL!
OF WOOLIX
!
EXCUSE ME...
!
THE BOSS THERE BOUGHT THE LOT.
WELL, DON'T YOU HAVE ANYTHING TO SAY?
UH?
YOU HEAP BIG DEAD LOSS!

BY JUPITER! LOOK AT THAT!
OBELIX & CO.
SPLENDID! WELL DONE! COME INTO MY TENT AND WE'LL GET DOWN TO BUSINESS. MENHIRS ARE GOING UP AGAIN.
BUT I HAVE TO UNLOAD MY MENHIRS...
NO, NO! THAT'S NO JOB FOR A CAPTAIN OF INDUSTRY.
OBELIX & CO.
UNLOAD THE MENHIRS, YOU LOT!
UH?
UNLOAD HEAP BIG MENHIRS! YOU SAVVY?
JOIN UP, THEM SAY! IT HEAP BIG MAN'S LIFE, THEM SAY...
CRAAASH!
SOON AFTERWARDS...
HULLO, OBELIX!
I JUST WANTED TO CONGRATULATE YOU ON BECOMING THE MOST INFLUENTIAL MAN IN THE VILLAGE.
YOU DID? ER... WELL...
BY THE WAY... YOU COULDN'T DO SOMETHING FOR ME, COULD YOU?
OF COURSE!

POM TIDDLEY POM
SUPPER READY, MY LOVE?
NO, SUPPER IS NOT READY! GET IT YOURSELF. I'M BUSY!
BUSY DOING WHAT, MY PET?
OBELIX ASKED ME TO MAKE HIM SOME CLOTHES. HE'S GOING TO PAY HAND-SOMELY...
I HAVEN'T A THING TO WEAR! AND SINCE I CAN'T COUNT ON YOU, I HAVE TO FIND SOME WAY TO EARN A BIT OF MONEY!
24A
A LITTLE LATER...
NOW THAT FAT FOOL OBELIX IS MAKING A PILE WITH HIS MENHIRS MY WIFE'S BECOMING A REAL SEW-AND-SEW. I CAN'T GO ON LIKE THIS!
CALM DOWN! AFTER ALL, OBELIX IS MY FRIEND!
WELL, MY WIFE IS MAKING EYES AT YOUR FRIEND!
AND SHE'S NEVER LOOKED AT ANYONE BUT ME... IT'S INCREDIBLE!
YES, I'VE OFTEN THOUGHT SO MYSELF...
SO WHAT AM I TO DO?
NOTHING. I'LL TRY TO TALK TO OBELIX!
YOU JUST DO THAT, OR I SHALL MAKE YOUR FINE FRIEND EAT MY STICK!
24B

?!?
?!?
HARF! HARF! HARF!
HAHAHA! HAHA!
WHAT'S THE BIG JOKE?
JUST LOOK AT YOU, OBELIX!
NOT BAD, EH? YOU HAVE TO DRESS WELL WHEN YOU GET TO BE A BIG MAN IN MENHIRS.
HARRF! HARRF!
SPEAKING OF MENHIRS, DON'T YOU THINK THE JOKE'S WEARING A BIT THIN?
LOOK, I'M IN A HURRY... IF YOU LIKE WE'LL HAVE A WORKING LUNCH SOME DAY.
OBELIX! OBELIX! NOTHING BUT OBELIX! I'M SICK OF OBELIX!
YOU MAY BE SICK OF OBELIX, BUT HE'S MR BIG AROUND HERE. HE MAY NOT BE BRINGING HOME BOARS, BUT HE'S BRINGING HOME THE BACON.
I CAN'T HELP IT IF THERE'S MORE DEMAND FOR MENHIRS THAN FISH JUST NOW, CAN I?
WHY NOT TRY MAKING MENHIRS?
?

MAKING MENHIRS? BUT I DON'T KNOW HOW TO MAKE MENHIRS!
OH, YOU DON'T NEED A DRUID'S DEGREE TO LEARN.
THE THING IS, MENHIRS ARE HEAVIER THAN HERRINGS! NOW OBELIX IS STRONG...
I'M FED TO THE BACK TEETH WITH OBELIX! IF I CAN CARRY A HERRING I CAN CARRY A MENHIR!
VERY WELL SAID, UNHYGIENIX!
WELL, HAVE YOU BEEN TALKING TO YOUR FAT FOOL OF A FRIEND?
I'VE GOT A BETTER IDEA: YOU CAN FIGHT HIM WITH HIS OWN WEAPONS. YOU CAN MAKE MENHIRS!
MENHIRS!
26A
THE FACT IS...
DON'T WORRY, I'LL SEE TO EVERYTHING!
OHO! THAT GLEAM IN YOUR EYE TELLS ME YOU HAVE AN IDEA!
YES, I HAVE! IF THE ROMANS WANT MENHIRS, WE'LL PROVIDE THEM!
WILL YOU LAY ON MAGIC POTION FOR EVERYONE WHO WANTS TO MAKE MENHIRS?
BY ALL MEANS! LET US PROMOTE THE GROWTH OF THE MENHIR INDUSTRY! OUR VILLAGE WILL BECOME THE BIGGEST MENHIR PRODUCTION CENTRE IN THE ENTIRE ANCIENT WORLD!
AND THE FUNNY THING IS, WE STILL DON'T KNOW WHAT MENHIRS ARE FOR!
26B

NEXT DAY...
?
WHAT'S THAT?
FUNNY QUESTION, COMING FROM YOU! IT'S A MENHIR.
YOU MEAN YOU'RE DELIVERING MENHIRS THESE DAYS?
WHY NOT? THEY'RE NO HEAVIER THAN HERRINGS.
WELL, REALLY!
WHERE'S FULLIAUTOMATIX?
OUT DELIVERING HIS MENHIRS.
FULLIAUTOMATIX
BEST MENHIRS IN THE VILLAGE
DELIVERING HIS...? BUT I'M THE ONE WHO...
OUT OF THE WAY!
GERIATRIX
SPECIALLY MATURED MENHIRS
!?!

THIS HEAP GOOD START!
YOU NOT 'ARF SAID IT!
HEY, MATES! HERE'S ANOTHER OF 'EM!
IT STRIKES ME YOUR SENTRY'S MILITARY PARLANCE IS DETERIORATING.
YOU'VE GOT A NERVE! IT'S SINCE YOU ARRIVED MY MEN HAVE BEEN TALKING FUNNY...
...THEIR INTELLECTUAL LEVEL WAS NEVER ANYTHING GREAT, BUT STILL...
YOU'RE BUYING MENHIRS HERE, RIGHT?
YES, INDEED! LET US HELP YOU UNLOAD THEM, VENERABLE OLD GENTLEMAN!
OLD? I'LL SHOW YOU IF I'M OLD, ROMAN!
28A
WHERE DO I PUT THEM?
?!?
WATCH OUT, YOU LOT! HERE'S ANOTHER WEIRDO COMING!
UNHYGIENIX FRESH MENHIRS
THIS MENHIR BUSINESS IS STARTING TO GET ON MY NERVES!
28B

JUST WHERE DO YOU THINK ALL THESE MENHIRS WILL GET YOU?
I DON'T WANT THEM TO GET ME ANYWHERE. I'VE ALREADY TOLD YOU, I CAME AND I CONQUERED!
THE GAULS ARE ALL USING THEIR MAGIC POWERS TO MAKE MENHIRS, INSTEAD OF THUMPING OUR LEGIONARIES...
THEY HAVE BEEN DEFEATED BY THE PROFIT MOTIVE! GOLD AND HIGH LIVING WILL WEAKEN THEIR MORAL FIBRE. DON'T YOU AGREE?
WELL... MAYBE...
BUT TAKE A LOOK AT THIS!
WHAT ARE WE GOING TO DO WITH THIS BIG HEAP OF MENHIRS?
REDDE CAESARI QUAE SUNT CAESARIS.
UH?
RENDER UNTO CAESAR HEAP BIG HEAP MENHIRS THAT ARE CAESAR'S
DON'T SPEAK TO ME LIKE THAT! YOUR MENHIRS ARE CAUSING SOFTENING OF THE BRAIN ALL ROUND!
CAESAR HAS PAID FOR THESE MENHIRS, SO IT'S ONLY RIGHT FOR ME TO DELIVER THEM. WHILE I'M AWAY, CARRY ON BUYING MENHIRS, AND KEEP RAISING THE PRICE. SI VIS PACEM, BUY MENHIRS!
29

WHAT DOES THE CHIEF WANT US FOR?
WE'LL SOON SEE.
WHAT HAPPENED TO HIM?
HE WANTED TO WORK IN FULLIAUTOMATIX'S QUARRY, BUT FULLIAUTOMATIX DOESN'T CARE FOR MUSIC WHILE HE WORKS.
I ASKED YOU TO COME BECAUSE IT STRIKES ME YOU'RE THE LAST SANE PEOPLE LEFT IN THIS VILLAGE...
THEY'VE ALL GONE NUTS! HALF OF THEM ARE HUNTING BOAR TO FEED THE OTHER HALF, WHO ARE MAKING MENHIRS! WHAT ON EARTH IS ALL THIS IN AID OF?
DON'T WORRY, O CHIEF!
I'M NOT WORRIED...
...I'VE KNOWN THEY WERE ALL NUTS FOR AGES. BUT NOW IMPEDIMENTA KEEPS TELLING ME I OUGHT TO BE MAKING MENHIRS TOO...
...SAYS SHE CAN'T FACE HER FRIENDS THESE DAYS. THEIR HUSBANDS ARE ROLLING IN SESTERTII...
BE PATIENT...
THE ROMANS' TROUBLES AREN'T OVER. THEY'LL FIND US AND OUR MENHIRS TOUGH NUTS TO CRACK!
HOHOHO! HOHOHO!
NOW THEY'RE NUTS TOO!
WARF! WARF! WARF!
SLAP! SLAP SLAP!

IN JULIUS CAESAR'S PALACE IN ROME...
AND JUST WHAT AM I SUPPOSED TO DO WITH ALL THESE MENHIRS?
BUT CAESAR, THOSE MENHIRS ARE THE PROOF OF MY SUCCESS! THE GAULS ARE TOO BUSY MAKING MENHIRS TO FIGHT, SO...
MAYBE, BUT YOU'RE DRAINING MY TREASURY TO KEEP A FEW MADMEN BUSY!
PEACE IS BEYOND ALL PRICE... SI VIS PACEM...
YOUNG MAN, I MAKE THE CLASSICAL REMARKS AROUND HERE, ALEA JACTA EST AND ALL THAT, AND WHAT'S MORE, YOU HAVEN'T ANSWERED MY QUESTION: WHAT AM I SUPPOSED TO DO WITH ALL THESE MENHIRS?
SELL THEM O CAESAR.
SELL THEM?
THAT'S RIGHT. THAT WAY, YOU NOT ONLY RECOVER YOUR EXPENSES, YOU MAKE A PROFIT TOO.
BUT WHO'D WANT MENHIRS? THEY'RE NO GOOD FOR ANYTHING!
PRECISELY! WE MUST DRAW UP A PLAN OF CAMPAIGN, DECIDE ON OUR STRATEGY, SET OUR SIGHTS ON THE RIGHT TARGET!
CAMPAIGN? STRATEGY? TARGET? THAT'S THE KIND OF THING I LIKE TO HEAR! I'LL GIVE ORDERS FOR THE LEGIONS TO PREPARE FOR BATTLE!
NO, NO! LET ME EXPLAIN...

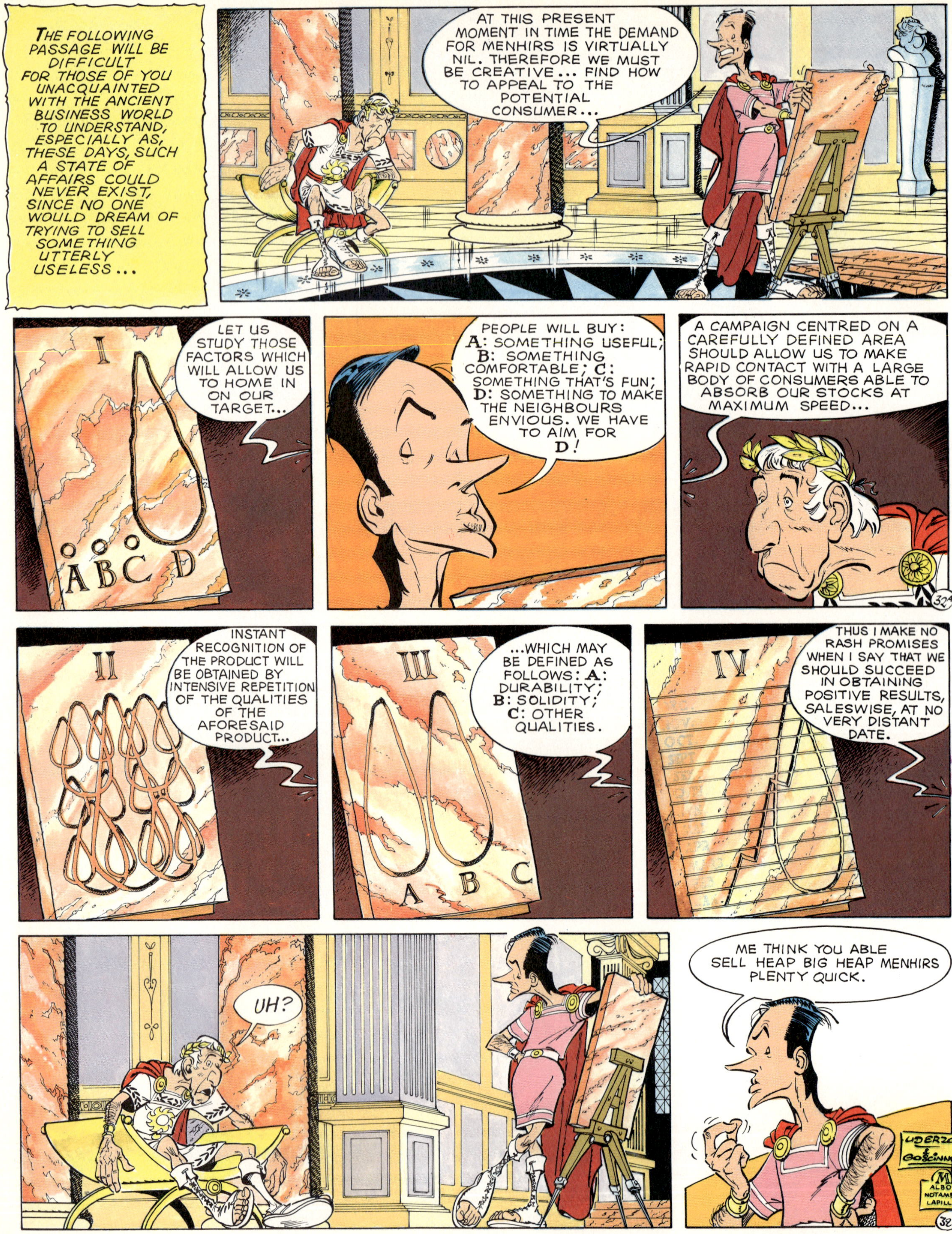
THE FOLLOWING PASSAGE WILL BE DIFFICULT FOR THOSE OF YOU UNACQUAINTED WITH THE ANCIENT BUSINESS WORLD TO UNDERSTAND, ESPECIALLY AS, THESE DAYS, SUCH A STATE OF AFFAIRS COULD NEVER EXIST, SINCE NO ONE WOULD DREAM OF TRYING TO SELL SOMETHING UTTERLY USELESS...
AT THIS PRESENT MOMENT IN TIME THE DEMAND FOR MENHIRS IS VIRTUALLY NIL. THEREFORE WE MUST BE CREATIVE... FIND HOW TO APPEAL TO THE POTENTIAL CONSUMER...
I
ABCD
LET US STUDY THOSE FACTORS WHICH WILL ALLOW US TO HOME IN ON OUR TARGET...
PEOPLE WILL BUY: A: SOMETHING USEFUL; B: SOMETHING COMFORTABLE; C: SOMETHING THAT'S FUN; D: SOMETHING TO MAKE THE NEIGHBOURS ENVIOUS. WE HAVE TO AIM FOR D!
A CAMPAIGN CENTRED ON A CAREFULLY DEFINED AREA SHOULD ALLOW US TO MAKE RAPID CONTACT WITH A LARGE BODY OF CONSUMERS ABLE TO ABSORB OUR STOCKS AT MAXIMUM SPEED...
32A
II
INSTANT RECOGNITION OF THE PRODUCT WILL BE OBTAINED BY INTENSIVE REPETITION OF THE QUALITIES OF THE AFORESAID PRODUCT...
III
ABC
...WHICH MAY BE DEFINED AS FOLLOWS: A: DURABILITY; B: SOLIDITY; C: OTHER QUALITIES.
IV
THUS I MAKE NO RASH PROMISES WHEN I SAY THAT WE SHOULD SUCCEED IN OBTAINING POSITIVE RESULTS, SALESWISE, AT NO VERY DISTANT DATE.
UH?
ME THINK YOU ABLE SELL HEAP BIG HEAP MENHIRS PLENTY QUICK.
UDERZO - GOSCINNY
ALBO NOTAMBA LAPILLO
32B

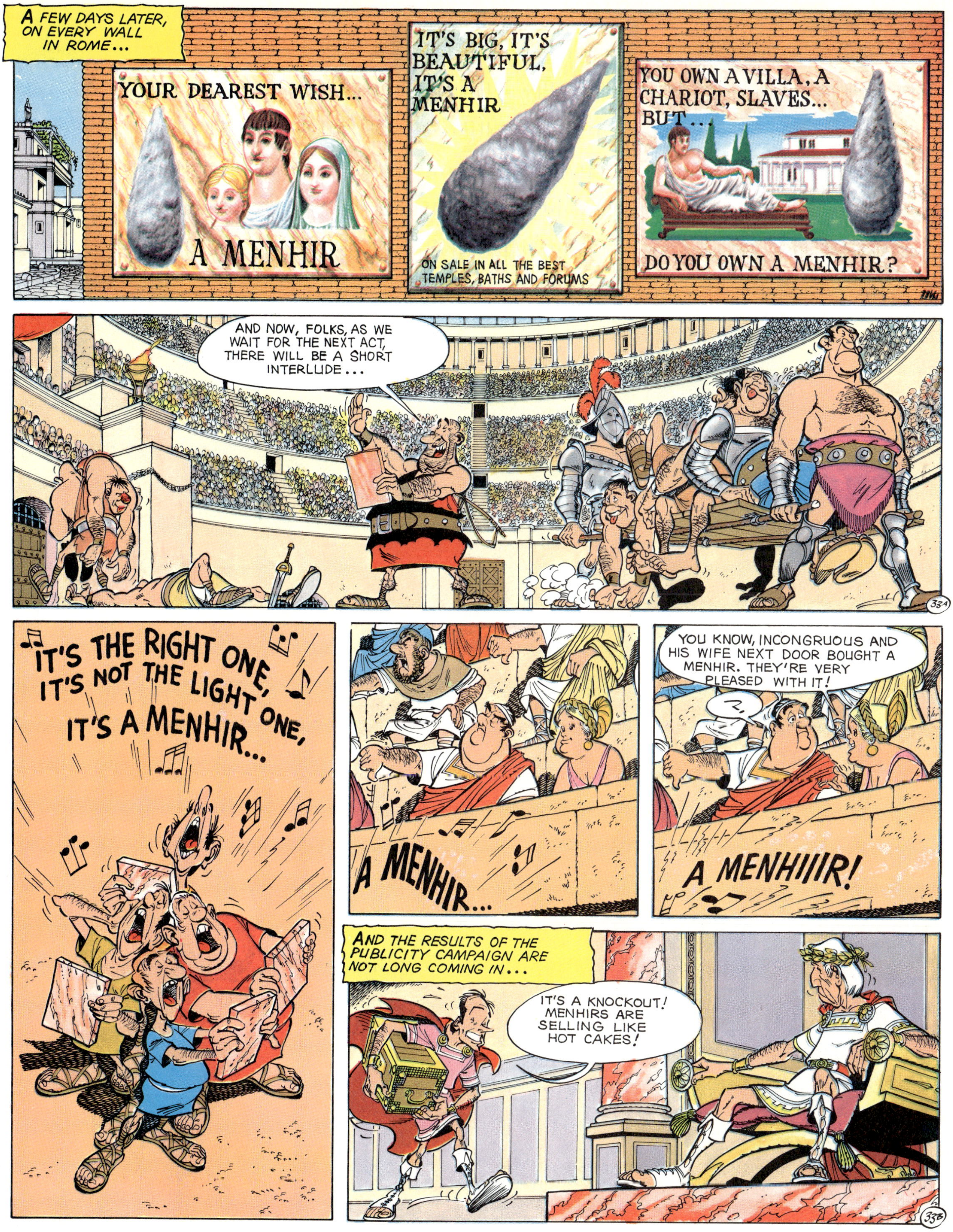

A FEW DAYS LATER, ON EVERY WALL IN ROME...
YOUR DEAREST WISH...
A MENHIR
IT'S BIG, IT'S BEAUTIFUL, IT'S A MENHIR
ON SALE IN ALL THE BEST TEMPLES, BATHS AND FORUMS
YOU OWN A VILLA, A CHARIOT, SLAVES... BUT...
DO YOU OWN A MENHIR?
AND NOW, FOLKS, AS WE WAIT FOR THE NEXT ACT, THERE WILL BE A SHORT INTERLUDE...
IT'S THE RIGHT ONE, IT'S NOT THE LIGHT ONE, IT'S A MENHIR...
A MENHIR...
YOU KNOW, INCONGRUOUS AND HIS WIFE NEXT DOOR BOUGHT A MENHIR. THEY'RE VERY PLEASED WITH IT!
A MENHIIIR!
AND THE RESULTS OF THE PUBLICITY CAMPAIGN ARE NOT LONG COMING IN...
IT'S A KNOCKOUT! MENHIRS ARE SELLING LIKE HOT CAKES!

I'VE HAD SOME MORE IDEAS, CAESAR!
TOGAS!
SUNDIALS!
JEWELLERY!
AND THIS DO-IT-YOURSELF MENHIR KIT!!
WE HAVE PEACE WITH THE GAULS, AND THANKS TO THEM WE'RE GOING TO MAKE A REAL KILLING TOO!
34A
BY JUPITER, I'M PLEASED WITH YOU!
WE OUGHT TO MAKE MENHIRS IN SOMETHING LESS DURABLE. BUILT-IN LACK OF OBSOLESCENCE ISN'T GOOD FOR BUSINESS, AND...
CAESAR!
THIS HAS BEEN STUCK UP ALL OVER ROME!
?!
GENUINE ROMAN MENHIRS CHEAPER THAN IMPORTED VARIETIES
BUY ROMAN
·MERETRICIUS · MENHIR MAKER
SOMEONE GO AND FIND THIS MERETRICIUS!
34B

SOON AFTERWARDS...
WHAT'S THE BIG IDEA, MERETRICIUS? SINCE WHEN HAVE ROMANS BEEN MANUFACTURING MENHIRS?
SINCE PEOPLE STARTED BUYING THEM, O CAESAR.
WELL, I FORBID YOU TO SELL ANY MORE MENHIRS!
I REPRESENT THE ENTIRE ROMAN MENHIR INDUSTRY, AND I CANNOT COUNTENANCE AN EDICT WHICH ENDANGERS THE JOBS OF SO MANY WORKERS!
BUT THE WORKERS ARE SLAVES!
EXACTLY! THE RIGHT TO WORK IS THE ONLY RIGHT A SLAVE HAS. HE MUST NOT BE DEPRIVED OF IT!
IF YOU GO ON CIRCULATING MENHIRS YOU'LL FIND YOURSELF IN THE CIRCUS!
RIGHT. YOU LEAVE ME NO ALTERNATIVE.
NEXT DAY, ON THE APPIAN WAY...
JOBS FOR THE SLAVES
BAN THE GAULISH MENHIR

THE ROMAN MANUFACTURERS DO HAVE THEIR FINGER ON THE PULSE OF PUBLIC OPINION... O CAESAR, I THINK YOU'LL HAVE TO LIFT YOUR BAN...
YOU BET I WILL! I'M NOT RISKING A CIVIL WAR JUST FOR YOUR STUPID MENHIRS!
ONLY WE'RE GOING TO HAVE TROUBLE UNLOADING THOSE GAULISH MENHIRS..
WE MUST TAKE THE OFFENSIVE...
SUMMON MY LEGIONS!
NO, NO! I MEAN TAKE THE OFFENSIVE IN THE PRICE WAR! WE MUST BE COMPETITIVE... UNDERCUT THEIR PRICES... LET THE MENHIR FLOAT...
CUT PRICE GAULISH MENHIRS
TWO ROMAN MENHIRS FOR THE PRICE OF ONE
BIGGER, BETTER, CHEAPER! THE SUPER DE LUXE ROMAN MENHIR
FREE GIFT OF TWO SLAVES WITH EVERY GAULISH MENHIR
HAVE YOU TRIED AN EGYPTIAN MENHIR
PRICES ARE FALLING! THE EGYPTIANS, GREEKS AND PHOENICIANS ARE FLOODING THE MARKET WITH THEIR MENHIRS!
SURE ENOUGH...
UTI, NON ABUTI. I TOLD YOU THE LOOT WOULD BE TOO HEAVY FOR OUR SHIP!
I THOUGHT MENHIRS WERE FLOATING THESE DAYS...
MAYBE THEY WERE, BUT THEY'RE GOING DOWN NOW.

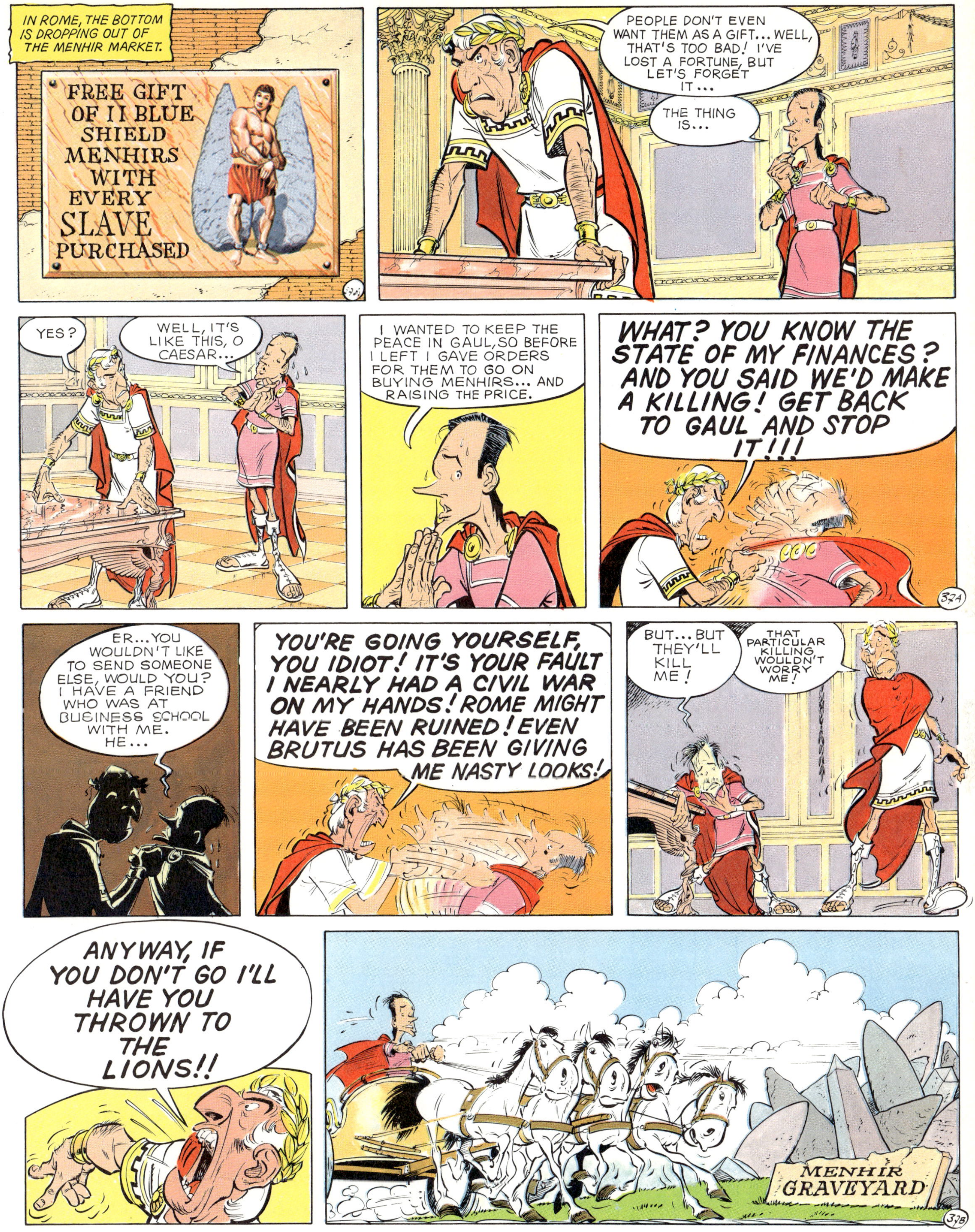
IN ROME, THE BOTTOM IS DROPPING OUT OF THE MENHIR MARKET.
FREE GIFT OF II BLUE SHIELD MENHIRS WITH EVERY SLAVE PURCHASED
PEOPLE DON'T EVEN WANT THEM AS A GIFT... WELL, THAT'S TOO BAD! I'VE LOST A FORTUNE, BUT LET'S FORGET IT...
THE THING IS...
YES?
WELL, IT'S LIKE THIS, O CAESAR...
I WANTED TO KEEP THE PEACE IN GAUL, SO BEFORE I LEFT I GAVE ORDERS FOR THEM TO GO ON BUYING MENHIRS... AND RAISING THE PRICE.
WHAT? YOU KNOW THE STATE OF MY FINANCES? AND YOU SAID WE'D MAKE A KILLING! GET BACK TO GAUL AND STOP IT!!!
ER... YOU WOULDN'T LIKE TO SEND SOMEONE ELSE, WOULD YOU? I HAVE A FRIEND WHO WAS AT BUSINESS SCHOOL WITH ME. HE...
YOU'RE GOING YOURSELF, YOU IDIOT! IT'S YOUR FAULT I NEARLY HAD A CIVIL WAR ON MY HANDS! ROME MIGHT HAVE BEEN RUINED! EVEN BRUTUS HAS BEEN GIVING ME NASTY LOOKS!
BUT... BUT THEY'LL KILL ME!
THAT PARTICULAR KILLING WOULDN'T WORRY ME!
ANYWAY, IF YOU DON'T GO I'LL HAVE YOU THROWN TO THE LIONS!!
MENHIR GRAVEYARD

BUT THE WORLD MENHIR CRISIS HAS NOT YET AFFECTED THE GAULISH VILLAGE...
ASTERIX! DOGMATIX!
LISTEN... CAN I GO HUNTING BOARS WITH YOU?
38A
WHAT, AN INFLUENTIAL MAN LIKE YOU? DON'T YOU HAVE A CONFERENCE? DON'T YOU HAVE A BUSINESS LUNCH?
PLEASE DON'T LAUGH AT ME. I KNOW I'VE BEEN SILLY. I'M BORED, AND I'VE HAD ENOUGH! EVERYONE HAS LOTS OF SESTERTII NOW! EVERYONE'S THE MOST INFLUENTIAL MAN IN THE VILLAGE!
I WANT TO BE FRIENDS AGAIN! I WANT TO HUNT BOAR! I WANT TO HAVE FUN...
BOOOHOOO!
WERE YOU THINKING OF HUNTING BOARS IN THAT GET-UP?
SNIFF... HMPH?
I'LL BE RIGHT BACK!
TEEHEE!
38B

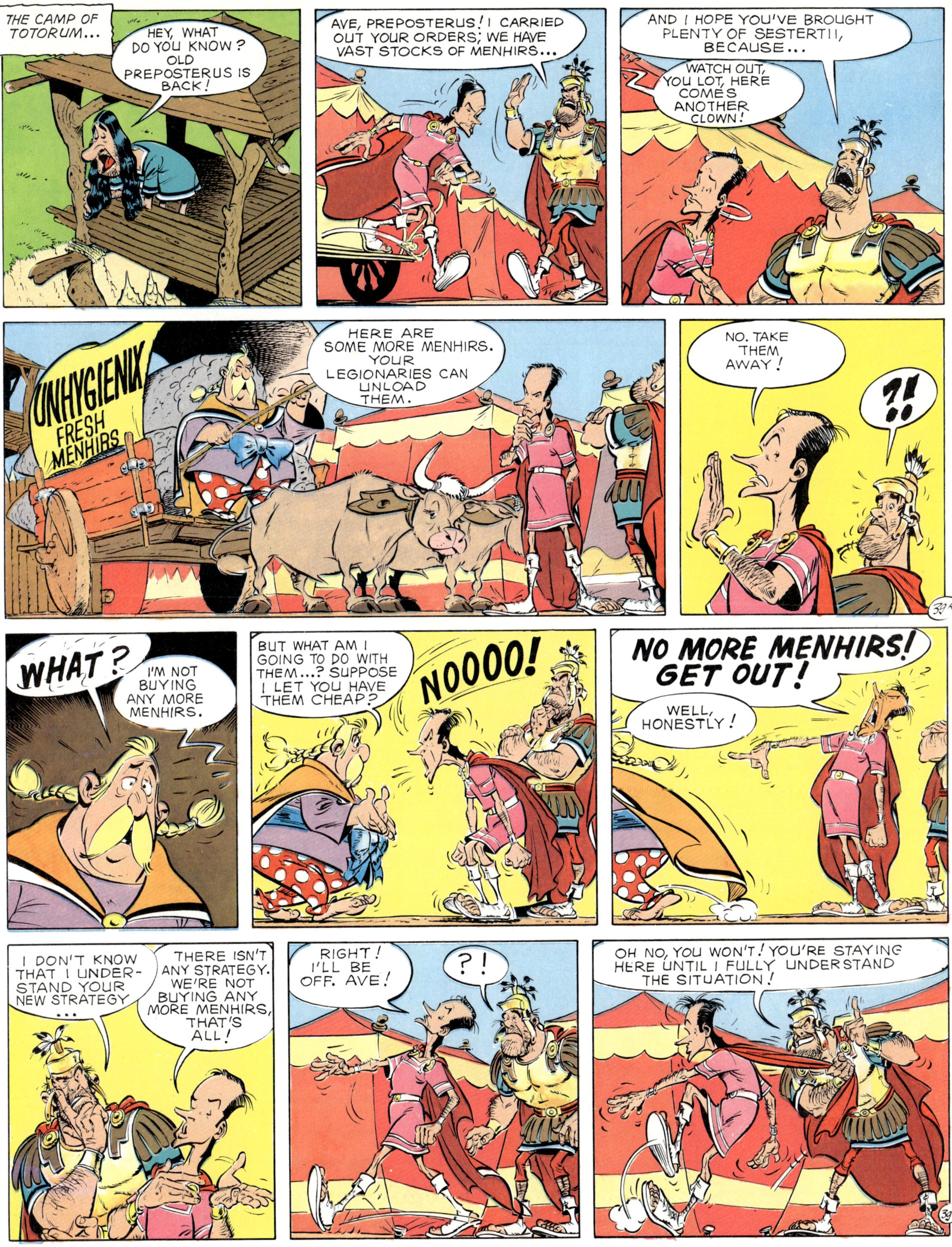
THE CAMP OF TOTORUM...
HEY, WHAT DO YOU KNOW? OLD PREPOSTERUS IS BACK!
AVE, PREPOSTERUS! I CARRIED OUT YOUR ORDERS; WE HAVE VAST STOCKS OF MENHIRS...
AND I HOPE YOU'VE BROUGHT PLENTY OF SESTERTII, BECAUSE...
WATCH OUT, YOU LOT, HERE COMES ANOTHER CLOWN!
UNHYGIENIX FRESH MENHIRS
HERE ARE SOME MORE MENHIRS. YOUR LEGIONARIES CAN UNLOAD THEM.
NO. TAKE THEM AWAY!
?!
WHAT?
I'M NOT BUYING ANY MORE MENHIRS.
BUT WHAT AM I GOING TO DO WITH THEM...? SUPPOSE I LET YOU HAVE THEM CHEAP?
NOOOO!
NO MORE MENHIRS! GET OUT!
WELL, HONESTLY!
I DON'T KNOW THAT I UNDERSTAND YOUR NEW STRATEGY ...
THERE ISN'T ANY STRATEGY. WE'RE NOT BUYING ANY MORE MENHIRS, THAT'S ALL!
RIGHT! I'LL BE OFF. AVE!
?!
OH NO, YOU WON'T! YOU'RE STAYING HERE UNTIL I FULLY UNDERSTAND THE SITUATION!

UNHYGIENIX FRESH MENHIRS
THEY'RE NOT BUYING ANY MORE MENHIRS!!!
!
YOU MEAN THEY'RE NOT BUYING ANY MORE OF YOUR MENHIRS!
AND WHY MY MENHIRS, MAY I ASK?
BECAUSE MY MENHIRS DON'T STINK OF ROTTEN FISH, THAT'S WHY... ANYWAY, I'M OFF TO DELIVER THEM. YOU'LL SOON SEE IF THEY'RE BUYING MENHIRS OR NOT!
?
WHAT'S GOING ON?
OH, NOTHING.
READY?
YOU BET!
OFF WE GO, THEN! WITH ALL THESE HUNTERS IN THE FOREST NOWADAYS WE HAVE TO GO QUITE A WAY TO FIND BOARS!
A LITTLE LATER...
FULLIAUTOMATIX TODAY'S MENHIRS
THEY DON'T EVEN WANT MINE ANY MORE!!!
C.O.D.
!

FULLIAUTOM
TODAY
THAT ROMAN TOLD ME HE NEVER WANTED TO SEE ANOTHER MENHIR IN HIS LIFE!
HO!
BUT... BUT... WHAT'S TO BE BECOME OF ME? HOW AM I GOING TO PAY ALL THE PEOPLE WORKING FOR ME?
I'M GLAD TO HEAR IT! NOW I'LL BE ABLE TO GET MY SHIELD-BEARERS BACK!
LOOK!
OBELIX HAS STOPPED MAKING MENHIRS!
SO HE KNEW THE ROMANS WOULDN'T BE BUYING ANY MORE ... AND HE DIDN'T WARN US!
AND IT'S ALL HIS FAULT WE STARTED MAKING MENHIRS IN THE FIRST PLACE!
HE'S A TRAITOR!
IT'S ALL HIS DOING!
WE OUGHT TO TEACH HIM A LESSON!
HOLD THIS, WILL YOU, ASTERIX?
WITH PLEASURE.
COME ON, DOGMATIX!
GRRROOAAARRR

HOW NICE TO SEE THE VILLAGE RETURN TO ITS GOOD OLD WAYS!
YES, THERE'S NOTHING LIKE THE DAILY ROUND, THE COMMON TASK...
YOU DID VERY WELL. I'M PLEASED WITH YOU.
WAIT A MINUTE. LET'S TIE ALL THIS UP!
42A
STOP, EVERYBODY! LISTEN TO ME!
SORRY TO DISTURB YOU, BUT WHY DON'T WE PAY A LITTLE CALL ON THE ROMANS INSTEAD OF FIGHTING EACH OTHER? AFTER ALL, THEY STARTED THE WHOLE THING!
YEAH!
HE'S RIGHT!
I WANT TO THANK YOU FOR YOUR LOVELY BIRTHDAY PRESENT, SO THIS TIME THE ROMANS ARE ON ME!
HOW ABOUT IT, O CHIEF VITALSTATISTIX?
LET'S GET THEM, BY TOUTATIS!
42B

I STILL DON'T GET IT... JUST TELL ME HOW THE GAULS ARE GOING TO REACT NOW YOU'RE NOT BUYING ANY MORE OF THEIR MENHIRS...?
BECAUSE BEFORE YOU CAME ALONG, PLAYING THE FOOL, WE WERE WAITING QUIETLY FOR OUR RELIEF, WE WERE!
I'VE COMPLETED MY MISSION! LET ME GO!
WATCH OUT, MATES! HERE COME THE...
?
?
POC!
?!
THE GAU... THE GAU...

THEY'VE FINISHED THEIR ATTACKS! RELIEF HERE, IS IT?
DUNNO, BUT WE SHOULD BE DUE FOR A TAX RELIEF ALL RIGHT AFTER THIS...
HEAP BIG WHIZZ-KID, EH? YOU SAVVY?
ALL OUR FRIENDS ARE ROLLING IN SESTERTII ... WHAT WILL THEY DO WITH THEM?
NOT MUCH...
I HERE THERE'S A GRAVE FINANCIAL CRISIS IN ROME, THOUGH I DON'T KNOW WHAT CAUSED IT. ANYWAY, THEY'VE DEVALUED THE SESTERTIUS.
UH?
BIG HEAP MENHIR MAKERS STONY BROKE!
44A
BUT ALL SUCH COMPLICATED PROBLEMS MELT AWAY UNDER THE STARS, LIKE SNOW MELTING IN THE SUN, AND THE GAULS CELEBRATE THE RE-ESTABLISHMENT OF THEIR FRENDSHIP WITH A QUIET MIND...
44B
THE END
UDERZO & GOSCINNY

ASTERIX THE GLADIATOR

TEXT BY GOSCINNY

DRAWINGS BY UDERZO

TRANSLATED BY ANTHEA BELL AND DEREK HOCKRIDGE

HODDER DARGAUD
LONDON SYDNEY AUCKLAND

Asterix the Gladiator

Copyright © Dargaud Editeur 1964, Goscinny-Uderzo
English language text copyright © Brockhampton Press Ltd 1969
(now Hodder Children's Books)

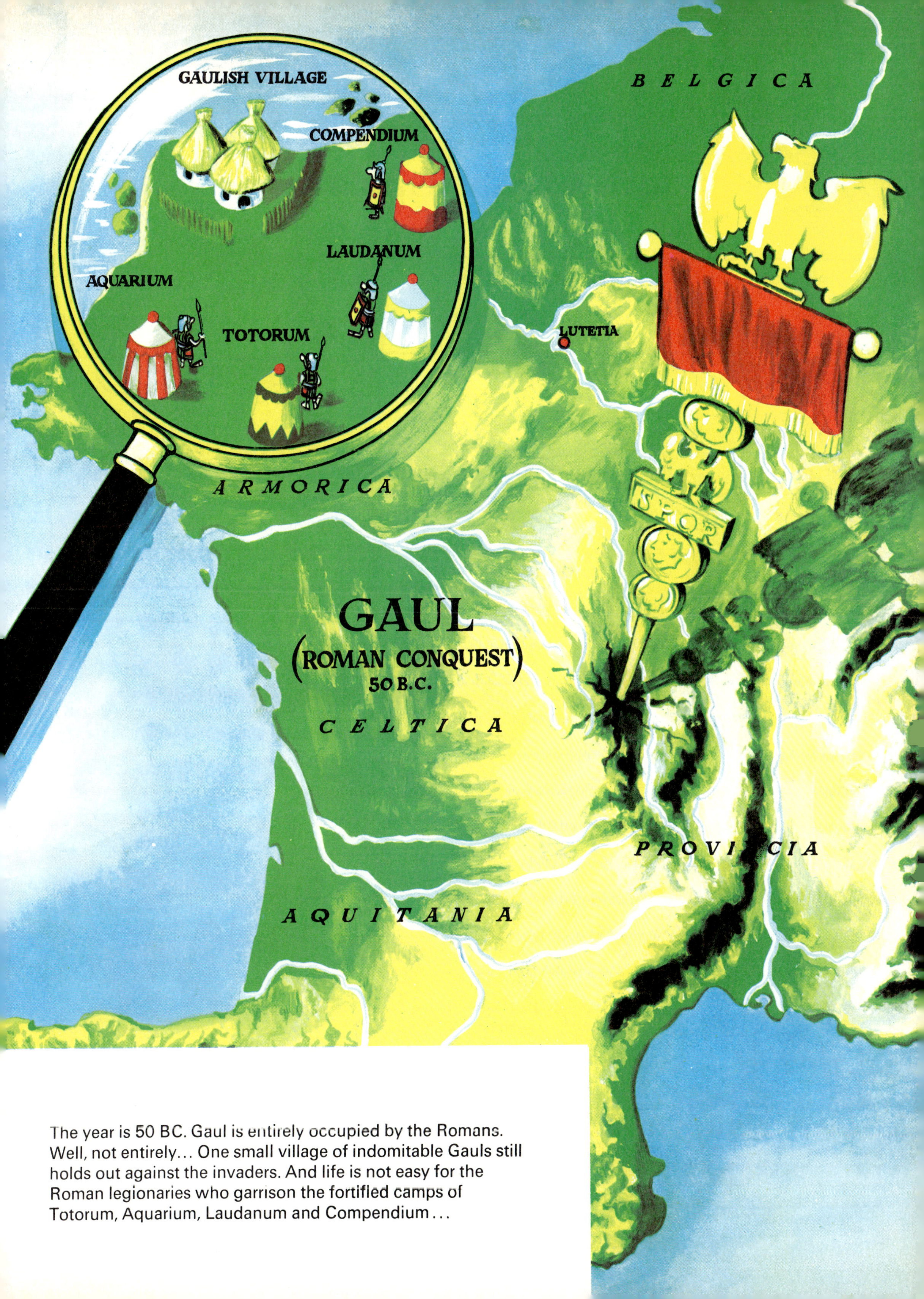

The year is 50 BC. Gaul is entirely occupied by the Romans. Well, not entirely... One small village of indomitable Gauls still holds out against the invaders. And life is not easy for the Roman legionaries who garrison the fortified camps of Totorum, Aquarium, Laudanum and Compendium...

a few of the Gauls

Asterix, the hero of these adventures. A shrewd, cunning little warrior; all perilous missions are immediately entrusted to him. Asterix gets his superhuman strength from the magic potion brewed by the druid Getafix...

Obelix, Asterix's inseparable friend. A menhir delivery-man by trade; addicted to wild boar. Obelix is always ready to drop everything and go off on a new adventure with Asterix – so long as there's wild boar to eat, and plenty of fighting.

Getafix, the venerable village druid. Gathers mistletoe and brews magic potions. His speciality is the potion which gives the drinker superhuman strength. But Getafix also has other recipes up his sleeve...

Cacofonix, the bard. Opinion is divided as to his musical gifts. Cacofonix thinks he's a genius. Everyone else thinks he's unspeakable. But so long as he doesn't speak, let alone sing, everybody likes him...

Finally, Vitalstatistix, the chief of the tribe. Majestic, brave and hot-tempered, the old warrior is respected by his men and feared by his enemies. Vitalstatistix himself has only one fear; he is afraid the sky may fall on his head tomorrow. But as he always says, 'Tomorrow never comes.'

THE ROMAN CAMP OF COMPENDIUM IS IN A FERMENT. THE PREFECT OF GAUL, ODIUS ASPARAGUS, IS PAYING A CALL ON CENTURION GRACCHUS ARMISURPLUS. THE PREFECT ARRIVES FROM THE NEARBY COAST WHERE HIS GALLEY HAS PUT IN...
PRESENT... PILUM!...
AVE, PREFECT! THIS IS A GREAT HONOUR FOR ME!
AVE, CENTURION! YOU'RE TELLING ME!
AND NOW FOR THE PURPOSE OF MY VISIT, CENTURION! I'M GOING TO ROME ON LEAVE, AND CUSTOM DECREES THAT I TAKE CAESAR A HANDSOME PRESENT... SOMETHING UNUSUAL AND VERY VALUABLE...
... I DID THINK OF TAKING HIM A PRESENT FROM LUTETIA, MAYBE A MARBLE MEMO TABLET FOR HIM TO CARVE DOWN HIS APPOINTMENTS, BUT THAT'S TOO ORDINARY...
THEN I HAD A BRILLIANT IDEA! WHY NOT TAKE CAESAR ONE OF THE INVINCIBLE GAULS FROM HEREABOUTS?
WHAT?!
BUT, PREFECT, ABOUT THESE INVINCIBLE GAULS ... THERE'S JUST ONE SNAG!
WELL, WHAT IS IT?
THEY HAPPEN TO BE INVINCIBLE!
THAT'S WHAT MAKES THEM SO VALUABLE! GET ME ONE OF THESE GAULS, AND YOU WON'T REGRET IT!
THERE'S CERTAINLY ONE WHO'S A BIT MORE HARMLESS THAN THE OTHERS... CACOFONIX THE BARD. HE OFTEN GOES FOR WALKS IN THE FOREST BY HIMSELF LOOKING FOR INSPIRATION!
EXCELLENT! I MUST HAVE THIS BARD-AND FAST!
AND IN THE GAULISH VILLAGE...
GOODBYE, ASTERIX, I'M GOING FOR A WALK IN THE FOREST!
GOODBYE, CACOFONIX!

?!
?
NO, CACOFONIX! DON'T GO TO THE FOREST!
I AM TOUCHED BY YOUR SOLICITUDE, OBELIX!
IT'S NOT THAT! ONLY WHEN YOU SING IN THE FOREST YOU SCARE THE WILD BOARS AWAY!
BOOR! THE BOARS APPRECIATE MY MUSIC BETTER THAN YOU!
THAT'S ONLY NATURAL. YOU SING LIKE A PIG!
HAHAHA! HOHOHO!
BARBARIANS! PHILISTINES! SAVAGES!
IN THE FOREST...
GO AND CAPTURE A BARD, GO AND CAPTURE A BARD...IT'S EASY TO SAY THAT!
I'M ALWAYS PICKED ON TO VOLUNTEER FOR DANGEROUS MISSIONS! IT'S NOT FAIR!!!
QUIET! I HEARD A NOISE! TAKE COVER!
THIS WILL BE A GOOD PLACE TO SING...
maybe it's because I'm Armorican
that I love Armorica so...
THESE GAULISH SECRET WEAPONS OUGHT TO BE BANNED BY THE HELVETIA CONVENTION!

RIGHT! I'VE THOUGHT OF A WAY TO COUNTER THE BARD'S SECRET WEAPON... WE ALL STUFF OUR EARS
WHAT WITH?
PARSLEY. THERE'S PLENTY OF IT AROUND
PARSLEY IN MY EARS? I DON'T FANCY THAT. I'LL FEEL LIKE SOMETHING OUT OF A BUTCHER'S SHOP
NOW, BACK INTO AMBUSH! WHEN I GIVE THE SIGNAL WE ALL ATTACK THE BARD!
NOT UP YOUR NOSE, IDIOT!
SOON AFTERWARDS...
NOW... WHAT SHALL I SING NEXT?
COME ON, BOYS!
??? THE... THE OTHERS DIDN'T FOLLOW ME!
A FAN! AT LAST! SOMEONE WHO APPRECIATES GOOD MUSIC! STOP RIGHT THERE, FRIEND. I WILL NOW GIVE YOU A RECITAL!
??? WHAT DID HE...
I'm only a bard in a gilded cage...
POP!
STOP! STOP! I CAN'T BEAR IT! SHUT UP! SHUT UP!
WELL? COULDN'T YOU HEAR ME SHOUTING, YOU COWARDLY LOT?
PARDON?
3

PHEW! THAT'S THAT!
HMMMMM!
WHAT DID YOU SAY?
TAKE THAT PARSLEY OUT OF YOUR EARS!
?!
AVE! MISSION ACCOMPLISHED! WE CAPTURED THE GAULISH BARD AT THE RISK OF OUR LIVES, ESPECIALLY MINE!
EXCELLENT! EXCELLENT!
THERE, IT WASN'T ALL THAT DIFFICULT...
THE TROUBLE IS WE CAN NOW EXPECT REPRISALS FROM THE OTHERS...
OH... ER... WELL, YES... WELL, I REALLY MUST BE GOING! FETCH MY LITTER! THE PRISONER AND I WILL LEAVE AT ONCE TO GO ON BOARD THE GALLEY FOR ROME...
MEANWHILE...
OBELIX, OUR BARD CACOFONIX HASN'T COME BACK YET
THAT'S GOOD NEWS, BUT I DON'T SUPPOSE HE'LL BE LONG
TAC TAC!
ASTERIX! ASTERIX! I SAW SOME ROMANS CAPTURING CACOFONIX!
ARE YOU SURE, PICANMIX?
I WAS OUT HUNTING WILD PIGLETS IN THE FOREST, AND I SAW IT ALL!
WHAT A FUNNY IDEA OF THE ROMANS! WHYEVER SHOULD THEY WANT TO LUMBER THEMSELVES WITH CACOFONIX?
ANYWAY, WE MUST AVENGE THIS INSULT! I'M OFF TO TELL OUR CHIEF VITALSTATISTIX THE NEWS!
OBELIX QUARRY
CAUTION MENHIRS TURNING
HIGHER!
IV
4

O VITALSTATISTIX, OUR BARD CACOFONIX HAS DISAPPEARED!
YOU'RE JUST SAYING THAT TO PLEASE ME...
THE ROMANS HAVE CAPTURED HIM!
WHAT?
BY TOUTATIS! EVEN IF IT IS A FUNNY IDEA OF THE ROMANS, THAT'S NOT PLAYING FAIR! WE CAN'T HAVE THIS SORT OF THING!
A GAUL MUST KNOW HOW TO MAKE HIS ENEMY RESPECT HIM! WE SHALL ORGANIZE A PUNITIVE EXPEDITION! LET THE DRUID PREPARE THE MAGIC POTION!
SOON AFTERWARDS THE GAULISH WARRIORS ARE DRINKING THE MAGIC POTION WHICH GIVES THEM INVINCIBLE STRENGTH...
NO, OBELIX! NOT YOU! I'VE ALREADY TOLD YOU YOU DON'T NEED ANY POTION! YOU'RE STRONG ENOUGH AS YOU ARE!
WHAT, ME STRONG? NOT A BIT OF IT! I'M AS WEAK AS ANYTHING!
GO ON! I'LL GIVE YOU THIS NICE MENHIR!
NO, NO AND FOR THE THIRD TIME NO!
SILENCE! OUR CHIEF VITALSTATISTIX IS GOING TO MAKE A SPEECH!
FRIENDS, GAULS, COUNTRYMEN! WE MUST GIVE THESE ROMANS A GOOD LESSON, BY TOUTATIS!
AND REMEMBER, WE HAVE NOTHING TO FEAR BUT THE SKY FALLING ON OUR HEADS!
IN THE ROMAN CAMP OF COMPENDIUM THE TROOPS HAVE BEEN ALERTED...
AND REMEMBER, ROMANS, WE HAVE NOTHING TO FEAR BUT THE GAULS!

THIS IS THE FIRST TIME CACOFONIX HAS EVER GIVEN US ANY ENTERTAINMENT!
I SAY, ASTERIX! HOW ABOUT A BET? THE ONE WHO KNOCKS OUT MOST LEGIONARIES WINS, AND WE HAVE TO COLLECT THEIR HELMETS AS PROOF!
AT THIS VERY MOMENT, AT COMPENDIUM...
PUT YOUR HELMETS ON!!!
THE GAU... GAULS! SOUND THE ALARM!
HELP! THEY'RE COMING!
AND INSIDE THE CAMP WE OBSERVE THE IMPRESSIVE SPECTACLE OF LEGIONARIES MANOEUVRING IN ACCORDANCE WITH THE FAMOUS PRECISION OF THE ROMAN ARMY...
COHORTS INTO THREE LINES... FORM!
SOUND THE HORNS, TRUMPETS AND BUCINAS!
PILUM AT THE READY!
MANOEUVRE, BY JUPITER!!!
WHOOOOOOSH!
WE CAN'T! THE GAULS ARE IN THE WAY!
6

THE BATTLE IS SHORT...
CLINKCLANKCLONK!
BANG!
BIFF!
BUT SHARP...
SWOOOSH!
I CAN'T FIND CACOFONIX ANYWHERE... AH, THERE'S THE ROMAN COMMANDER!
BANG!
BING!
I SHALL FIGHT TO THE DEATH!
WANT ME TO THUMP YOU?
OH ALL RIGHT! ALL IS LOST! I SURRENDER! ALEA JACTA EST!
AND LET IT BE A LESSON TO YOU! NOW, GIVE US BACK OUR BARD, AND DON'T DO IT AGAIN!
THE FACT IS... YOUR BARD ISN'T HERE ANY MORE. AT THIS MOMENT HE'S ON BOARD A GALLEY, SAILING FOR ROME TO BE GIVEN TO CAESAR AS A PRESENT...
!!!
WE'RE WASTING OUR TIME...
A PRESENT? THAT'S A REALLY FUNNY IDEA!
LOOK AT THIS, ASTERIX! I'M SURE I'VE WON OUR BET! AND ONE LEGIONARY WAS FIGHTING BARE-HEADED TOO. IT'S AGAINST ALL THE RULES OF WARFARE TO GO INTO BATTLE IMPROPERLY DRESSED! I'VE A GOOD MIND TO REPORT HIM!
THE GAULS WITHDRAW, LEAVING BEHIND THEM THE AFTERMATH OF BATTLE...
THEY REALLY LET US HAVE IT, EH, SIR?
IN THE FIRST PLACE, GET THIS CAMP BACK INTO ORDER!!! WHAT'S ALL THIS UNTIDINESS IN AID OF? AND DON'T ANYONE EVER MENTION THIS BATTLE TO ME AGAIN!!!

LATER, IN THE GAULISH VILLAGE...
POOR CACOFONIX, PRISONER ON BOARD A ROMAN GALLEY!
HE WAS SO NICE! SCRUNCH! SO WELL BROUGHT UP! NEVER SANG WITH HIS MOUTH FULL! SCRUNCH! PITY HE DIDN'T EAT MUCH... SCRUNCH!
MEANWHILE...
I CAN'T WAIT TO GIVE YOU TO CAESAR!
YOUR CAESAR DOESN'T DESERVE ME, ROMAN!
MAKE THEM ROW FASTER!
BONG! BONG!
BONG! BONG!
CRACK! CRACK!
?!
STOP HAVING THOSE UNHAPPY SOULS WHIPPED, ROMAN! LOOSEN SOME OF MY BONDS! I WILL SING THEM A SONG TO LIVEN THEM UP!
farewell and adieu to you fair Celtic ladies...
farewell and adieu to you ladies of Gaul...
STOP! MERCY!
WE'D RATHER HAVE THE WHIP!
CLICK! CLACK! CLONK! CLUNK! BOING!
OUR WORK ISN'T ALL FUN AND GAMES, BUT THIS IS INHUMAN! IF THE GAUL WILL SHUT UP WE PROMISE TO ROW OUR HARDEST!
YOU IGNORANT LOT! YOU BRUTES! YOU'LL ALL END UP IN THE... WELL, YOU ALREADY HAVE!
BONG!
I'M BEGINNING TO WONDER IF CAESAR REALLY DOES DESERVE THIS...

OBELIX! WE MUST GO TO ROME AND RESCUE CACOFONIX!
THAT'S ALL RIGHT BY ME... SCRUNCH! SCRUNCH! ...BUT HOW DO WE GET THERE? IT'S A LONG WAY! SCRUNCH!
BONK
...AND SO WE'LL GO DOWN TO THE BEACH AND TAKE THE FIRST BOAT FOR ROME!
IT'S RISKY, ASTERIX, BUT YOU'RE RIGHT; WE CAN'T LEAVE OUR BARD IN THE LURCH. HE SINGS ATROCIOUSLY, BUT HE'S A GOOD SORT...
AN EXCELLENT SORT!
YOU COME WITH ME, ASTERIX, AND I'LL MAKE YOU A GOURD OF MAGIC POTION...
I'LL JUST GO AND FIND SOMEONE TO DELIVER MY MENHIRS WHILE I'M AWAY...
I DON'T KNOW THAT I'M CUT OUT FOR THIS SORT OF WORK...
I'M RELYING ON YOU. YOU NEEDN'T DELIVER MORE THAN ONE AT A TIME TO START WITH
COME ON, OBELIX, IT'S TIME TO LEAVE!
COMING, ASTERIX!
TAKE CARE!
DON'T WORRY! IF THE ROMANS AREN'T NICE TO US WE'LL LEAVE THEIR CITY FULL OF RUINS!
ASTERIX, WHAT'S THE LATIN FOR WILD BOAR?
SINGULARIS PORCUS, BUT I DON'T KNOW IF THEY HAVE THEM IN ROME
NOW WE HAVE TO WAIT FOR A SHIP...
LET'S HAVE A BET WHILE WE WAIT. WE SEE HOW MANY DOZEN OYSTERS WE CAN EAT, AND THE ONE WHO EATS MOST WINS A SINGULARIS PORCUS!
LOOK! A SHIP! WE'RE IN LUCK!
WHY DON'T WE WAIT FOR THE NEXT ONE? THEN WE COULD HAVE OUR BET!
8

NOW TO STOP THIS SHIP SAILING ALONG THE COAST!
ASTERIX AND OBELIX MAKE THE ANCIENT GAULISH SIGN INDICATING A WISH TO BE TAKEN ON BOARD... NOTE THE FOUR CLENCHED FINGERS AND THE THUMB JERKED IN THE DESIRED DIRECTION. IF YOU WISH TO GO TO ROME, THE DIRECTION OF THE THUMB IS IMMATERIAL, SINCE ALL ROADS LEAD THERE
N.B. THIS GESTURE IS STILL EMPLOYED TODAY, THOUGH NOT OFTEN TO STOP SHIPS
IT'S A PHOENICIAN GALLEY. THE PHOENICIANS ARE FAMOUS SAILORS AND MERCHANTS!
WHAT'S THE PHOENICIAN FOR SINGULARIS PORCUS?
WE'RE FROM TYRE IN PHOENICIA. MY NAME IS EKONOMIKRISIS. WOULD YOU LIKE TO BUY ANY GLASS, JEWELS, TEXTILES, PURPLE, FURNITURE?
NO, WE WANT TO GO TO ROME
HM...ER...ALL RIGHT, COME ON BOARD!
ARE THOSE SLAVES?
OH NO, THEY'RE PARTNERS... WHEN WE FLOATED THE COMPANY, I DREW UP THE CONTRACT AND THEY FAILED TO READ IT CAREFULLY BEFORE SIGNING. I'M CHAIRMAN AND MANAGING DIRECTOR
IT'S KIND OF YOU TO TAKE US TO ROME. I HOPE IT DOESN'T MEAN GOING OUT OF YOUR WAY?
AS IT HAPPENS, WE WERE PLANNING TO GO TO ROME. ONE OF MY PREDECESSORS ABANDONED HIS SHIP THERE...
IT SANK?
NO, HE SOLD IT. HE WAS A BETTER SALESMAN THAN SAILSMAN
10

A SAIL ON THE HORIZON, MR. CHAIRMAN!
IT MUST BE PIRATES! THEY MAY TAKE US PRISONER, KILL US, OR EVEN WORSE STEAL OUR MERCHANDISE!
SURE ENOUGH, ON BOARD THE PIRATE GALLEY...
SHIVER ME TIMBERS, WE'VE GOT 'EM, ME HEARTIES! PULL AWAY! THAT HEAVY PHOENICIAN SHIP WITH ALL ITS CARGO WILL NEVER ESCAPE US!
LET'S PUSH THE BOAT OUT!
TEEHEE HFF!
MY DEAR FELLOW DIRECTORS, I THINK WE SHALL BE OBLIGED TO FIGHT...
NO, NO, MR. CHAIRMAN! OUR CONTRACT SAYS WE HAVE TO ROW, BUT THERE'S NOTHING IN THE SMALL PRINT ABOUT FIGHTING!
NOW, I SUGGEST WE CHANGE THE CONTRACT. I HAVE AN IMPORTANT MODIFICATION TO MAKE
ME TOO!
ME TOO!
ME TOO!
ME TOO!
ME TOO!
ME TOO!
ME TOO!
WE CAN'T COUNT ON THESE CHATTER-BOXES TO FIGHT. WE'LL HAVE TO DEAL WITH THIS ON OUR OWN
GOODY! THERE'LL BE MORE ROOM! LOOK, HERE COME THE PIRATES. POOR THINGS!
THEY'RE WEARING HELMETS! WE CAN HAVE ANOTHER BET LIKE WE DID WITH THE LEGIONARIES!
GIDDY GOAT'S HORNS, WE'LL MAKE JUST ONE MOUTHFUL OF THEM!
VANITAS VANITATUM ET OMNIA VANITAS!
WE MIGHT ON THE ONE HAND HOLD AN EXTRAORDIN-ARY GENERAL MEETING TO DISCUSS TERMS OF CONTRACT, WHILE ALTERNATIVELY, ON THE OTHER HAND...
WELL, I THINK THIS WOULD BE A VERY GOOD MOMENT TO...

AT 'EM ME HEARTIES!
BOING!
COME ON, OBELIX!
OO, YES!
WHAM!
BONK
HEY! THAT'S AGAINST THE RULES! JUMPING INTO THE SEA IS AGAINST THE RULES!
NO! NO! HI, NO!
CREEAAK!
I THINK THIS IS THE FIRST TIME I'VE FOUGHT ON A BOAT... MAKES A NICE CHANGE...
I SAY, WOULD YOU LEND ME THAT ONE TO FINISH OFF?
NOOOOOO!
CRASH!
THERE, THAT'S THAT. WE'D BETTER GET BACK TO THE PHOENICIANS
I THOUGHT THEY HAD A BIGGER CREW ON THESE GALLEYS
AND WHEN OUR FRIENDS HAVE LEFT THE GALLEY...
THOSE GAULS NEVER MISS THE BOAT.
12

YOU HAVE SAVED WHAT IS DEAREST TO OUR HEARTS — OUR CARGO! NOW WE'RE BOSOM FRIENDS!
I ORIGINALLY INTENDED TO SELL YOU AS SLAVES WHEN WE CALLED AT THE NEXT PORT. BUT NOW I'LL TAKE YOU TO ROME AS AGREED
YOU CERTAINLY DO HAVE BUSINESS ACUMEN!
WHAT CAN YOU EXPECT? AS I WAS SAYING TO MY PARTNERS, WE'RE ALL IN THE SAME BOAT, AND WE MUSTN'T REST ON OUR OARS IF OUR OVERHEADS ARE NOT TO MAKE US GO UNDER!
MEANWHILE, IN ROME...
AVE, CAESAR!
AVE, ODIUS ASPARAGUS, PREFECT OF GAUL
HERE'S MY PRESENT, O CAESAR! A GAULISH BARD FROM THE TRIBE OF INDOMITABLE GAULS IN THE COMPENDIUM AREA
I'VE BEEN BROUGHT HERE AS A SOUVENIR... JUST AS IF I WAS A VULGAR PAINTED SHELL!
A BARD? HOW INTERESTING!
YOU CAN WAIT TILL THE COWS COME HOME BEFORE I'LL SING FOR YOU... AND YOU DON'T KNOW WHAT YOU'RE MISSING!
THANKS FOR THIS ORIGINAL LITTLE PRESENT, PREFECT. YOU MAY GO!
SEND FOR CAIUS FATUOUS, THE LANISTA*
SNAP!
* TRAINER OF THE GLADIATORS
CAIUS FATUOUS, CAN YOU MAKE A GLADIATOR OF THIS BARD?
DEAR ME, NO, O CAESAR! HE'S TOO WEAK... NOT ENOUGH MEAT ON HIM
IF I WASN'T RESTRAINING MYSELF...
VERY WELL THEN, THROW HIM TO THE LIONS AT THE NEXT GAMES. TAKE HIM AWAY!
13

WE'RE NEARING THE END OF OUR VOYAGE. ROME IS A FEW HOURS' WALK FROM THE PLACE WHERE WE'RE GOING TO LAND...
WE'LL BE STAYING HERE FOR A WHILE TO BUY AND SELL GOODS. IF YOU FINISH YOUR BUSINESS IN TIME WE'LL TAKE YOU BACK TO GAUL...
THANKS, EKONOMI-KRISIS!
HOIST THE FLAG!
SALE
FINAL CLEARANCE
JUST LOOK AT THIS, OBELIX! IF THE ROADS ARE SO WIDE AND STRAIGHT HERE, WHAT MUST IT BE LIKE IN ROME?
DANGER
SLIPPERY FLAGSTONES
WE'RE THERE!
VIA APPIA
ROMA
?!?
HOW ABOUT THAT HELMET GAME AGAIN? WE COULD HAVE A LOVELY FIGHT WITH ALL THESE ROMANS!
WE MUST START MAKING INQUIRIES... AND I THINK I SEE WHAT WE NEED!
14

WE SHALL FIND SOME OF OUR FELLOW COUNTRYMEN IN THERE!
AND WILD BOAR!
GAULISH RESTAURANT
WINES OF AQUITANIA AND NARBONNE
LUGDUNUM SAUSAGE
BOAR ON THE SPIT
RECLINE AT THIS TABLE. I'LL BE WITH YOU IN A MINUTE
WE'RE GAULS!
WELL, FANCY THAT! FELLOW COUNTRYMEN! MY NAME'S INSTANTMIX. I'VE BEEN LIVING IN ROME SOME TIME...
I'M TRYING TO SAVE UP, AND THEN I SHALL OPEN A ROMAN RESTAURANT IN LUTETIA
WE'RE LOOKING FOR A FRIEND. A BARD WHO WAS GIVEN TO JULIUS CAESAR AS A PRESENT
?!?
HE WENT OFF WITHOUT A WORD!
YES, HE NEVER TOOK OUR ORDER!
COME AND SEE ME THIS EVENING... I SLIPPED MY ADDRESS INTO ONE OF THE BOARS...
OH, THAT MUST HAVE BEEN THE BIT THAT WAS DIFFICULT TO SWALLOW... BRING US YOUR ADDRESS AGAIN INSIDE ANOTHER BOAR!
?!

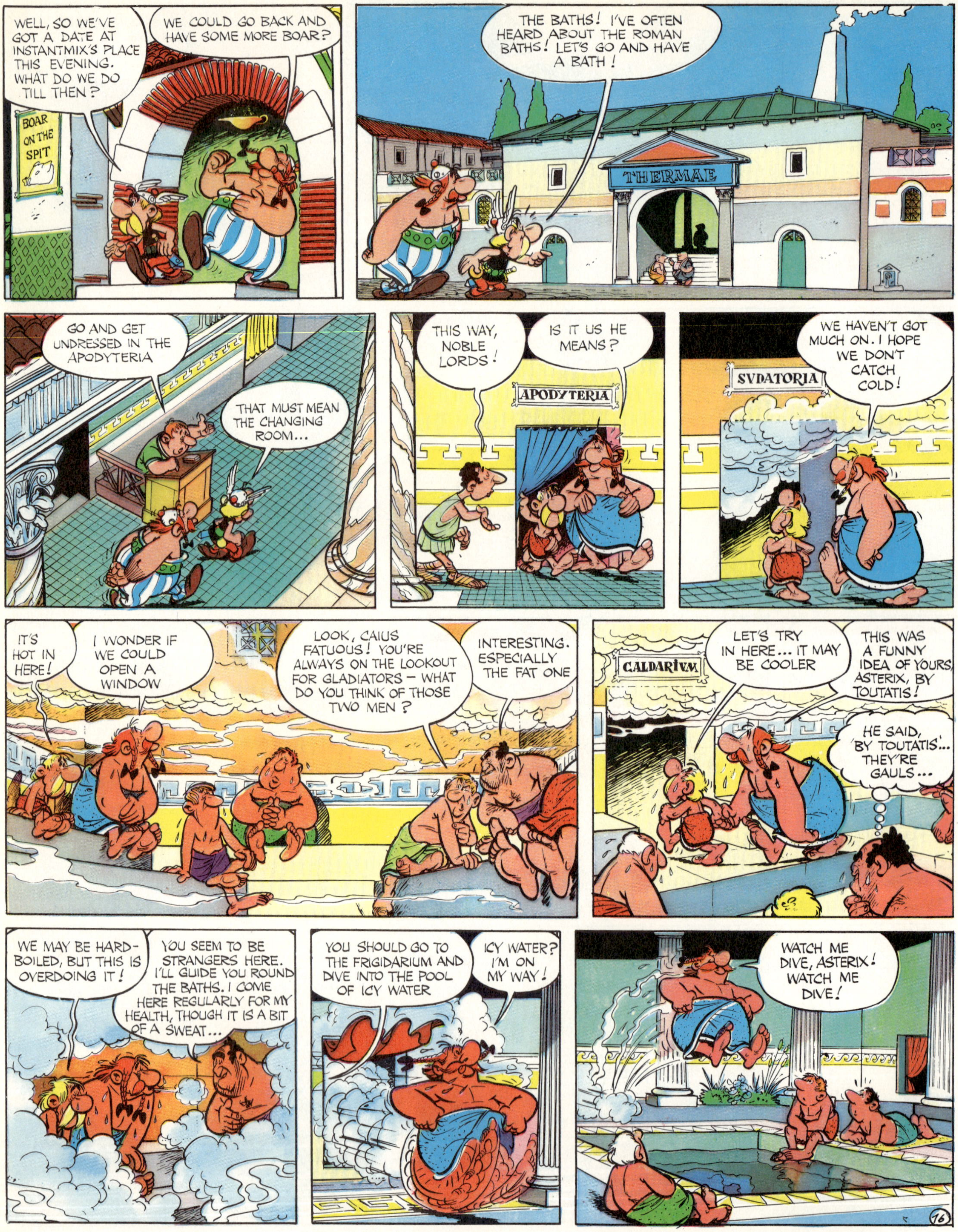

WELL, SO WE'VE GOT A DATE AT INSTANTMIX'S PLACE THIS EVENING. WHAT DO WE DO TILL THEN?
WE COULD GO BACK AND HAVE SOME MORE BOAR?
BOAR ON THE SPIT
THE BATHS! I'VE OFTEN HEARD ABOUT THE ROMAN BATHS! LET'S GO AND HAVE A BATH!
THERMAE
GO AND GET UNDRESSED IN THE APODYTERIA
THAT MUST MEAN THE CHANGING ROOM...
THIS WAY, NOBLE LORDS!
IS IT US HE MEANS?
APODYTERIA
SVDATORIA
WE HAVEN'T GOT MUCH ON. I HOPE WE DON'T CATCH COLD!
IT'S HOT IN HERE!
I WONDER IF WE COULD OPEN A WINDOW
LOOK, CAIUS FATUOUS! YOU'RE ALWAYS ON THE LOOKOUT FOR GLADIATORS – WHAT DO YOU THINK OF THOSE TWO MEN?
INTERESTING. ESPECIALLY THE FAT ONE
CALDARIVM
LET'S TRY IN HERE... IT MAY BE COOLER
THIS WAS A FUNNY IDEA OF YOURS, ASTERIX, BY TOUTATIS!
HE SAID, 'BY TOUTATIS'... THEY'RE GAULS...
WE MAY BE HARD-BOILED, BUT THIS IS OVERDOING IT!
YOU SEEM TO BE STRANGERS HERE. I'LL GUIDE YOU ROUND THE BATHS. I COME HERE REGULARLY FOR MY HEALTH, THOUGH IT IS A BIT OF A SWEAT...
YOU SHOULD GO TO THE FRIGIDARIUM AND DIVE INTO THE POOL OF ICY WATER
ICY WATER? I'M ON MY WAY!
WATCH ME DIVE, ASTERIX! WATCH ME DIVE!
16

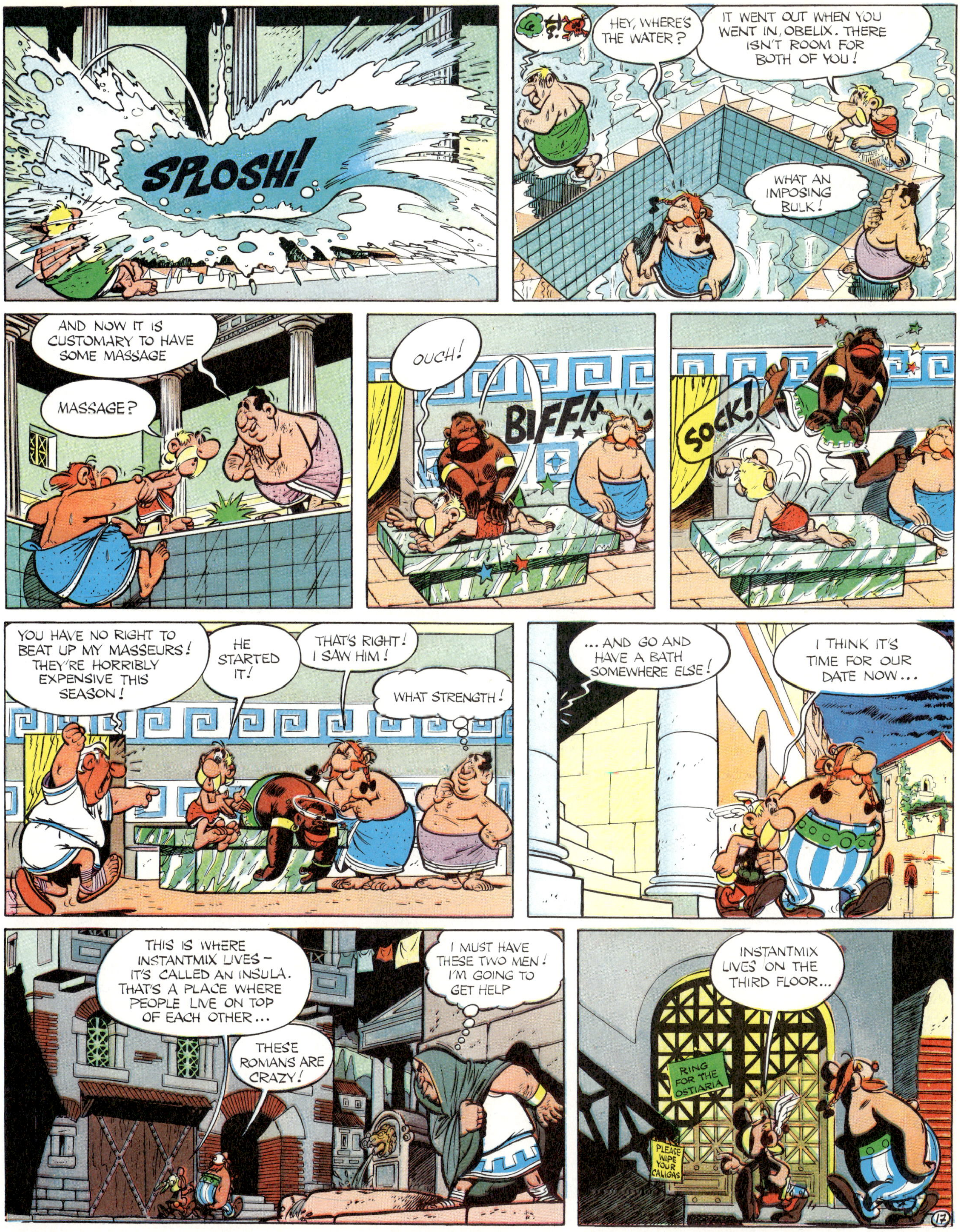
SPLOSH!
HEY, WHERE'S THE WATER?
IT WENT OUT WHEN YOU WENT IN, OBELIX. THERE ISN'T ROOM FOR BOTH OF YOU!
WHAT AN IMPOSING BULK!
AND NOW IT IS CUSTOMARY TO HAVE SOME MASSAGE
MASSAGE?
OUCH!
BIFF!
SOCK!
YOU HAVE NO RIGHT TO BEAT UP MY MASSEURS! THEY'RE HORRIBLY EXPENSIVE THIS SEASON!
HE STARTED IT!
THAT'S RIGHT! I SAW HIM!
WHAT STRENGTH!
... AND GO AND HAVE A BATH SOMEWHERE ELSE!
I THINK IT'S TIME FOR OUR DATE NOW...
THIS IS WHERE INSTANTMIX LIVES – IT'S CALLED AN INSULA. THAT'S A PLACE WHERE PEOPLE LIVE ON TOP OF EACH OTHER...
THESE ROMANS ARE CRAZY!
I MUST HAVE THESE TWO MEN! I'M GOING TO GET HELP
INSTANTMIX LIVES ON THE THIRD FLOOR...
RING FOR THE OSTIARIA
PLEASE WIPE YOUR CALIGAS
17

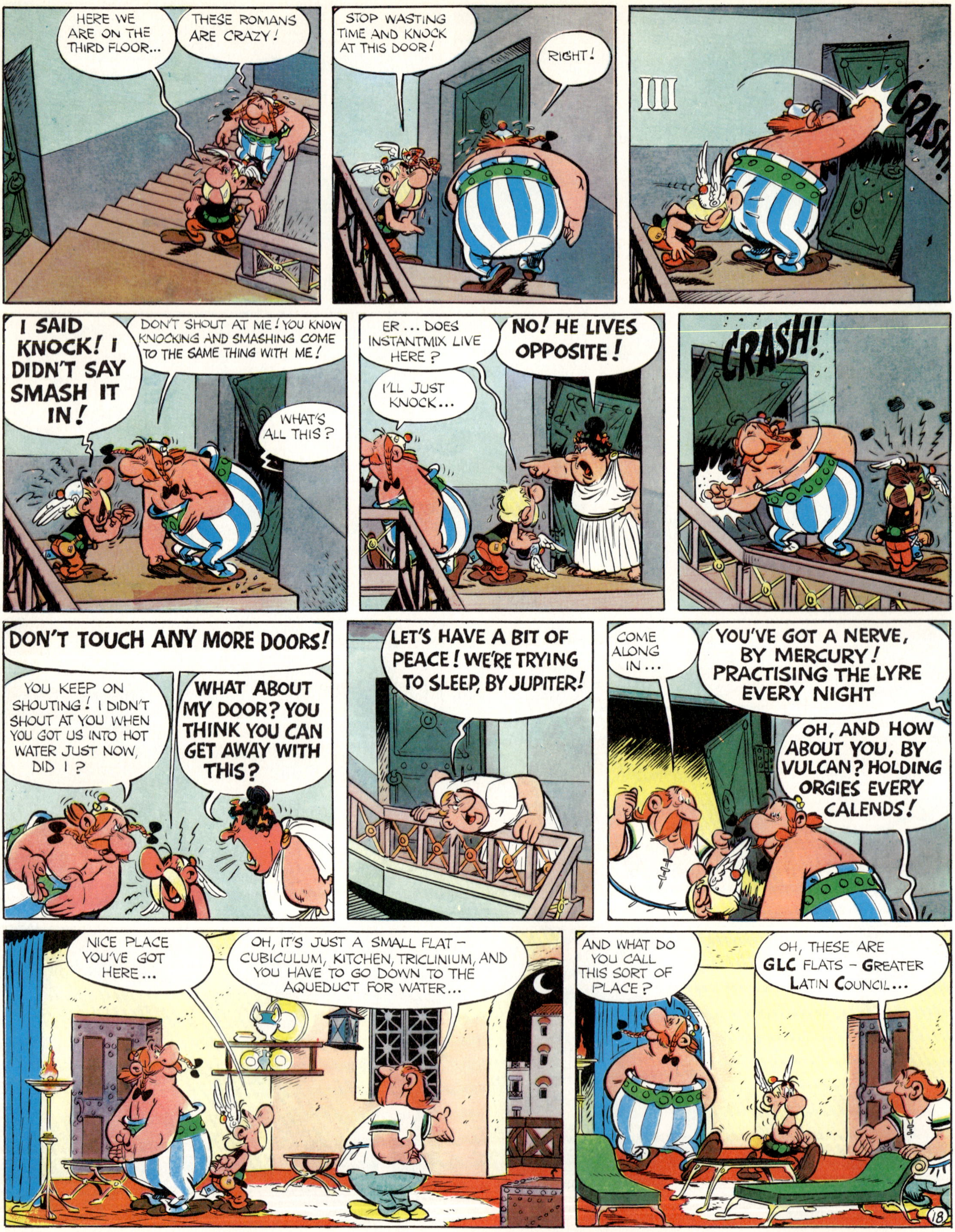
HERE WE ARE ON THE THIRD FLOOR...
THESE ROMANS ARE CRAZY!
STOP WASTING TIME AND KNOCK AT THIS DOOR!
RIGHT!
III
CRASH!
I SAID KNOCK! I DIDN'T SAY SMASH IT IN!
DON'T SHOUT AT ME! YOU KNOW KNOCKING AND SMASHING COME TO THE SAME THING WITH ME!
WHAT'S ALL THIS?
ER... DOES INSTANTMIX LIVE HERE?
NO! HE LIVES OPPOSITE!
I'LL JUST KNOCK...
CRASH!
DON'T TOUCH ANY MORE DOORS!
YOU KEEP ON SHOUTING! I DIDN'T SHOUT AT YOU WHEN YOU GOT US INTO HOT WATER JUST NOW, DID I?
WHAT ABOUT MY DOOR? YOU THINK YOU CAN GET AWAY WITH THIS?
LET'S HAVE A BIT OF PEACE! WE'RE TRYING TO SLEEP, BY JUPITER!
COME ALONG IN...
YOU'VE GOT A NERVE, BY MERCURY! PRACTISING THE LYRE EVERY NIGHT
OH, AND HOW ABOUT YOU, BY VULCAN? HOLDING ORGIES EVERY CALENDS!
NICE PLACE YOU'VE GOT HERE...
OH, IT'S JUST A SMALL FLAT – CUBICULUM, KITCHEN, TRICLINIUM, AND YOU HAVE TO GO DOWN TO THE AQUEDUCT FOR WATER...
AND WHAT DO YOU CALL THIS SORT OF PLACE?
OH, THESE ARE GLC FLATS – GREATER LATIN COUNCIL...
18

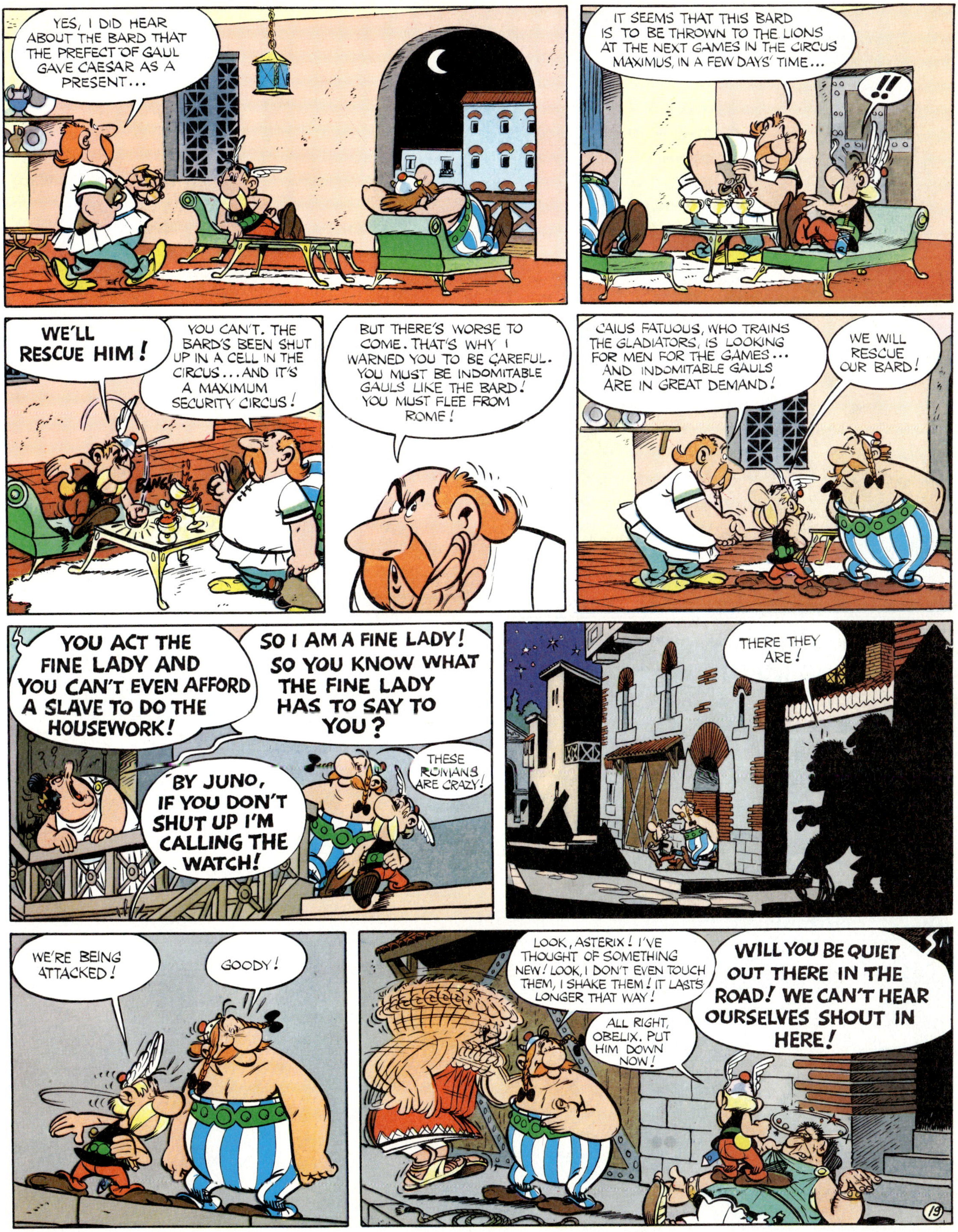
YES, I DID HEAR ABOUT THE BARD THAT THE PREFECT OF GAUL GAVE CAESAR AS A PRESENT...
IT SEEMS THAT THIS BARD IS TO BE THROWN TO THE LIONS AT THE NEXT GAMES IN THE CIRCUS MAXIMUS, IN A FEW DAYS' TIME...
!!
WE'LL RESCUE HIM!
YOU CAN'T. THE BARD'S BEEN SHUT UP IN A CELL IN THE CIRCUS... AND IT'S A MAXIMUM SECURITY CIRCUS!
BANG
BUT THERE'S WORSE TO COME. THAT'S WHY I WARNED YOU TO BE CAREFUL. YOU MUST BE INDOMITABLE GAULS LIKE THE BARD! YOU MUST FLEE FROM ROME!
CAIUS FATUOUS, WHO TRAINS THE GLADIATORS, IS LOOKING FOR MEN FOR THE GAMES... AND INDOMITABLE GAULS ARE IN GREAT DEMAND!
WE WILL RESCUE OUR BARD!
YOU ACT THE FINE LADY AND YOU CAN'T EVEN AFFORD A SLAVE TO DO THE HOUSEWORK!
SO I AM A FINE LADY! SO YOU KNOW WHAT THE FINE LADY HAS TO SAY TO YOU?
BY JUNO, IF YOU DON'T SHUT UP I'M CALLING THE WATCH!
THESE ROMANS ARE CRAZY!
THERE THEY ARE!
WE'RE BEING ATTACKED!
GOODY!
LOOK, ASTERIX! I'VE THOUGHT OF SOMETHING NEW! LOOK, I DON'T EVEN TOUCH THEM, I SHAKE THEM! IT LASTS LONGER THAT WAY!
ALL RIGHT, OBELIX. PUT HIM DOWN NOW!
WILL YOU BE QUIET OUT THERE IN THE ROAD! WE CAN'T HEAR OURSELVES SHOUT IN HERE!
19

THIS INN OPPOSITE THE CIRCUS WILL SUIT US NICELY. LET'S SEE IF THEY HAVE ANY ROOM
RIGHT
CIRCUS INN
I WONDER IF THEY'LL LET US IN AT THIS TIME OF NIGHT...
INN
I'LL JUST KNOCK...
SOON AFTERWARDS...
THAT WILL BE 20 SESTERTII FOR THE NIGHT AND 40 SESTERTII FOR THE DOOR
TAP! TAP! TAP!
MEANWHILE IN THE HOUSE OF CAIUS FATUOUS THE GLADIATOR TRAINER...
WELL, DID YOU GET THEM?
ER... NO, BOSS... THEY DIDN'T WANT TO COME
I MUST HAVE THOSE TWO MEN! JUMP TO IT, EVERY-ONE!
AND NEXT MORNING...
SLEEP WELL, ASTERIX?
YES, THANK YOU, OBELIX. LET'S GO AND HAVE BREAKFAST NOW
WE MUST TRY TO GET INTO CONVERSATION WITH ONE OF THE CIRCUS GUARDS AND FIND OUT EXACTLY WHERE CACOFONIX IS IMPRISONED!
WAITER! HAVE YOU BY ANY CHANCE GOT SOME PARSLEY?
PARSLEY? WHAT FOR?
FOR PUTTING IN MY EARS! I'VE GOT A PRISONER WHO KEEPS ON SINGING, SOMETHING HORRIBLE!
THAT'S CACOFONIX!
THE DESCRIPTION FITS, ANYWAY!
20

LET'S TRY A FEW CRAFTY QUESTIONS ON THIS GUARD. WE MUSTN'T AROUSE HIS SUSPICIONS...
NO...
HEY, YOU! WHERE'S CACOFONIX IMPRISONED?
?!
CELL XVIII FIRST BASEMENT DOWN, BUT IT'S A SECRET!
THERE!
SOON AFTERWARDS...
AND NOW FOR THE CIRCUS. I'LL DRINK A LITTLE MAGIC POTION
HERE'S MY PLAN—WE KNOCK DOWN EVERYONE AND EVERYTHING UNTIL WE FIND CACOFONIX AND THEN WE MAKE OFF WITH HIM!
THAT'S A CLEVER PLAN!
HALT! NO...
ENTRY!
CELL XV... CELL XVI... CELL XVII... WE'RE GETTING WARM!
OUR BET ABOUT THE HELMETS IS STILL ON, ISN'T IT?
CELL XVIII IS EMPTY!
HEY! WHAT ARE YOU TWO DOING HERE?
POP!
21

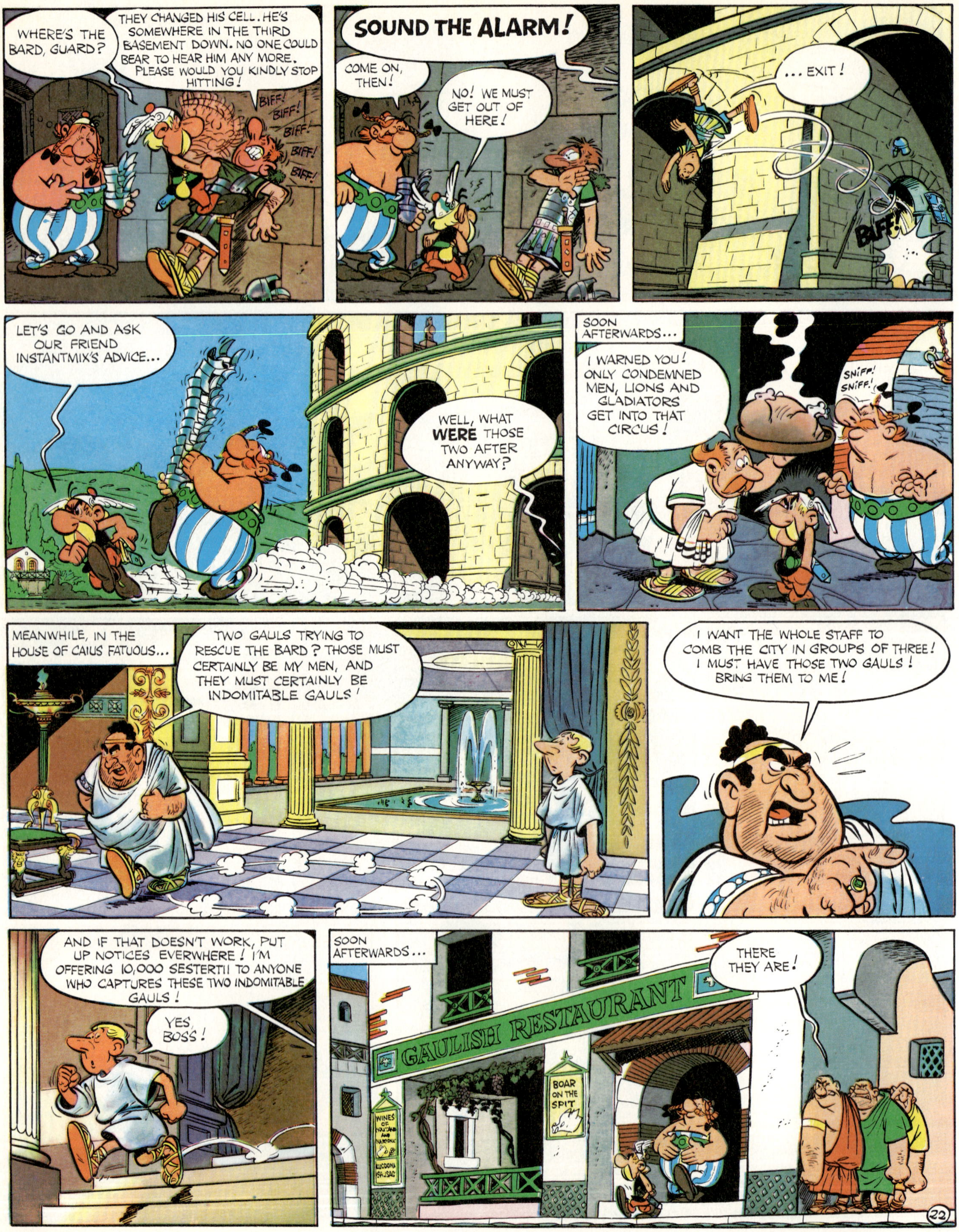
WHERE'S THE BARD, GUARD?
THEY CHANGED HIS CELL. HE'S SOMEWHERE IN THE THIRD BASEMENT DOWN. NO ONE COULD BEAR TO HEAR HIM ANY MORE. PLEASE WOULD YOU KINDLY STOP HITTING!
BIFF! BIFF! BIFF! BIFF! BIFF!
SOUND THE ALARM!
COME ON, THEN!
NO! WE MUST GET OUT OF HERE!
... EXIT!
BAFF!
LET'S GO AND ASK OUR FRIEND INSTANTMIX'S ADVICE...
WELL, WHAT WERE THOSE TWO AFTER ANYWAY?
SOON AFTERWARDS...
I WARNED YOU! ONLY CONDEMNED MEN, LIONS AND GLADIATORS GET INTO THAT CIRCUS!
SNIFF! SNIFF!
MEANWHILE, IN THE HOUSE OF CAIUS FATUOUS...
TWO GAULS TRYING TO RESCUE THE BARD? THOSE MUST CERTAINLY BE MY MEN, AND THEY MUST CERTAINLY BE INDOMITABLE GAULS!
I WANT THE WHOLE STAFF TO COMB THE CITY IN GROUPS OF THREE! I MUST HAVE THOSE TWO GAULS! BRING THEM TO ME!
AND IF THAT DOESN'T WORK, PUT UP NOTICES EVERWHERE! I'M OFFERING 10,000 SESTERTII TO ANYONE WHO CAPTURES THESE TWO INDOMITABLE GAULS!
YES, BOSS!
SOON AFTERWARDS...
GAULISH RESTAURANT
BOAR ON THE SPIT
THERE THEY ARE!
22

LET'S GET THEM!
SPLAT!
IT'S A NUISANCE, WHAT INSTANTMIX TOLD US...
CLONK!
YES, HEARING THINGS LIKE THAT MAKES ME COME OVER ALL FAINT...
HE SAID ONLY CONDEMNED MEN, LIONS AND GLADIATORS GET INTO THE CIRCUS...
SUPPOSE WE DRESSED UP AS LIONS?
GAULISH RESTAURANT
POF!
HERE THEY COME!
YOU'RE TOO FAT FOR A LION!
IF ONLY I'D KNOWN...
ALL THE SAME, WE MUST SAVE OUR BARD!
OF COURSE!
LET'S BEAT IT! HERE COME THE COPS!
NOW, NOW, NOW, WHAT'S ALL THIS 'ERE? YOU COME ALONG QUIETLY TO THE STATION! AND NO FUNNY BUSINESS–WE'RE SEVEN TO TWO!
LET'S GET BACK TO OUR INN!
FORWARD, MEN...OUFF!
I SAY, ASTERIX, DON'T YOU THINK IT'S FUNNY, ALL THESE PEOPLE ATTACKING US?
PEOPLE? WHAT PEOPLE?
CIRCUS INN
23

TEN THOUSAND SESTERTII
FOR THE CAPTURE OF TWO DANGEROUS INDOMITABLE GAULS: ONE SMALL FAIR MAN, BIG MOUSTACHE, WINGED HELMET, ONE FAT GINGER-HAIRED MAN, BIG MOUSTACHE, PIGTAILS
CAIUS FATUOUS
LANISTA
IN THE CIRCUS INN...
OBELIX, I'VE JUST HAD AN IDEA! WE'LL BECOME GLADIATORS!
OH?
AND HOW DO WE GET TO BE GLADIATORS?
WE'LL ASK A ROMAN... THE ONLY ONE WE KNOW IS THAT ONE WHO HAS A LOT OF BATHS. LET'S GO TO THE BATHS!
AND OUTSIDE THE BATHS...
THERMAE
10,000 SESTERTII... THAT'S A LOT OF MONEY!
I COULD JUST DO WITH THAT!
LOOK!
I SAW THEM FIRST!
NO, ME!
IT'S A LIE! THE 10,000 SESTERTII ARE MINE!
?!???
HERE, LET US BY! WE'RE IN A HURRY
THESE ROMANS ARE CRAZY!
OH, SO IT'S YOU TWO BACK AGAIN. I THOUGHT I TOLD YOU BEFORE...
OI! TAKE YOUR SANDALS OFF IF YOU WANT TO COME IN THE BATH!
SPLOSH!
24

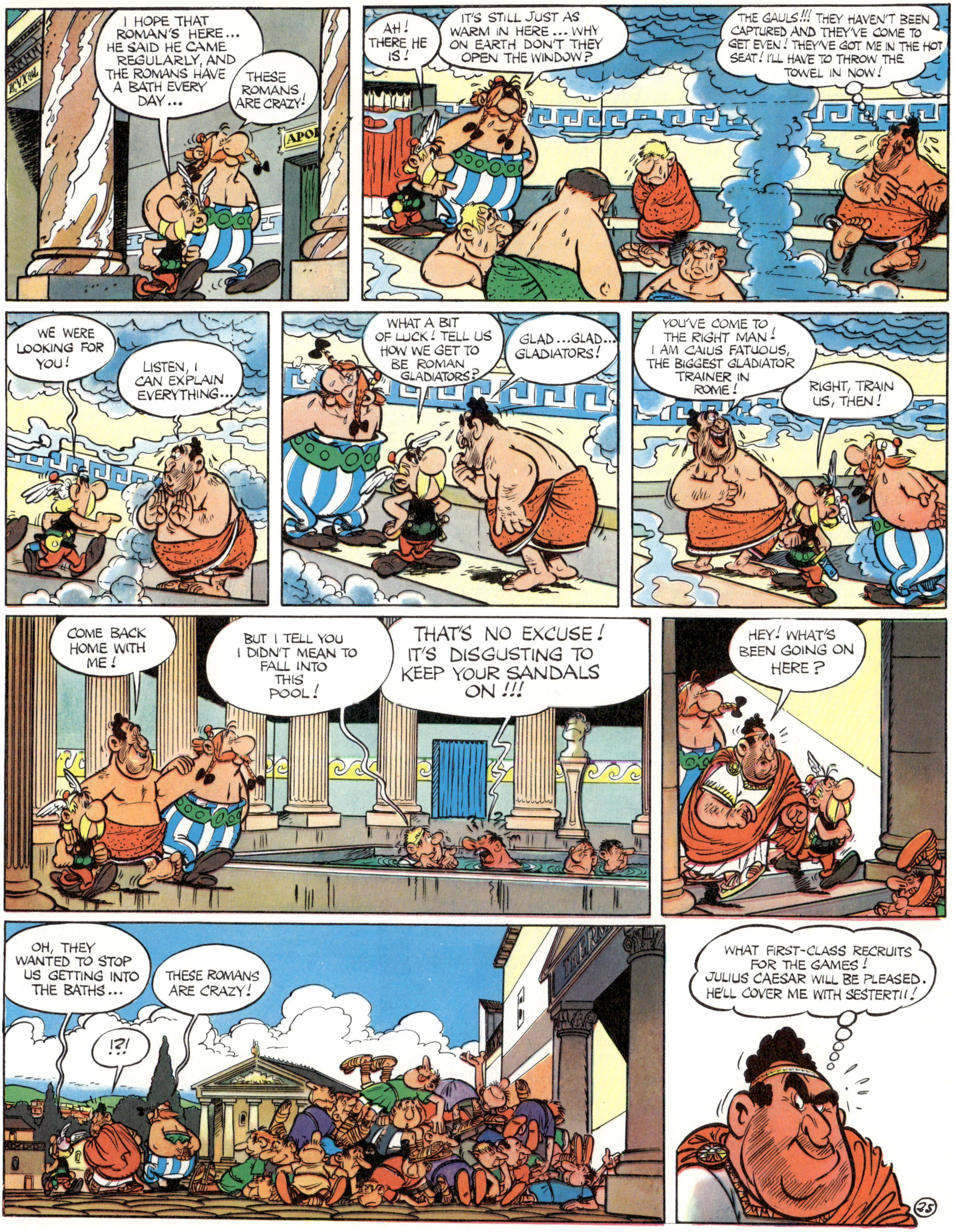
I HOPE THAT ROMAN'S HERE... HE SAID HE CAME REGULARLY, AND THE ROMANS HAVE A BATH EVERY DAY...
THESE ROMANS ARE CRAZY!
AH! THERE HE IS!
IT'S STILL JUST AS WARM IN HERE... WHY ON EARTH DON'T THEY OPEN THE WINDOW?
THE GAULS!!! THEY HAVEN'T BEEN CAPTURED AND THEY'VE COME TO GET EVEN! THEY'VE GOT ME IN THE HOT SEAT! I'LL HAVE TO THROW THE TOWEL IN NOW!
WE WERE LOOKING FOR YOU!
LISTEN, I CAN EXPLAIN EVERYTHING...
WHAT A BIT OF LUCK! TELL US HOW WE GET TO BE ROMAN GLADIATORS?
GLAD...GLAD... GLADIATORS!
YOU'VE COME TO THE RIGHT MAN! I AM CAIUS FATUOUS, THE BIGGEST GLADIATOR TRAINER IN ROME!
RIGHT, TRAIN US, THEN!
COME BACK HOME WITH ME!
BUT I TELL YOU I DIDN'T MEAN TO FALL INTO THIS POOL!
THAT'S NO EXCUSE! IT'S DISGUSTING TO KEEP YOUR SANDALS ON!!!
HEY! WHAT'S BEEN GOING ON HERE?
OH, THEY WANTED TO STOP US GETTING INTO THE BATHS...
THESE ROMANS ARE CRAZY!
!?!
WHAT FIRST-CLASS RECRUITS FOR THE GAMES! JULIUS CAESAR WILL BE PLEASED. HE'LL COVER ME WITH SESTERTII!
25

I MUST FIRST WIN THEIR CONFIDENCE SO THAT THEY'LL SIGN THE CONTRACT WHICH WILL GET THEM INTO MY HOT LITTLE HANDS...
COME ALONG IN... WE'LL HAVE A LIGHT MEAL
COULDN'T WE HAVE A HEAVY MEAL INSTEAD?
NICE PLACE YOU'VE GOT HERE!
JUST TASTE THESE PASTIES! THEY'RE A NEW RECIPE – THEY COST A FORTUNE! NIGHTINGALES' TONGUES IMPORTED FROM THE NORTH OF GAUL, STURGEONS' EGGS FROM THE FARTHEST BARBARIAN LANDS, COCKROACHES' GUMS FROM MONGOLIA...
WELL, WHAT DO YOU THINK OF THEM?
GULP!
SALTY
!
RIGHT! THE FUN'S OVER, BY JUPITER! MAKE YOUR MARKS ON THESE CONTRACTS!
EXCELLENT! UP YOU GET! INSALUBRIUS!
INSALUBRIUS, HERE ARE THE TWO NEW GLADIATORS! TRAIN THEM FOR THE CIRCUS – AND JUMP TO IT!
THEY'LL JUMP TO IT ALL RIGHT, LANISTA, THEY'LL JUMP TO IT!
I SAY, ASTERIX, DO YOU THINK THE LIGHT MEAL'S OVER?
SALTY! HUH! THESE BARBARIANS DON'T APPRECIATE GOOD FOOD! BRING ME THE GIBLET JAM!
SNAP!
26

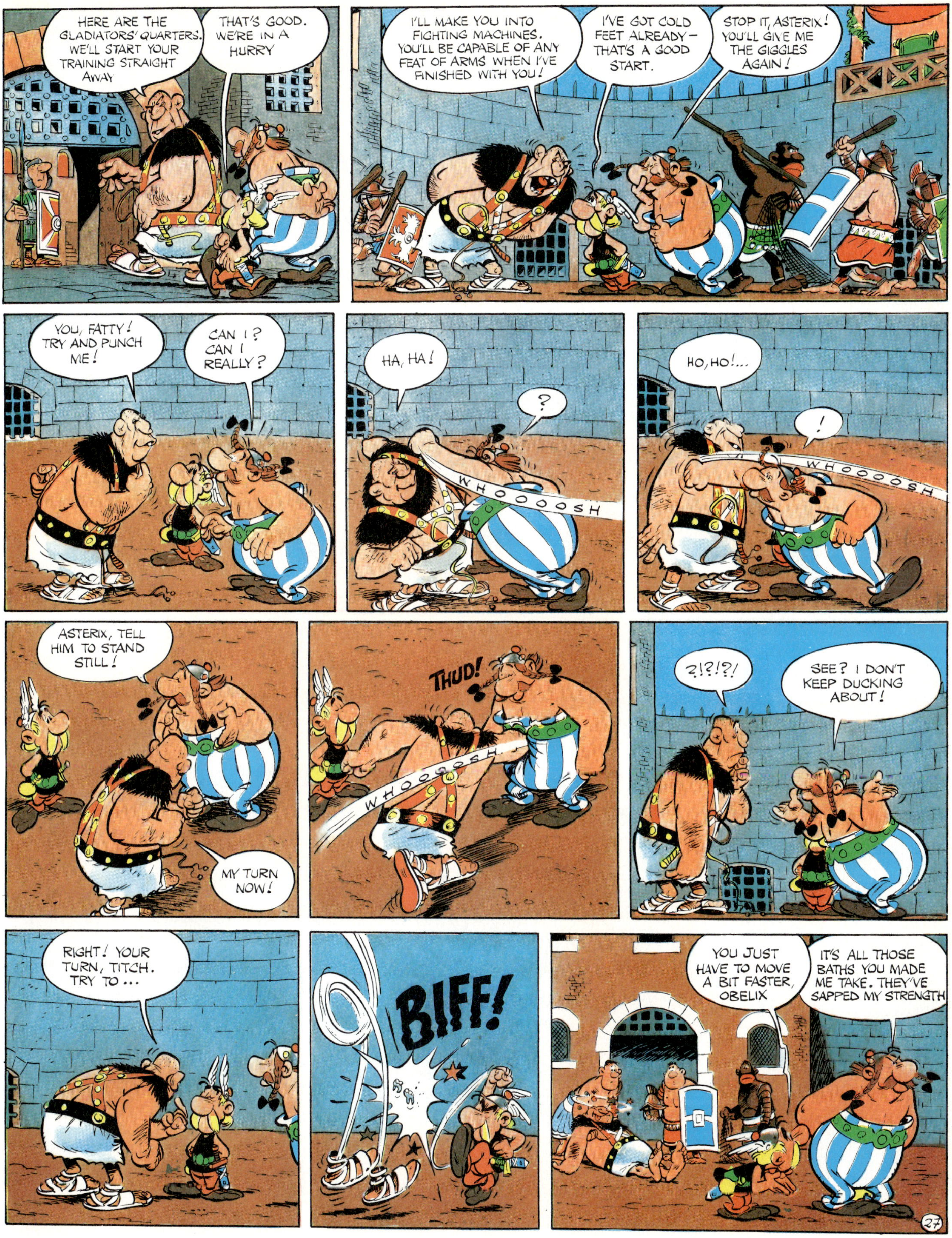
HERE ARE THE GLADIATORS' QUARTERS. WE'LL START YOUR TRAINING STRAIGHT AWAY
THAT'S GOOD. WE'RE IN A HURRY
I'LL MAKE YOU INTO FIGHTING MACHINES. YOU'LL BE CAPABLE OF ANY FEAT OF ARMS WHEN I'VE FINISHED WITH YOU!
I'VE GOT COLD FEET ALREADY – THAT'S A GOOD START.
STOP IT, ASTERIX! YOU'LL GIVE ME THE GIGGLES AGAIN!
YOU, FATTY! TRY AND PUNCH ME!
CAN I? CAN I REALLY?
HA, HA!
?
WHOOOOOSH
HO, HO!...
!
WHOOOOOSH
ASTERIX, TELL HIM TO STAND STILL!
MY TURN NOW!
THUD!
WHOOOOOSH
?!?!?!
SEE? I DON'T KEEP DUCKING ABOUT!
RIGHT! YOUR TURN, TITCH. TRY TO ...
BIFF!
YOU JUST HAVE TO MOVE A BIT FASTER, OBELIX
IT'S ALL THOSE BATHS YOU MADE ME TAKE. THEY'VE SAPPED MY STRENGTH
27

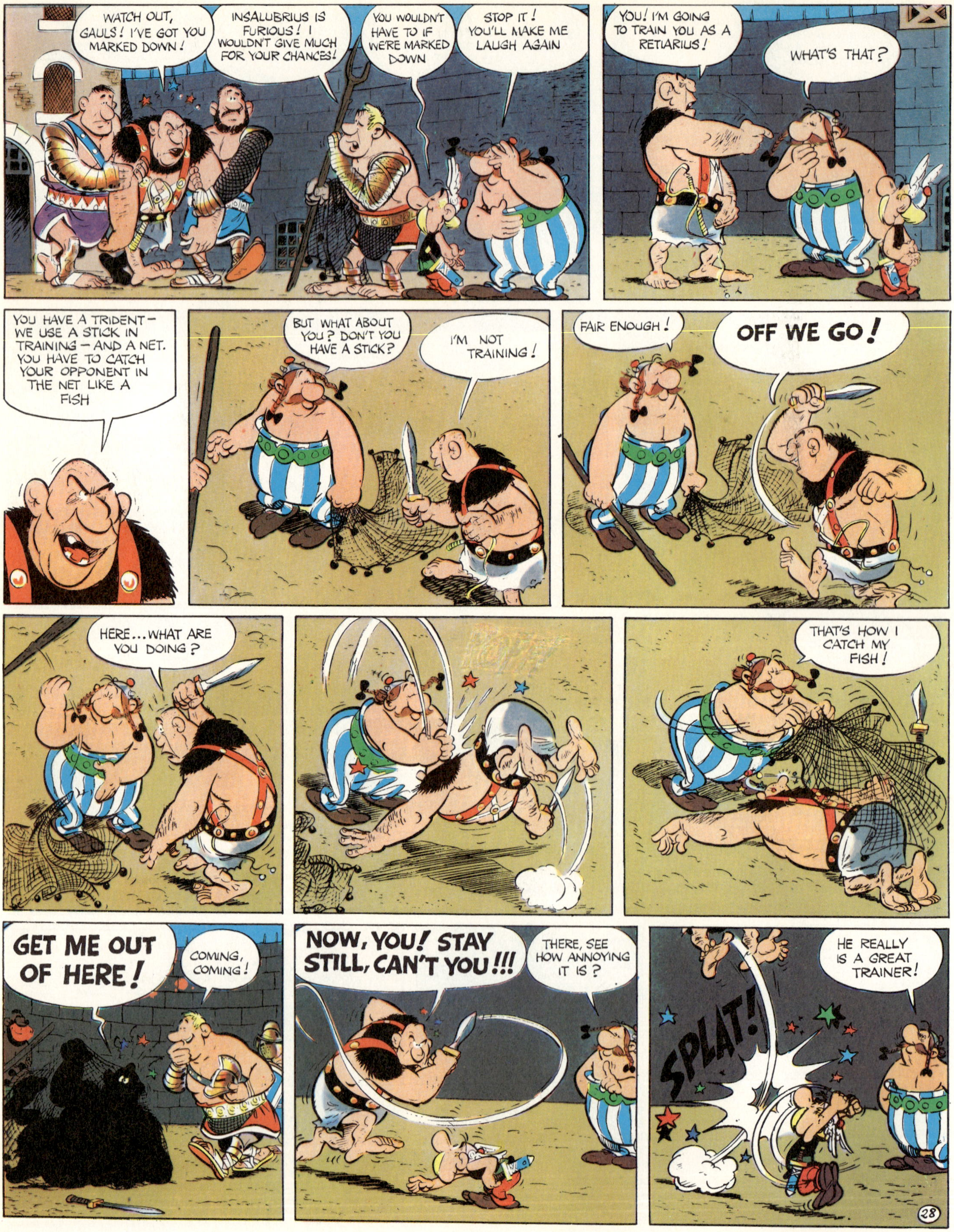

WATCH OUT, GAULS! I'VE GOT YOU MARKED DOWN!
INSALUBRIUS IS FURIOUS! I WOULDN'T GIVE MUCH FOR YOUR CHANCES!
YOU WOULDN'T HAVE TO IF WE'RE MARKED DOWN
STOP IT! YOU'LL MAKE ME LAUGH AGAIN
YOU! I'M GOING TO TRAIN YOU AS A RETIARIUS!
WHAT'S THAT?
YOU HAVE A TRIDENT – WE USE A STICK IN TRAINING – AND A NET. YOU HAVE TO CATCH YOUR OPPONENT IN THE NET LIKE A FISH
BUT WHAT ABOUT YOU? DON'T YOU HAVE A STICK?
I'M NOT TRAINING!
FAIR ENOUGH!
OFF WE GO!
HERE... WHAT ARE YOU DOING?
THAT'S HOW I CATCH MY FISH!
GET ME OUT OF HERE!
COMING, COMING!
NOW, YOU! STAY STILL, CAN'T YOU!!!
THERE, SEE HOW ANNOYING IT IS?
SPLAT!
HE REALLY IS A GREAT TRAINER!
28

ALL RIGHT! I GET THE MESSAGE!
INSALUBRIUS IS OFF!
BUT HE HASN'T FINISHED OUR TRAINING!
I KNOW A VERY GOOD GAME! I ASK QUESTIONS AND YOU HAVE TO ANSWER WITHOUT SAYING YES, NO, BLACK OR WHITE. ANYONE WHO SAYS ANY OF THOSE WORDS IS OUT. ALL RIGHT?
OH YES! OH YES! OH YES! OH YES!
YOU'RE OUT!
NO!
YOU'RE OUT AGAIN!
IT'S NOT FAIR. I'M GOING TO SULK!
HA! HA! HA!
MEANWHILE...
I WANT MY WAGES. I'M PACKING IT IN! THOSE GAULS ARE TOO MUCH FOR ME. I'M GOING BACK TO MY FATHER'S LACE FACTORY!
?!
HO, HO! LET'S HAVE A LOOK AT THESE AMAZING RECRUITS WHO MANAGED TO GET THE TERRIBLE INSALUBRIUS DOWN!
WHAT THE... WHAT ARE YOU DOING?
WE'RE PLAYING A GAME. IT'S GREAT FUN. WANT TO JOIN IN?
NO!
HE'S OUT! HE'S OUT! HE'S OUT!
I DON'T PAY YOU FOR GAMES LIKE THAT!!!
ALL RIGHT THEN, WHAT ABOUT CHARADES?
POF! POF! POF! POF!
29

AND YOU GLADIATORS, GET BACK TO YOUR TRAINING, I HAVE TO GO AND SEE CAESAR ...
I SAY, OBELIX, SUPPOSE WE TOOK A LITTLE STROLL ROUND TOWN TOO?
NOT A BAD IDEA!
HALT, GLADIATORS! YOU AREN'T ALLOWED OUT OF YOUR QUARTERS!
PUT THAT HELMET DOWN, OBELIX! YOU'LL HAVE TO GET OUT OF THAT SILLY HABIT!
WHAT FOR? IT DOESN'T HURT ANYONE!
THESE MODERN CITIES ARE ALL VERY WELL, BUT THEY'RE NOT WHAT I'D CALL FRIENDLY
LET'S GO AND SEE WHAT'S HAPPENING OVER THERE WHERE ALL THOSE PEOPLE ARE READING THAT NOTICE
MEANWHILE ...
HERE'S THE PROGRAMME FOR THE GAMES, O CAESAR. I'VE HAD THESE TABLETS PUT UP ALL OVER ROME
IF THE PEOPLE LIKE THE GAMES, I SHALL TREAT YOU GENEROUSLY. IF NOT, THE LIONS GET THE TREAT!
GRAND CIRCUS GAMES
IMPRESARIO, CAIUS FATUOUS
CHARIOT RACES
GAULISH BARD THROWN TO THE LIONS
GLADIATORIAL CONTESTS WITH ASTERIX & OBELIX THE INDOMITABLE GAULS
(BOOKING OFFICE NOW OPEN)
NOT BAD ... BUT YOU'D BETTER NOT LET THE GAULS ESCAPE. THEY'RE THE STAR ATTRACTION
DON'T YOU WORRY, O CAESAR, THEY'RE SAFELY LOCKED AWAY!
AT LAST I'LL BE ABLE TO BUY THAT LITTLE FARM AT ALBUM IN THE PROVINCE OF STERNUM!
LOOK! IF IT ISN'T GOOD OLD FATUOUS!
?!
SO IT IS! THERE'S A BIT OF LUCK!
30

WH... WHAT'S THIS? YOU'VE GOT OUT??
NOT A BAD PROGRAMME, BUT WE'LL WANT TO MAKE A FEW ALTERATIONS...
ASTERIX & OBELIX
HE DOES SEEM SURPRISED TO SEE US! AND PLEASED!
YOU TURNED UP JUST AT THE RIGHT MOMENT! WE WERE LOOKING FOR A GUIDE TO SHOW US THE TOWN!
A GUI... A GUI... A GUIDE!
SLAP!
KEEP A STIFF UPPER LIP... THE MAIN THING IS NOT TO LOSE SIGHT OF THEM...
ALL RIGHT
TOURIST GUIDE
... AND THIS IS THE FORUM
PITY WE CAN'T TAKE PICTURES OF ALL THIS BACK TO GAUL WITH US...
SOUVENIRS
YOU SEEM VERY SURE YOU'LL GET OUT OF THE CIRCUS ALIVE!
WELL, OF COURSE!
DON'T YOU WORRY ABOUT US!
?!?
SUPPOSE I WENT CARVING MY NAME ON YOUR PYRAMIDS, EH?
NOW LET'S GO BACK TO YOUR PLACE FOR DINNER!
AND NO BORING LITTLE PASTIES THIS TIME – JUST BOARS!
DINNER IS MUCH ENJOYED BY EVERYONE – WELL, NEARLY EVERYONE...
I'LL SAY ONE THING FOR THE ROMANS, THEY KNOW HOW TO ENTERTAIN! ISN'T THAT RIGHT, OBELIX?
YUM! GULP! 'SRIGHT! SCRUNCH!
PATIENCE, PATIENCE! THEY'LL BE LAUGHING THE OTHER SIDE OF THEIR FACES IN THE ARENA!
COME ALONG, IT'S TIME TO GO BACK TO OUR QUARTERS! I HOPE WE HAVEN'T OVERSTAYED OUR WELCOME?
I SHOULD HAVE HAD A BOAR FOR THE ROAD...
31

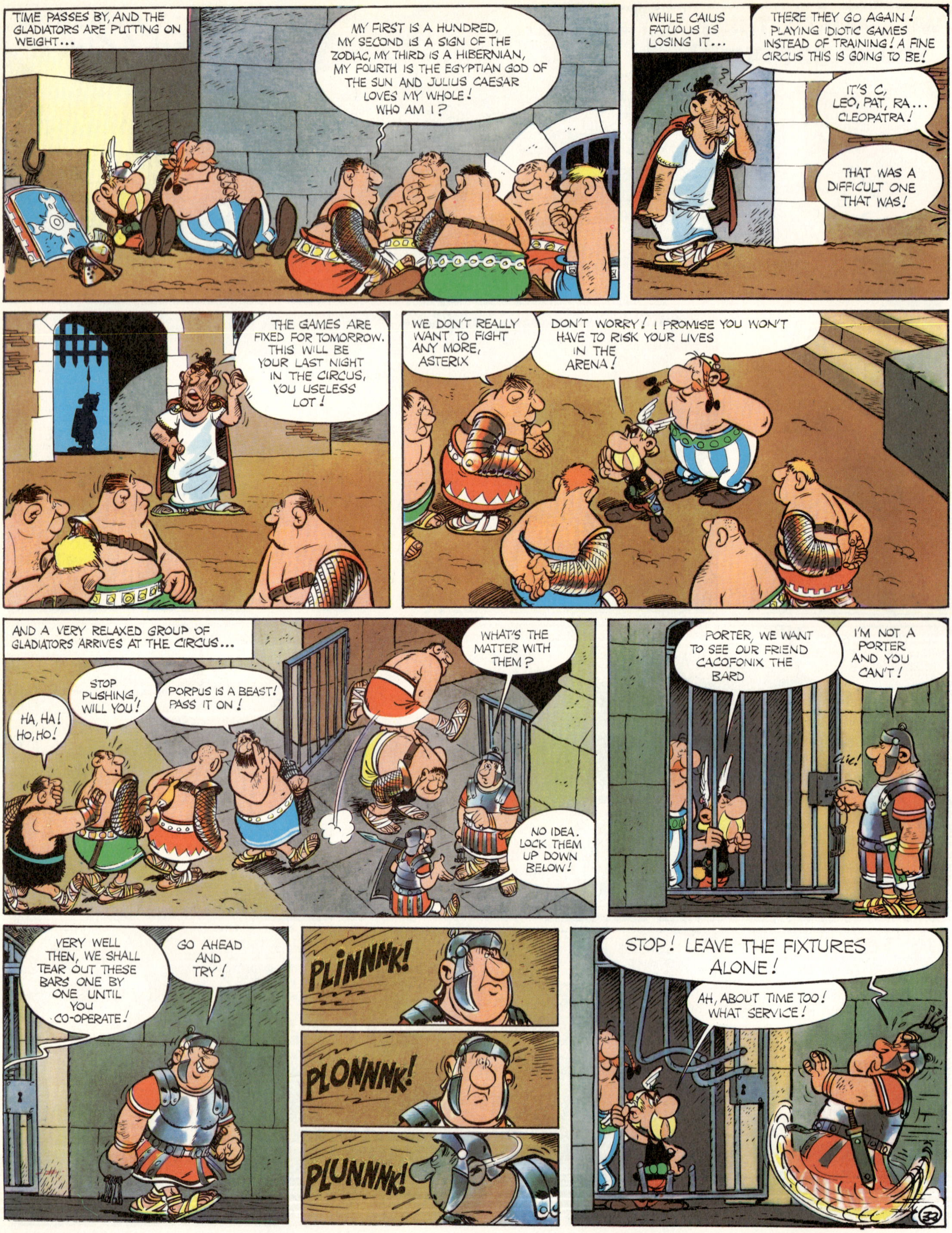
TIME PASSES BY, AND THE GLADIATORS ARE PUTTING ON WEIGHT...
MY FIRST IS A HUNDRED, MY SECOND IS A SIGN OF THE ZODIAC, MY THIRD IS A HIBERNIAN, MY FOURTH IS THE EGYPTIAN GOD OF THE SUN AND JULIUS CAESAR LOVES MY WHOLE! WHO AM I?
WHILE CAIUS FATUOUS IS LOSING IT...
THERE THEY GO AGAIN! PLAYING IDIOTIC GAMES INSTEAD OF TRAINING! A FINE CIRCUS THIS IS GOING TO BE!
IT'S C, LEO, PAT, RA... CLEOPATRA!
THAT WAS A DIFFICULT ONE THAT WAS!
THE GAMES ARE FIXED FOR TOMORROW. THIS WILL BE YOUR LAST NIGHT IN THE CIRCUS, YOU USELESS LOT!
WE DON'T REALLY WANT TO FIGHT ANY MORE, ASTERIX
DON'T WORRY! I PROMISE YOU WON'T HAVE TO RISK YOUR LIVES IN THE ARENA!
AND A VERY RELAXED GROUP OF GLADIATORS ARRIVES AT THE CIRCUS...
HA, HA! HO, HO!
STOP PUSHING, WILL YOU!
PORPUS IS A BEAST! PASS IT ON!
WHAT'S THE MATTER WITH THEM?
NO IDEA. LOCK THEM UP DOWN BELOW!
PORTER, WE WANT TO SEE OUR FRIEND CACOFONIX THE BARD
I'M NOT A PORTER AND YOU CAN'T!
VERY WELL THEN, WE SHALL TEAR OUT THESE BARS ONE BY ONE UNTIL YOU CO-OPERATE!
GO AHEAD AND TRY!
PLINNNK!
PLONNNK!
PLUNNNK!
STOP! LEAVE THE FIXTURES ALONE!
AH, ABOUT TIME TOO! WHAT SERVICE!

I'M RESPONSIBLE FOR THE FIXTURES, I AM!
OPEN UP, SENDERVICTORIUS. IT'S ME, APPIANGLORIUS!
TAP! TAP! TAP! TAP!
THAT'S FUNNY, THERE'S NO ANSWER...
LET ME HAVE A GO...
CRAASH
NO! OUR DOOR!
WHAT'S GOING ON HERE? WHY DON'T YOU ANSWER WHEN WE KNOCK?
PARDON?
POP!
Love is a menhir splendid thing...
HE'S OFF AGAIN!
I CAN'T BEAR IT! I CAN'T BEAR IT! (SOBS)
CACOFONIX!
ASTERIX! OBELIX! WHAT BRINGS YOU HERE?
WE'VE COME TO RESCUE YOU!
OH, I'M NOT AFRAID OF THESE MISERABLE ROMANS! BUT IT'S NICE TO SEE YOU!
WE PROMISED TO GET OUR GLADIATOR FRIENDS OUT OF A SPOT. WE'LL BE LEAVING FOR GAUL STRAIGHT AFTER THE GAMES!
THAT'S FINE. I'D LIKE TO SEE THE GAMES. I'VE HEARD SO MUCH ABOUT THEM SINCE I GOT HERE...
JUST ONE MORE THING... WAIT TILL WE'VE GONE BEFORE YOU START SINGING AGAIN
WHA... WHAT?
PHILISTINES! BRUTES! BARBARIANS!
SOON AFTERWARDS...
Roman in the gloamin'...
MERCY! MERCY! I'LL DO ANYTHING YOU LIKE, BUT STOP THAT AWFUL NOISE!
33

A HUGE CROWD IS FORMING OUTSIDE THE CIRCUS...
WASH YOUR TOGAS IN SUPER PERSIC! SUPER PERSIC WASHES EVEN PURPLER!
SUPER PERSIC
WASHES EVEN PURPLER
SCORE CARD! SCORE CARD!
CUSHIONS! CUSHIONS!
CHIPOLATAE! CANES CALIDI! CHIPOLATAE!
AND INSIDE THE IMPOSING ARENA THE TRUMPETS ANNOUNCE THE ARRIVAL OF CAESAR IN THE IMPERIAL BOX...
TANTAN TARA!!!!
PANEM ET CIRCENSES
LONG LIVE CAESAR!
CAESAR FOR EVER!
EVERYONE APPLAUDS THE DICTATOR...
CLAP! CLAP! CLAP! CLAP! CLAP! CLAP!
CLAP! CLAPCLAP! CLAP! CLAP! CLAP! CLAP!
ET TU BRUTE!
CLAP! CLAP! CLAP!
CLAP! CLAP! CLAP! CLAP! CLAP!
* YOU TOO, BRUTUS!
THAT BRUTUS... I CAN SEE I'M GOING TO HAVE TROUBLE WITH HIM *
CLAPCLAP! CLAPCLAP! CLAPCLAP! CLAPCLAP!
* AN EXAMINATION OF ACT III, SCENE 1 OF JULIUS CAESAR BY WILLIAM SHAKESPEARE WILL INDICATE THE PROPHETIC NATURE OF THIS REMARK
THIS WILL BE A GREAT SHOW, O CAESAR!
I HOPE SO, CAIUS FATUOUS. IF NOT, YOU'LL BE IN ON THE ACT
LET THE GAMES BEGIN!
GULP!
34

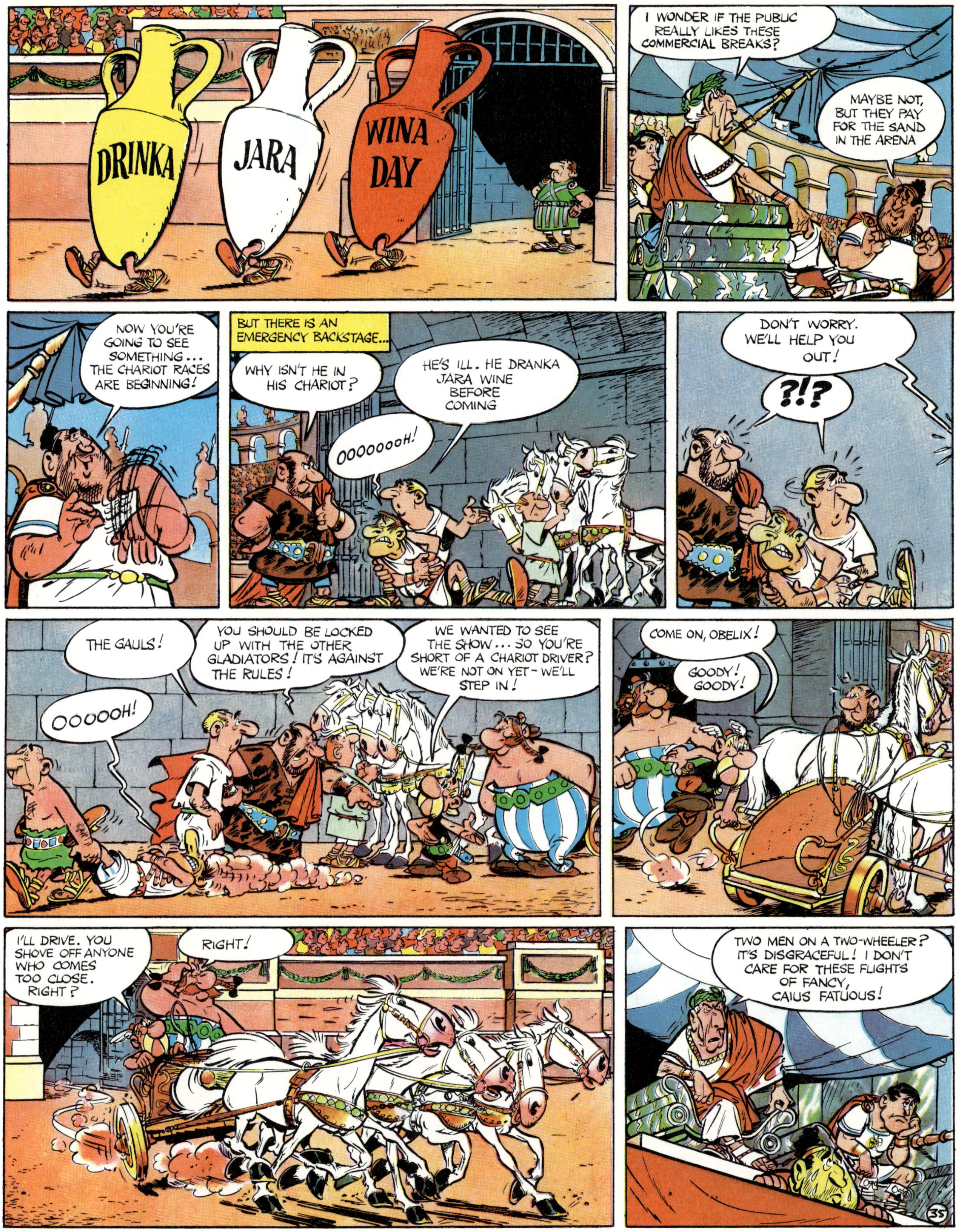
DRINKA
JARA
WINA DAY
I WONDER IF THE PUBLIC REALLY LIKES THESE COMMERCIAL BREAKS?
MAYBE NOT, BUT THEY PAY FOR THE SAND IN THE ARENA
NOW YOU'RE GOING TO SEE SOMETHING... THE CHARIOT RACES ARE BEGINNING!
BUT THERE IS AN EMERGENCY BACKSTAGE...
WHY ISN'T HE IN HIS CHARIOT?
HE'S ILL. HE DRANKA JARA WINE BEFORE COMING
OOOOOOOH!
DON'T WORRY. WE'LL HELP YOU OUT!
?!?
THE GAULS!
YOU SHOULD BE LOCKED UP WITH THE OTHER GLADIATORS! IT'S AGAINST THE RULES!
WE WANTED TO SEE THE SHOW... SO YOU'RE SHORT OF A CHARIOT DRIVER? WE'RE NOT ON YET - WE'LL STEP IN!
OOOOOH!
COME ON, OBELIX!
GOODY! GOODY!
I'LL DRIVE. YOU SHOVE OFF ANYONE WHO COMES TOO CLOSE. RIGHT?
RIGHT!
TWO MEN ON A TWO-WHEELER? IT'S DISGRACEFUL! I DON'T CARE FOR THESE FLIGHTS OF FANCY, CAIUS FATUOUS!
35

THE CHARIOTS ARE OFF...
THAT ONE IN FRONT WON'T LET US OVERTAKE!
POC!
AAAAARGH!
IF THOSE TWO COME NEAR ME, BY MERCURY, THEY'LL GET A TASTE OF MY WHIP!
CRACK!
LAST LAP
YOU GO ON– LEAVE THIS TO ME! WE'LL HAVE SOME FUN!
?!
LET GO, WILL YOU! LET GO THIS MINUTE!
YOU CAN LET GO NOW, OBELIX. I'VE WON!
NOOOOO!
WHOOSH
CRUNCH!
HURRAH! BY JUPITER! PLAUDITE CIVES!
AVE CAESAR!
THE PEOPLE ARE PLEASED... AND THAT PLEASES ME!
ER... THAT'S IT... I GOT UP A LITTLE COMIC TURN! I THOUGHT THE PEOPLE WOULD LIKE IT!
BUT WE DON'T WANT THE GAMES TO BE ALL COMIC TURNS!
NO, NO! AND NOW WE PRESENT A MAN BEING EATEN ALIVE BY THE LIONS!
36

WE'LL WAIT HERE, READY TO STEP IN! I'M GOING TO TAKE A LITTLE MAGIC POTION, JUST IN CASE...
DON'T WORRY, IT'S ALWAYS ALL RIGHT ON THE NIGHT. I'VE GOT A TOUCH OF STAGE FRIGHT, THAT'S ALL...
HI, JULIUS!
THEY... ER... THEY'RE NOT VERY POLITE!
RELEASE THE LIONS!
RRROAAOOO!
GRRRAOOR!
THEY'RE RAVENOUS, AS YOU MAY WELL IMAGINE... ALL THEY'VE HAD SINCE WE CAPTURED THEM IS A YOGHOURT A DAY!
Goodbye to the Forum, farewell Colosseum...
RUN FOR YOUR LIFE!
WILL YOU SHUT UP, GAUL?
YELP! YELP! YELP!
MiiiAOOO
MiAOOOOW!
YELP! YELP! YELP! YELP!
I WILL SING, YOU IGNORANT LOT! THIS IS THE FIRST TIME I'VE EVER SUNG IN FRONT OF SUCH A VAST AUDIENCE AND I'M GOING TO MAKE THE MOST OF IT!
ALL TOGETHER NOW...
For Gau-aul Lang Syne, My Dears...
TAKE HIM AWAY, BY JUNO!
POF! POF! POF!
LET ME GO, I SAY! LET ME GO!!!
HA! HA! HA! HO! HO! HO!
37

I CAME, I SAW AND I COULDN'T BELIEVE MY EYES! IS IT GOING ON LIKE THIS? IF SO I'LL EAT YOU MYSELF IF THE LIONS HAVEN'T GOT OVER THEIR FRIGHT!
OH, THE SERIOUS PART'S COMING NEXT... AND NOW WE PRESENT THE GLADIATORS! BLOOD, MORTAL COMBAT, SAVAGERY, THE LOT...
LET'S HOPE SO, FOR YOUR SAKE... OR ELSE...
EE-AI-ADDIO!
THAT'S SETTLED, THEN? YOU LET ME DO THE TALKING AND I'LL FIX EVERYTHING
AVE CAESAR! MORITURI TE SALUTANT!
HI, JULIUS, OLD BOY!
OH NO! THEY REALLY ARE **NOT** VERY POLITE!
LET THE FIGHTING BEGIN... BEFORE I LOSE MY TEMPER!
JUST A MINUTE. THERE'S A CHANGE IN THE PROGRAMME. THE GLADIATORS HAVE A NEW GAME TO SHOW YOU. WE FEEL SURE IT WILL AMUSE YOU ALL!
THROW YOUR WEAPONS DOWN!
CLING!
CLANG!
CLING!
CLONK! TING!
THAT'S A GOOD START!
38

THE MIRMILLO IN THE MIDDLE ASKS THE QUESTIONS AND THE OTHERS HAVE TO REPLY WITHOUT SAYING THE WORDS: YES, NO, BLACK OR WHITE. IF THEY DO THEY'RE OUT
YOU, THRACIAN! WHAT COLOUR IS SAND?
IT'S LIGHT!
YOU SAID WHITE!
NO, I DID NOT! I DIDN'T SAY WHITE!
?!?
?!!??
YOU'VE LOST! YOU'VE LOST! YOURE OUT!
HA! HA!
HA! HA! HA! HA!
EXCUSE ME! I HAVE THE RIGHT TO APPEAL TO CAESAR!
ARE YOU TRYING TO MAKE A FOOL OF ME, BY JUPITER? THE BIGGEST CIRCUS IN ROME, 250,000 SPECTATORS, AMONG THEM JULIUS CAESAR HIMSELF–ALL THIS JUST TO WATCH HALFWITS PLAYING SILLY ATRIUM GAMES!
GET FIGHTING!!!
39

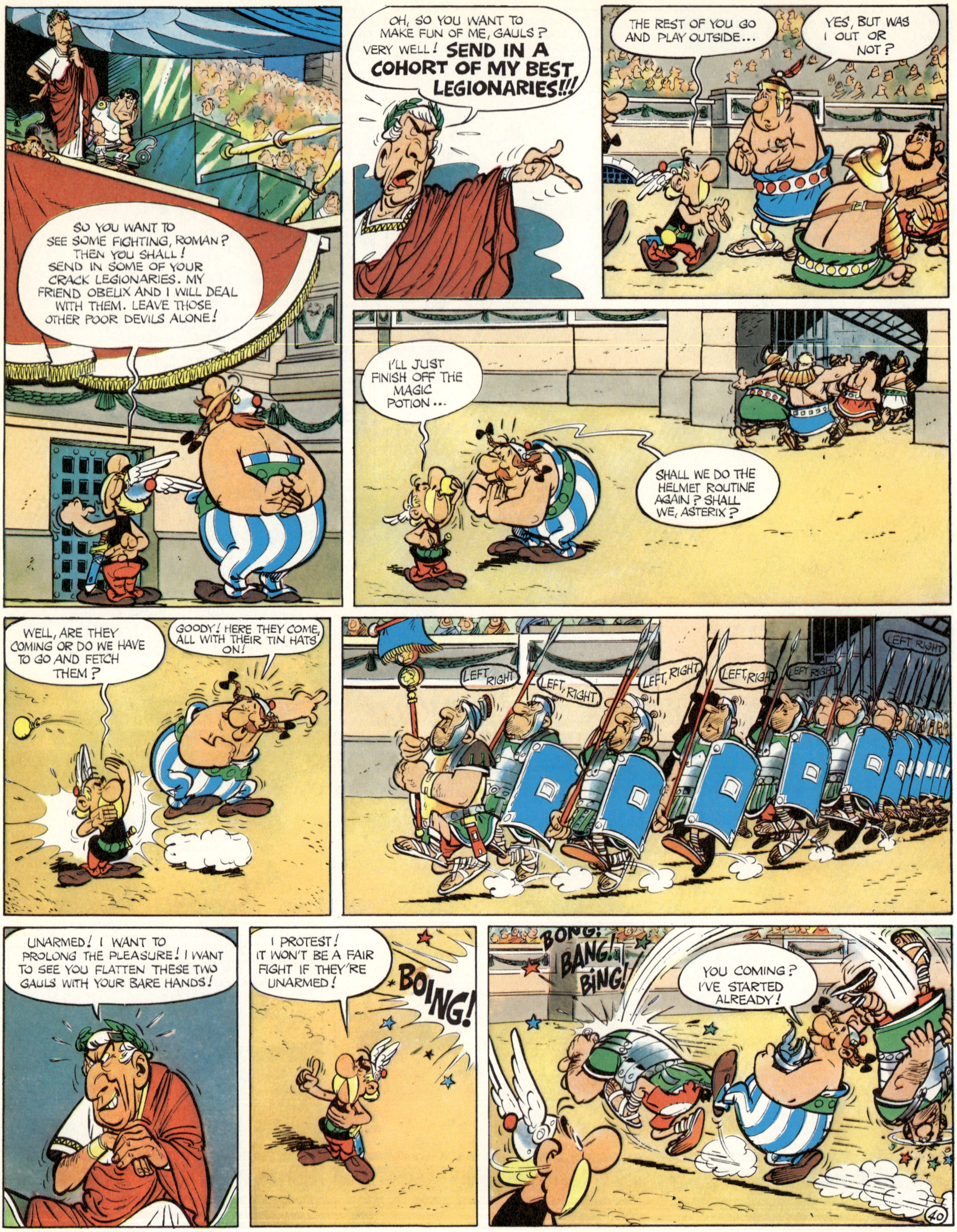
OH, SO YOU WANT TO MAKE FUN OF ME, GAULS? VERY WELL! SEND IN A COHORT OF MY BEST LEGIONARIES!!!
THE REST OF YOU GO AND PLAY OUTSIDE...
YES, BUT WAS I OUT OR NOT?
SO YOU WANT TO SEE SOME FIGHTING, ROMAN? THEN YOU SHALL! SEND IN SOME OF YOUR CRACK LEGIONARIES. MY FRIEND OBELIX AND I WILL DEAL WITH THEM. LEAVE THOSE OTHER POOR DEVILS ALONE!
I'LL JUST FINISH OFF THE MAGIC POTION...
SHALL WE DO THE HELMET ROUTINE AGAIN? SHALL WE, ASTERIX?
WELL, ARE THEY COMING OR DO WE HAVE TO GO AND FETCH THEM?
GOODY! HERE THEY COME, ALL WITH THEIR TIN HATS ON!
LEFT, RIGHT
LEFT, RIGHT
LEFT, RIGHT
LEFT, RIGHT
LEFT, RIGHT
LEFT, RIGHT
UNARMED! I WANT TO PROLONG THE PLEASURE! I WANT TO SEE YOU FLATTEN THESE TWO GAULS WITH YOUR BARE HANDS!
I PROTEST! IT WON'T BE A FAIR FIGHT IF THEY'RE UNARMED!
BOING!
BONG! BANG! BING!
YOU COMING? I'VE STARTED ALREADY!
40

CLANG!
CLINKCLONKCLANK!
CRUNCH!
WHAT HAVE YOU DONE WITH YOUR HELMET THEN? WHERE'S YOUR HELMET, EH?
SMACK! SMACK! SMACK! SMACK!
I WILL NOW GIVE YOU A SONG TO INSPIRE YOU WITH COURAGE...
?
WHAM!
NOOO!
AVE! LONG LIVE THE GAULS! ENCORE! ENCORE!
THE PEOPLE SEEM HAPPY!
?!
GAULS, YOU ARE BRAVE MEN, AND I SHOULD KNOW! I DECLARE YOU THE WINNERS, AND AS YOU HAVE MANAGED TO ENTERTAIN MY PEOPLE, I WILL GIVE YOU ANYTHING YOU ASK. SUCH IS THE GENEROSITY OF CAESAR!
LONG LIVE CAESAR! THAT'S WHAT I CALL A CIRCUS! AVE!
WAKE UP, CACOFONIX! WE'VE RESCUED YOU!
ANYWAY, I WON! YOU'LL NEVER BE ABLE TO CAP THAT!
41

I ASK YOU TO FREE THE BARD WE CAME TO RESCUE, AND LET US GO HOME TO GAUL BEFORE WE HAVE TO BEAT YOUR ARMY UP AGAIN...
... AND FINALLY I ASK YOU TO FREE THE GLADIATORS. THEY'RE GIVING UP THEIR BLOODTHIRSTY JOB!
GRANTED, O GAUL!
MMPH? IS THE SHOW OVER YET?
AND I HAVE ONE LAST FAVOUR TO ASK YOU, JULIUS...
YOU SAW THAT? NOT A BAD PROGRAMME, EH?
LEND US CAIUS FATUOUS THE GLADIATOR TRAINER FOR OUR JOURNEY BACK TO GAUL. WE'LL SEND HIM BACK BY RETURN
GRANTED, BY JUPITER!
BUT... BUT...
WHAT ARE YOU GOING TO DO WITH ME?
WE'RE GOING TO TEACH YOU A LITTLE LESSON, BY BELENOS!
LONG LIVE THE GAULS!
LONG LIVE THE GLADIATORS!
LONG LIVE CAESAR!
WHAT HAPPENED TO ME?
EXACTLY WHAT WILL HAPPEN AGAIN IF YOU DARE SING A NOTE BEFORE WE GET BACK TO GAUL!
NO FEAR! I'M NOT SINGING FOR ANY MORE ROMAN BARBARIANS, AND MOREOVER I'M TAKING NO FURTHER INTEREST IN THE MATTER!
HEY, WHERE ARE THE RUINS? DIDN'T A HOUSE FALL ON ME?
42

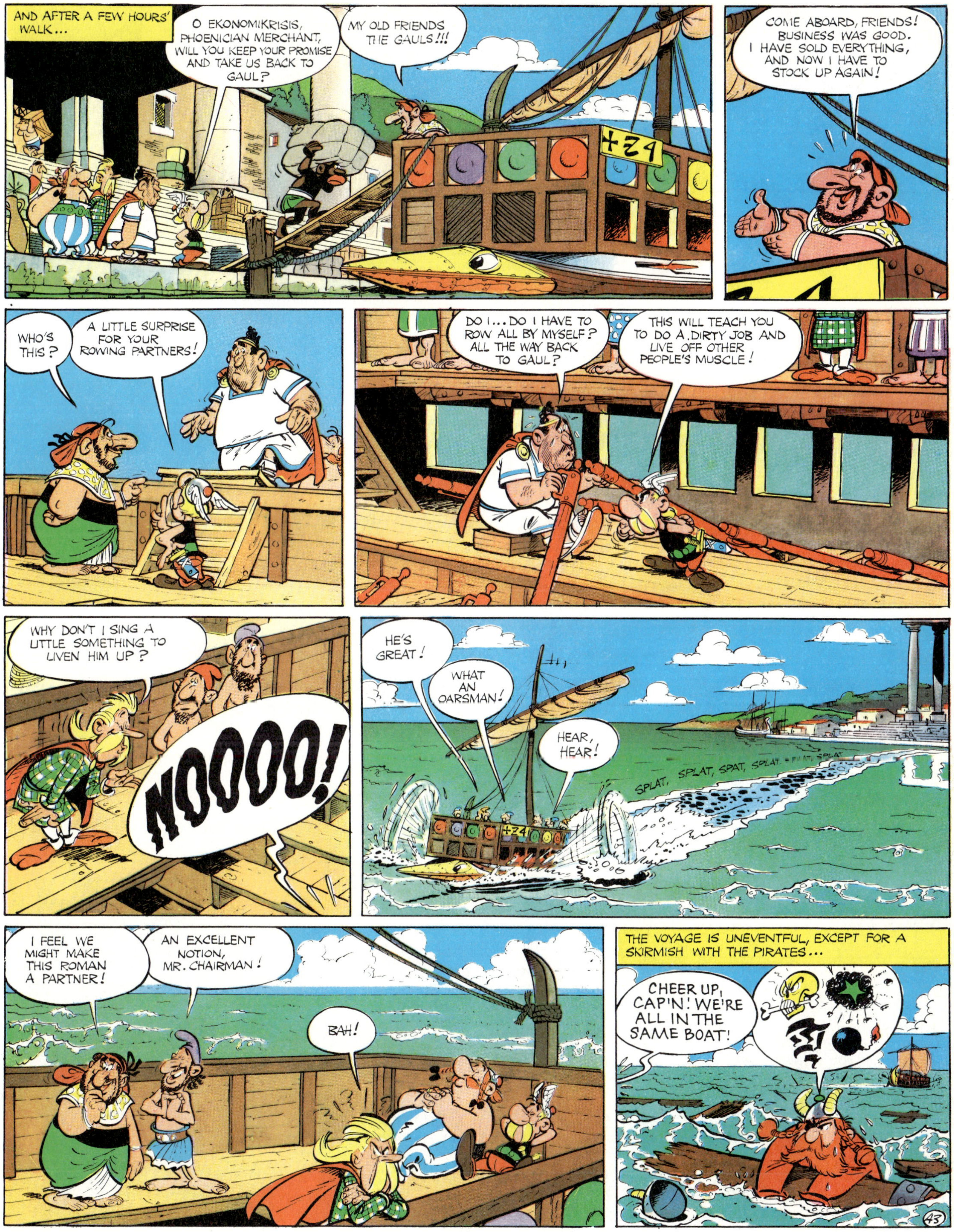
AND AFTER A FEW HOURS' WALK...
O EKONOMIKRISIS, PHOENICIAN MERCHANT, WILL YOU KEEP YOUR PROMISE AND TAKE US BACK TO GAUL?
MY OLD FRIENDS THE GAULS!!!
COME ABOARD, FRIENDS! BUSINESS WAS GOOD. I HAVE SOLD EVERYTHING, AND NOW I HAVE TO STOCK UP AGAIN!
WHO'S THIS?
A LITTLE SURPRISE FOR YOUR ROWING PARTNERS!
DO I... DO I HAVE TO ROW ALL BY MYSELF? ALL THE WAY BACK TO GAUL?
THIS WILL TEACH YOU TO DO A DIRTY JOB AND LIVE OFF OTHER PEOPLE'S MUSCLE!
WHY DON'T I SING A LITTLE SOMETHING TO LIVEN HIM UP?
NOOOO!
HE'S GREAT!
WHAT AN OARSMAN!
HEAR, HEAR!
SPLAT, SPLAT, SPAT, SPLAT
I FEEL WE MIGHT MAKE THIS ROMAN A PARTNER!
AN EXCELLENT NOTION, MR. CHAIRMAN!
BAH!
THE VOYAGE IS UNEVENTFUL, EXCEPT FOR A SKIRMISH WITH THE PIRATES...
CHEER UP, CAP'N! WE'RE ALL IN THE SAME BOAT!
43

PRINTED IN BELGIUM BY proost INTERNATIONAL BOOK PRODUCTION